TAKING THE RISK

ADVENTURES IN
TRAVEL & PUBLISHING

HILARY BRADT

Bradt Guides Ltd
Globe Pequot Press

First published in the UK in May 2024 by
Bradt Guides Ltd
31a High Street, Chesham, HP5 1BW, England
www.bradtguides.com

Print edition published in the USA by The Globe Pequot Press Inc,
PO Box 480, Guilford, Connecticut 06437-0480

Edited by Samantha Cook
Project management by Samantha Cook and Anna Moores
Cover illustration by Clover Robin
Cover design by Pepi Bluck, Perfect Picture
Layout and typesetting by Ian Spick
Maps by David McCutcheon FBCart.S. FRGS
Drawings by Hilary Bradt

All photos © Hilary Bradt except for:
Author photo © Lee Miller
Animal market, Otavalo, Ecuador © Barna Tanko/Shutterstock
Blue-footed booby © Rene Baars/Shutterstock
Third-generation Welsh-speaking brothers, Patagonia © John Pilkington
Cape dwarf chameleon © Piece of peace/Shutterstock
Giraffes © Tim Smith
Janet Mears © Anna Moores

Production managed by Sue Cooper, Bradt Guides & Jellyfish Print Solutions

ISBN: 9781804691847

British Library Cataloguing in Publication Data
A catalogue record for this book is available from the British Library

Digital conversion by www.dataworks.co.in
Printed in the UK by Jellyfish Print Solutions

Paper used for this product comes from sustainably managed forests, recycled and
controlled sources.

Interrupting her career as an occupational therapist with ever-lengthening periods of budget travel, **Hilary Bradt**, with former husband George, self-published her first guidebook in 1974 while journeying through South America. Thus Bradt Travel Guides was born. For 25 years she combined writing  guidebooks and running the company with leading tours to South America and Madagascar, her in-depth knowledge bringing her lecture engagements at the Royal Geographical Society, the Smithsonian Institution and expedition cruise ships. Under her watch, Bradt Travel Guides grew to become one of the most respected names in travel, with a reputation for championing sustainable travel – long before it became fashionable – and 'getting there first': publishing guides to destinations ignored by other publishers. This approach has garnered a host of accolades, including the *Sunday Times* Small Publisher of the Year Award and regular Best Guidebook Series awards from organisations like the British Guild of Travel Writers and *Wanderlust* magazine. The company now has over 200 books in print – but remains proudly independent and fiercely committed to Hilary's founding ethos.

In 2008, Hilary received an MBE for her contribution to the tourism industry. This was followed by four Lifetime Achievement awards and, in 2018, she was made an Officer of the National Order of Madagascar for her contribution to tourism in that country, having written and published the first guide to the island in 1984. Now in her eighties, Hilary lives in Devon where she writes, sculpts… and still hitch-hikes.

ACKNOWLEDGEMENTS

Thanks are due to the hard-working Bradt team for getting the book to press in time for our fiftieth anniversary, and especially to my wonderful editor and project manager Samantha Cook for her meticulous eye and unfailing tact. Also to Anna Moores for sorting out the visuals, including working with the talented Clover Robin on the book's jacket.

DEDICATION

This book is dedicated to the memory of three people: my parents, Janet and Brian Cross, who put up with so much for so long, and who never told their adventurous daughter to 'take care', and to Janet Mears who gave up not only her time but her house to this fledgling publisher.

CONTENTS

FOREWORD
BY KATE HUMBLE

In 1996 I received a letter in response to an article I had written for a broadsheet newspaper. The article – the first I had ever had published – was about the island of Madagascar. It had been chosen as the front page piece for that weekend's travel section. I couldn't believe it. I was so excited to see my words in print, my name in bold beneath the headline. As career highlights go, I thought, this couldn't be bettered.

But then the letter arrived; a letter thanking me for writing about Madagascar, an island that was, back then, not somewhere considered a holiday destination, even for the relatively adventurous. It was undeveloped, transport around the island was limited and haphazard, accommodation for tourists largely non-existent. 'You really got under the skin of the island. You understood it,' the letter said.

I'd spent two magical, if not always comfortable, months in Madagascar. The trip hadn't been sponsored by a travel company. It was taken after years and years of obsessing about this strange, faraway island, with its unique, somewhat bizarre, flora and fauna, mysterious cultural practices and dramatic, diverse landscapes. I had worked and worked and saved and saved to get there. I read every book and article I could find about the island, its people and wildlife. And there was one writer in particular whose knowledge, insight and passion for Madagascar was particularly infectious. And it was this same writer who had written to me, congratulating me on what was my very first piece of travel writing. It was signed 'Hilary Bradt'.

I read and reread Hilary's letter, probably a hundred times, hardly able to believe that the person I so admired – not just for her writing, but for the way she travelled – had not just read my article, but had made the effort to write and tell me I'd done justice to a place she knew probably better than anyone. My career highlight was catapulted into the stratosphere!

Hilary's evocative writing style, her skilful ability to transport her readers to the place she is describing – so they don't just picture a place in their imaginations, but hear it, smell it, sense it – comes largely from the way she chooses to travel. In the late '60s and early '70s, before the era of travel guides and long before the internet and social media, Hilary was travelling to places that today have become iconic tourist destinations, but back then were little known and often very hard to reach. She would never describe herself as an intrepid explorer. She wasn't setting off in the style of a Victorian expedition, with an entourage of porters, cases of claret and an elephant gun. Her formative journey along the length of South America was undertaken in a pair of lace-up Clarks shoes, with an old metal-framed rucksack and a small suitcase, which was almost immediately stolen, leaving her with only the clothes she stood up in. Yet she was among the earliest tourists to visit the Galápagos Islands. She walked the Inca Trail when it was barely more than a faint track. She endured lengthy bus rides which, thanks to unforeseen weather, natural disasters, or just the dilapidated state of the buses and roads, often ended before they reached their intended destination, leaving her stranded. She hitched rides on the decks of boats, slept in storerooms on sacks of potatoes, ate unfamiliar, not always very palatable, food. But her endless curiosity and fascination for people and places superseded the challenges and discomforts of those pioneering days of independent travel, and inspired her, not only to want to keep travelling, but to help other like-minded travellers experience new countries in a similar way. Her South American journeys gave rise to 'the Little Yellow Book', a guidebook written by her and her then husband and travelling companion George. It made them a profit of $200, and became the forerunner of the eponymous guides, beloved by backpackers – and non-backpackers –

everywhere. They have been my go-to travel companions since that first trip to Madagascar, two decades after the island first captured Hilary's heart and spawned the guide that encouraged me – and now so many others – to experience it for themselves.

The book you are about to read is not a guide, but the memoir of a true traveller and consummate storyteller. It will take you on an unforgettable journey, introduce you to countries and cultures, to curious creatures and extraordinary people. It will make you laugh, gasp, cringe, wonder. But most of all, it will make you want to sling a few things in a bag, lace up your shoes, and head out into the big, wide, wonderful world for an adventure.

Kate Humble, Wye Valley, Wales, 2024

PROLOGUE

To come straight to the point: this book is focused on quite a narrow subject, or pair of subjects – travel and publishing – which have occupied a good bit of my life but by no means all of it.

My oldest friend, Susie, who's known me since college days, was the first to read the manuscript. She commented: 'What about films, theatre, books, Shakespeare, exhibitions, sculpture, courses, cultural life in general? You are so much more than "just" a traveller!' Well yes, but because I co-founded Bradt Guides fifty years ago and kept it going during the bleak years, I *am* defined by travel and publishing to a large number of people. I could admit that a small part of me has a touch of envy for Casanova who published *The Story of My Life* in twelve volumes, at a total number of 3,600 pages. And he'd only reached the age of forty-nine, so be grateful.

More than fifty years of very eventful travel, not to mention building up a publishing company from scratch, is still a lot of happenings. A lot of words, even though so much has had to be left out. To give the book dip-in-ability I've devised the formula of interspersing the travel experiences with complete stories – Interludes – most of which were written originally as Christmas letters or other long-ago narratives. If you don't want to read the whole book, these will give you a good taste of the chronological progress of a naïve youngster to a rather surprised publisher.

I couldn't have written this book if my parents hadn't kept, and returned to me, every letter I sent them in the form of a day-to-day diary. I have quoted copiously from these throughout.

PART 1

YOUTHFUL ADVENTURES

1

EARLY DAYS

I was just three when I had my first solo adventure. Like many that followed, it was unintentional.

In 1944, during the last year of the War, I was on Bournemouth beach with my mother, aunt, baby sister and older brother. While Mother chatted to Auntie Kitty, I trotted back and forth to the sea with my bucket and poured water on my mother's toes. Then one time I returned and my family wasn't there. Gone. Vanished. So I set off down the beach to look for them. It's a long beach – seven miles long – and I walked and walked. Three hours passed. The sun was low in the sky and the crowds on the beach had thinned when a kindly woman caught sight of me and thought it a bit odd to see such a small child on her own. She eventually reunited me with my distraught mother and brother Andrew (who after about an hour of frantic searching had grumbled, 'Don't let's bother any more'). It was soon clear that it was me, rather than my family, who had disappeared, having walked back from the sea at an angle and apparently not even looked around before setting off in the wrong direction. And far from flinging myself into my mother's arms at being reunited, instead I said crossly, 'You lost me!'

I've been getting lost, and blaming other people, ever since. But this adventure does also illustrate something that I think might be one of my characteristics – dogged perseverance. Pity when it's heading in the wrong direction, though.

The idea that I could make a career in travel would have been inconceivable in 1956 when I reluctantly took my first trip abroad at the age of fifteen. I had been obediently and laboriously corresponding with my penfriend in Germany for a year despite, surely, realising that Christa and I had nothing whatsoever in common. She was a normal teenager with normal interests, whereas I had postponed adolescence in favour of an extended childhood taken up with the natural world and ponies.

That week in north Germany has faded into a blur of misery, with a few stabbing memories: a ghastly dance in the village hall; attending Christa's English class at school and being unable to answer the only question put to me. And, most vividly, the time I was happily alone in the house with my book when someone came knocking. Christa's mother, Frau Dr Schmidt, was a formidable woman, a busy GP, who had told me – honestly she had – that I could ignore any callers. So when there was a loud banging on the front door I took no notice. It continued for some time and then, to my alarm, the visitor moved around the house to knock on the windows. I hid under the dining room table. Cringing there I could glimpse the agitated face of the intruder, but hoped I was invisible. Eventually the banging stopped and the person went away. That evening Dr Schmidt told me that she had forgotten her key but 'unfortunately, you didn't hear me knock'.

Then came the '60s, the famous, fabulous '60s. What better decade to be a student in Oxford (not *at* Oxford – there's a subtle difference that I haven't always bothered to point out) – except that I was too bumbling, anxious and immature to make the most of it. I was training to be an occupational therapist, and we first-year students lived in a hostel at the end of a rural lane in Headington. Compared with today's teenagers, we were extraordinarily compliant, accepting the 11 o'clock curfew which meant that we could rarely see the ending of an evening film, and every aspect of our lives was controlled. In our shared dorm we planned our escape for the summer holiday which boiled down to one option: Brian Hughes's train to Greece.

Brian was an enterprising Oxford undergraduate who booked whole railway compartments to transport students to and from

Athens, travelling non-stop from Calais via Yugoslavia to Greece. My friend Val and I managed to save up for the trip, with a bit of help from our parents, in our first student summer in 1961. Each train compartment had seating for six. During the day we travelled conventionally, watching the passing scenery and people become ever more exotic to our youthful eyes, but at night, in order to gain a tolerable night's sleep, we had to rearrange the entire compartment. As Brian explained: 'The luggage goes on the floor to provide a bed for two, then two on the seats and two aloft on the luggage racks.' In a postcard home I commented wryly on the latter: 'because of the bars I woke up segmented like a worm'. Greece was a revelation. You stepped out into a blast of heat clutching your Blue Guide and doing your best to act grown up and be interested in ruins but really longing to plunge into the Mediterranean and eat mysterious meals. No need to understand the menu, you just walked into the kitchen and pointed to the bubbling pot that most took your fancy.

We hitchhiked. It's what you did in those days. And we slept on the flat roofs of hotels for free or for a nominal cost. It was wonderful! An undeveloped country, utterly foreign, with scabby, grubby children following us around, and leering old men trying to get us into bed. I turned twenty on my first Greece trip in 1961, and I returned twice; the third time en route to the Middle East with Val.

That trip to the Middle East was the real thing: travel not holiday, the journey not the destination, the final fling before settling down to become responsible professionals (we had already secured jobs in Scotland to take up on our return) – and to celebrate our irresponsibility we were honour-bound to hitchhike every mile of the way. This was before the days of lightweight travel gear. I borrowed my father's horrible Bergen rucksack which had a steel frame which dug into my hips and weighed as much empty as a high-tech one does these days when full. Val had a small canvas

4

rucksack and carried a sleeping bag in one hand and a large wicker basket in the other.

The couple who stopped for us a few miles from Dover were from Peru. 'Where's that?' I muttered to Val. 'Africa, isn't it?' Well, geography *was* the first subject I gave up at school. Three months and £90 later I walked up the hill to my parents' house with sixpence in my pocket and a much better understanding of geography and politics. It had been a life-changing trip, with the real benefit being what I had learned about people. Hitchhiking teaches you that most people, worldwide, are astonishingly kind and generous, and even the dodgy ones can be dealt with diplomatically. I'm afraid, however, that we made too much use of the kindness of drivers as we travelled through Europe, and the traditional hospitality of the Arabs as we made our way through the countries in the Near East. In Beirut we met up with Walter, an American, who was a useful chaperone. 'I've travelled with them for three weeks and I haven't *touched* them,' he was constantly intoning. What did touch us was the utter foreignness of Lebanon, Syria and Jordan (which was considerably bigger in 1963) and at the same time the sheer familiarity of so many of the place names for someone who had studied Divinity at O level: Jerusalem, Nazareth, the Sea of Galilee… We visited Petra when the Rose Red City was inhabited by Bedouin, not tourists, and wrote a postcard to my parents from Amman – the last they heard from me before I appeared at the front door – 'We're off to Baghdad tomorrow with the Iraqi army'. The soldiers went without us, perhaps fortunately.

Those were 'my salad days, when I was young and green in judgement'. After the trip, now a grown-up occupational therapist, I moved to Edinburgh with Val and Roz, another college friend, to take up our first jobs. We shivered in our freezing flat and pretended we knew what we were doing in our respective OT departments. One Scottish summer was enough and in 1964 I moved south to work at the London Hospital and share a flat in Kensington for £6 a month. Yes, my privileged generation could not only afford to live in London but we could indulge in an orgy of free evening classes and cheap theatre tickets. It was one of these that changed my life. Literally. And it was all a mistake.

It was largely because I was in love... in love with Laurence Olivier. I made sure I saw every play at the new National Theatre that he appeared in. I rather liked a newcomer called Maggie Smith too, so the production of Ibsen's *The Master Builder* with the two of them playing the lead parts was a must. I invited my brother to join me. When we took our seats we were a bit surprised at the set. It didn't look much like nineteenth-century Norway. I picked up a cast list and, oh dear, it wasn't *The Master Builder* at all, it was a preview of a new play, *The Royal Hunt of the Sun* by Peter Shaffer. That sort of thing seemed to happen to me more than to other people, but never have I been happier with this flaw in my character. I was enthralled by the story of the betrayal and murder of the supreme Inca, Atahualpa, by the conquistador Pizarro. It remains one of my best evenings in the theatre ever, and I was now besotted with the Incas, who I hadn't even heard of before (remember, only the previous year I had thought Peru was in Africa).

I read everything I could find about the Incas and started to work out how I could get to Peru and see the remains of their empire for myself. I would never save enough money working for the NHS, so there was only one thing for it: I had to get a job in America. But how? And where?

The where surely had to be New York – the only city I knew anything about – but when I was chatting to someone knowledgeable about my plans they took on a serious, caring expression. 'Oh I don't think so! New York gets terribly, horribly hot in the summer. About 95 degrees. You'll hate it.' Hmm. I hauled out the atlas and looked for a biggish town to the north of New York. North equals cooler, right? Boston! I'd heard of it and it seemed as good as anywhere, so

I took myself off to the American Embassy in Grosvenor Square and asked to look at Boston's telephone Yellow Pages. Turning to the letter 'H' I found plenty of hospitals and noted down all their addresses. Only one replied to my letter: the Robert B. Brigham hospital, which specialised in arthritis, and they bravely offered me a job without an interview.

Friends and family speculated that I would marry an American and disappear forever, an unwelcome thought considering how much I loved England. So as a sort of insurance I bet a friend £5 (a significant sum on money in those days) that I would not marry an American. I still have the relevant piece of paper.

It was a big adjustment being alone in a new country, in a new city and in a new job, but slowly, very slowly, I learned what to do and how to behave. I learned that you can't just walk into a café and plonk yourself down at a table, you must wait to be seated, and you can't leave the library through the wrong door without being roughly searched by a man with a gun on his hip. I learned how to do my job and made lifelong friends. And an extraordinarily large amount of money was paid into my bank account each month. I had a black-and-white photo of Machu Picchu on my wall to remind myself why I was there, and after eighteen months I set out with a friend and her VW Beetle to see America.

To arrive in San Francisco in 1967, the Summer of Love, was quite something. Far out. Groovy. The trees in Golden Gate Park had curiously flat tops; on closer inspection it transpired that it was because the hippies were roosting there. The flower beds were bare because at every step an earnest young person with long hair would offer me a bloom. I learned to recognise the smell of marijuana smoke, and to travel by cable car (often the two went together).

And I shared an apartment with two English friends from the olden days. What I didn't do is find a job. No one wanted an OT, even though by now I had my American registration. As Christmas approached I was down to my last $5, so applied for a job at Macy's department store. First I had to take a maths test. I failed. Crestfallen, I applied the next day in disguise and failed again. Clearly it was OT or penury.

I eventually settled for a split job in two 'convalescent hospitals' in Menlo Park and Palo Alto, both a train ride south of the city. Actually they were care homes, pretending to be for convalescents, and my early efforts at rehabilitation were not what was wanted. My job was to oversee the two Activities Directors who ran the daily hobbies and entertainment sessions, working two days in each place. So I had Mondays off – quite a bonus in San Francisco. I supplemented my income by babysitting and learned to relax. Then my new room-mate, Linda, arrived.

Linda was a true Californian. She took LSD, she seduced every man who ventured on her radar, and she cooked a batch of hash brownies which I saw cooling in the kitchen, thought 'Oh goody, brownies' and stole two for my breakfast before heading for the train station. I was high as a kite, fell asleep on the train thinking I was in a hammock, and wobbled into the hospital trying to focus. No one said anything – except for a furious Linda when I got home. But possibly that led one of my favourite residents, Charlie, who was having the time of his old age with a new respite patient, The Judge, to call me to one side with a question. Could I get hold of some marijuana? 'The Judge and I think we ought to try it before we die.' I rather regret, now, saying no.

INTERLUDE
HITCHHIKING WITH VAL

Hitchhiking teaches you about the kindness of strangers, but also to be suspicious, sometimes, of the kindness of strangers if you are young women. We acquired a sort of sixth sense of who to trust and who to be wary of...

Across Europe, down through Italy, and thence to Greece and on to Lebanon, Syria, Jordan and Israel, we got into hundreds of cars and lorries, and got out of them unscathed, although there were indeed a few dodgy moments. Here's one.

One golden rule was never to hitch after dark, and the sun had already set when a car stopped for our final ride into Athens, about 100 miles away. It was driven by an old man (who knows how old he really was – maybe only in his sixties) and he drove very, very slowly. We started to get anxious. We needed to find a flat roof to sleep on or maybe a room in a private house. We shared our anxieties with the driver. It was all right, he told us, he had a warehouse that we could sleep in. What he didn't tell us was that he planned to join us.

When he opened the warehouse door and turned on the light there was a mass scuttle and dozens of cockroaches fled behind the stacks of cardboard boxes. It was not looking promising. When he sat down on the one bed it looked even less promising. We moved hastily to another section of the building and laid out our sleeping bags. And then we heard it: the sound of undressing. And then we saw it: a skinny hand appeared round a pile of boxes and beckoned. 'Come on!'

Val and I looked at each other in horror. Hastily, and quietly, we packed up our sleeping bags, shouldered our packs, and slipped out into the dark. It was after midnight, we had no idea where we were – we just knew we needed to get away. We walked in the direction of some lights. Then we heard a motor and saw his car. He was coming after us! We dodged behind a newspaper stand. The car passed, stopped, and reversed. Oh God, he'd seen us! We retreated into a shop doorway. We heard the car door open. But... but what was it that had just been dropped on the pavement?

It was my small overnight bag which, in our haste to leave, I had left in the warehouse.

2

LATIN AMERICA

During my eighteen months in San Francisco I was planning my trip to Peru, the land of the Incas, and saving every cent that I could earn. Linda, infected by my enthusiasm, announced that she was coming too, providing we could travel down the length of the Amazon. Oh yes, let's factor that in. I relished the thought of having company, being more nervous about this trip into the unknown than I let on. In the 1960s the only guidebook that was any use to overland travellers was the iconic *How to travel without being rich*, by Norman Ford, first published in the 1950s. Covering the world, it wasn't exactly detailed on South America, but it did describe how to travel down the Pan-American Highway.

On March 14 1969 I boarded a flight from San Francisco to Mexico City, without Linda. She had decided she couldn't be away for such a long time (I reckoned we'd need at least three months), but she assured me we would meet in Lima. So instead my travel companion for two weeks was Peter, a middle-aged doctor I'd worked with in Boston. I was horribly impatient with this poor man who'd never travelled on a tight budget, and who fell in with my plans every step of the way – and, after all, if he was obsessed with cleanliness and his health it was a reasonable preoccupation given his profession.

Revisiting my record of that Latin American journey after a gap of more than fifty years I'm surprised and rather impressed at how self-reliant I was. Not at all the gauche, socially inept young woman I remember. America had changed me. I relished the pleasure that comes with engaging with interesting people, the sort I'd never normally meet: naturalists, anthropologists, professors. Among travellers there is a an undertone of disapproval if you seek out people who share your language and culture but most people need this relief from otherness when travelling for months.

Peter and I travelled together through Mexico to Lake Atitlán in Guatemala. The downside was that we had to stay in rather more expensive hotels than I had budgeted for – sometimes as much as $3 a night – but the upside was his arrangement to stay at Trudi Blom's place, Casa Na Bolom (the House of the Jaguar), in San Cristóbal de las Casas. Trudi was an extraordinary Swiss woman, a social anthropologist and photographer with a love for the culture of the Lacandon Maya people in Chiapas. Later in the '70s, she became a passionate environmentalist and an early activist against the destruction of the rainforest. After her husband died she ran her home as an exclusive guesthouse for 'students of serious intent'. She was quite fussy about this, so I don't know how we qualified. It was probably Peter's profession that convinced her. One time a fellow guest answered the doorbell. 'It was a hippie with a faraway look in his eyes. I sent him on his way.' Peter and I stayed there for a week. During the day we visited the nearby villages, astonished at the cultural integrity of the people in their different costumes. No one wore Western clothes. I discovered the benefit of sketching people rather than photographing them. Children loved it, adults were fascinated, I could give the rather unflattering portrait to the sitter, and there was none of the obtrusiveness of photography. Finding ways to look without intruding was always an issue. Peter had – quite rightly – reprimanded me for staring at people as though at a zoo. Dinner time was for conversation around the large table. I noted in my journal that I would never normally have dared talk to these erudite people but in this relaxed atmosphere it was no problem.

Each day we walked or got a lift to a different village.

Today we hitched a ride to Chamula, the village for the tribe of the same name… The church was one of the most spiritual I have ever been in. Pine needles had been scattered on the floor and small groups of Chamulas, mainly women wearing their heavy black embroidered woollen skirts, were squatting near their candles, either silent, or whispering, or breaking out into an individual chant. The candles are offerings to God in return for granting a request. One poor woman was distraught because her transistor radio had broken and was offering a candle to the deity in return for a quick repair job. The sides of the church were lined with painted wooden saints, thick with clothing. A new garment is provided each year, and the old one is never removed. Some had 14 or 15.

Peter left for home from Guatemala, a country I instantly fell in love with, so I was more excited than scared to find myself alone. Actually not true, I was very scared, but the antidote was Lake Atitlán, which Aldous Huxley described as 'exceeding the limit of the permissibly picturesque' and Holy Week in Antigua, watching the processions of wooden saints – one of whom carried his own umbrella against sudden rainstorms – and marvelling at the intricate 'carpets' created from coloured sawdust and flower petals. And there were the Guatemalan markets, always interesting, sometimes a challenge.

There was also a covered market, the entrance to which resembled a rugby scrum. Instead of forming two orderly streams, the goers-in and the comers-out faced each other in two opposing forces and shoved. The numbers being more or less equal, nothing happened for some time except sudden bulges to the sides which were controlled by the women traders on the perimeter who pushed hard at anyone likely to bulge on to her wares. It was a bit like dough being kneaded, but with everyone in great humour except for the wailing babies on backs, who were being squashed. At least I assumed they were babies since they were completely covered; one turned out to be a lamb. Eventually something gave and we burst into the building to relative peace.

Thereafter I pretty much followed the Pan-American Highway, sometimes linking up with other travellers, and flying the short distance from Panama to Barranquilla in Colombia. Mostly I was on my own, stoically spending days and nights on buses which broke down as a matter of course, usually for at least three hours, and which stopped for inedible meals in rustic restaurants. In between were the evenings, or days, of luxury, because the South Americans were insistent that it was incredibly dangerous travelling on my own and the only way to avoid having my throat cut was to stay in their houses and let them protect me. This way I enjoyed endless hospitality, learned Spanish and had the opportunity really to get to know the people. And, from a purely practical point of view, all those free beds and dinners worked wonders for my $5-a-day budget.

The first and culturally the most memorable of these house-stays was in Colombia. The train from Santa Marta on the coast to Bogotá was entrancing, a rather bumpy 24-hour trip, but passing through jungle vegetation bright with flowers and birds including a flight of macaws. As we approached Bogotá a young lad with floppy black hair, laughing eyes, and callipers on his legs swung himself along the aisle, using the seats as supports, so he could have a conversation with me. My Spanish at that stage was pretty basic. Most of my vocabulary came from Californian place names and there's a limit to what you can do with 'tall stick', 'the angels' and 'big river'. But we managed and he re-emerged, with his crutches, when I had disembarked – clutching my bags for fear of thieves – and asking around for a cheap hotel. As so often happened, my presence soon became immaterial as the large crowd that surrounded me started to argue among themselves about my best course of action. The teenager took charge, whisked me into a taxi, and somewhat to my confusion I found myself in his house and learned, through his English-speaking brother, that I was to stay there. Fortunately they found me uproariously funny. This was a good thing because there were six siblings – four brothers and two sisters – and Mama, who beamed gently throughout, and the house was not large, so my entertainment value helped assuage my guilt. The two boys who shared the room that I was given moved into a communal bed, and another slept on the living room floor.

They were a remarkable family. The youngest boy, Pablo, had been disabled by polio as a young child but was such an extrovert that he scarcely seemed to notice his disability. Their father had died seventeen years earlier and although they employed a maid (though I'm not sure actually whether she just lived with them) they were clearly quite poor. The children ranged in age from about sixteen to twenty-seven, but only one was earning. I stayed there for three days, and the meals were the same each day, even for breakfast: maize soup, mounds of potatoes, rice, popcorn and, once a day, a small amount of meat and perhaps some fruit. The boys vied with each other to talk to me, with a particular interest in improving my Spanish. I asked the best phrase to deter unwanted attention and was taught 'No jodas'. It slowly dawned on me how this translated, but it gave them such huge pleasure to hear me say it that I used it frequently with them just to get a laugh. They also taught me the response to the frequent question 'Are you married?' – 'No, and at your service'. Shameless! More worthy were our conversations about literature and politics. They wanted to discuss Sartre, Dickens and Tolstoy – and Harold Wilson.

In complete contrast, the next stay of several days in a private home was near Quito with the Bukovskys. I had met Jorge when I treated his mother at the Robert Brigham in Boston and, when he heard of my long-term plans to travel in South America, he insisted that I keep his address for when I was in Ecuador. At dinner in a Quito restaurant I learned that his great passion in life was horses and that he had a stable of showjumpers. Sharing this passion, but without the stable of horses, there was no question of me *not* staying with his family. My journal is full of exclamation marks. 'A hot bath – an actual bath *tub*! A loo *seat*! A proper towel!' And as for the horses… These were thoroughbreds which competed in showjumping events all over Ecuador. I rode and jumped every day and under Jorge's critical eye improved significantly. I ate lots of cake, met some distinguished people, and felt quite discombobulated by the contrast with the rest of my travels. Time to move on.

In fact, I've got ahead of myself (or of my journey) because there was quite a bit of Colombia still to experience before I got to Ecuador. For instance, there was the time I was trying to get from Cali to Popayán by train. Finding myself alone in a train compartment with a young railway policeman I felt a bit uneasy and resisted his attempts at conversation. Then the train stopped in the middle of nowhere. A landslide had blocked the line, but I didn't know that. We were there for four hours and it grew dark outside. Then the lights went out and I was scared. Sitting in darkness, my heart thumping, I sought to distract him and pointed out the fireflies dancing outside the window. He muttered something, opened the carriage door and jumped on to the track. I couldn't imagine what he was doing and my anxiety increased. Then he reappeared, beaming with delight, with his scarf over his cap – which he whisked away to release half a dozen fireflies into the carriage. My fear dissolved into laughter, the lights came back on, the train started to move, and I spent the retreat back to Cali with my Spanish dictionary achieving a conversation of sorts. He became my guardian and insisted on carrying my bags, helping me find a hotel and checking that the price was appropriate. Then we shook hands warmly and he disappeared.

My positive feeling towards the Cali police was reinforced the following day when I made another attempt to leave the city, this time by bus, which I had been told went at 8am. Arriving at the bus station in good time I learned that it actually left at 10am so I had two hours to kill. As I strolled through the town lost in my own thoughts, a hand suddenly shot out from nowhere and wrenched my watch from my wrist. I watched the boy run up a side street and, always hating to make a scene, was in two minds as to whether to do anything. Then I thought what a nuisance it would be to travel without a watch, so I set off in hot pursuit, at a brisk walk, muttering 'the bastard took my watch' to the mildly curious onlookers, until one pointed out two policemen. One of these set off at a very commendable run, and to my astonishment returned with the boy – and my watch. Our little procession made its way to the police station – the two policemen, the boy and me, plus about fifty locals who were having their best day for quite a while. The boy and I were seated opposite each other. He muttered continuously and incomprehensively to me while I looked up words in my dictionary to indicate that I wasn't angry. The policeman returned with a form which I signed, though I have no idea what it said, and I had a police escort back to the bus station. I had very effectively killed those spare two hours.

Back to Quito, where I very reluctantly left the Bukovsky cocoon, which really *wasn't* the real South America, to continue on to Lima. I had kept in touch with Linda who, to my relief and some surprise, was indeed planning to meet me in the Peruvian capital. In our last communication we had even agreed on a date.

Attracted by the brochure depicting passengers lying back in their seats in an ecstasy of smiles, I decided to splash out on a Tepsa bus which apparently gave you forty hours of undiluted pleasure for the modest price of $25. The first part of the journey was indeed very enjoyable, winding over the Andes – with me peering nervously over the precipices at the wrecked cars below – and passing herds of llamas with their coloured ear tassels. There were only six of us on the bus, so the first night I curled up comfortably on my double seat, only drowsily aware that the surface of the road seemed to be deteriorating. At 2am I was woken by animated conversation. It seemed that the driver didn't like the look of the road ahead, and proposed to wait until dawn to proceed. He reached up to the first-aid box located reassuringly above my seat and produced some bananas to tide us over until first light. At six he still didn't like the look of the road, but thought that perhaps later... At eleven, when it was apparently still the same (I hadn't ventured out to see for myself since it had rained steadily for the whole nine hours), we turned back to the nearest town, Guayaquil, a steamy, banana-ridden port. After a free night in a hotel, we tried again the next morning. We six passengers were quite pally by then. I never knew what was going on but decided it didn't matter. Nothing I could do except read my James Bond book (thank goodness for Ian Fleming during all these breakdowns). 'The sun will help,' my new friends assured me, although since it was still raining I was a little sceptical. When we reached the troublesome stretch of road I could understand the problem. The rain had reduced it to a quagmire, two trucks were stuck in axle-deep mud and a cheery gang of volunteers were straining to get them out. Our bus driver roared his engine, drove straight in as fast as he could, and got stuck. Three hours later they were discussing the possibility of getting a tractor to pull us out, although it would mean waiting another five hours. I wandered off into the jungle to soothe my nerves and for a call of nature, not believing that the latest towing effort would succeed. I was amazed to hear a resounding cheer and the roar of engines which announced that the bus had been rescued.

The Peruvian frontier was closed. As I suppose it would be since it was late evening when we arrived. The other passengers slept on the bus but I'd had enough and stomped off to a dingy hotel. I felt almost cheerful after a night in a bed – of sorts – and loved the bleakness of the Peruvian desert landscape, the most desolate I'd seen since the Middle East. Dinner that evening was notable for the most revolting food and surroundings of the trip so far. The cockroaches were so thick on the ground you couldn't help treading on the creatures, and the loo was a stinking hole in the floor – or where the floor would be if you could see it through the seething mass of cockroaches. I had to shake them out of my clothes and hair when I emerged.

I deserved to splash out on a $2 hotel in Lima before embarking on the highlight of every capital – the trip to the American Express office to pick up my mail. Quite apart from the longed-for letters from friends and family I was anxiously hoping to hear from Linda, so was anguished when I received the message saying she'd given up waiting and had left the previous day. After reading the letters over a cup of coffee nearby I was standing vacantly in the plaza trying to get my bearings when I was hit by a shrieking, whirling tornado. Linda!

Of course we talked and talked, and planned and planned. The decision was that she would leave the next day for the Amazon – Pucallpa – having met an anthropologist who had invited her to stay in 'her' Shipibo village. Certainly not an offer to pass up. And I would finally – finally! – achieve that five-year ambition and see the Inca sites around Cusco. And visit Machu Picchu.

I was getting fed up with South American buses. The statutory three-hour breakdowns were no longer a novelty, and when they happened above 13,000ft, at night, it was *cold*. Two consecutive nights on crowded buses which arrived six hours late tried my patience but Cusco was, of course, worth it. I marvelled at the Inca stonework, taking pages in my letter home to describe the exact fit of stone on stone and the beauty of those ancient walls. I left out an incident at Sacsayhuamán, the fortress above Cusco, though it's in my journal:

I passed a man and greeted him in the usual way. He stopped, turned round and started following me. I walked quicker, so did he. We were quite a way from any other people. I slowed down and hoped he would pass me. He moved alongside and started talking. 'No entiendo.' So to make his meaning clear he patted my bottom. 'Stop that!' I said. He didn't and started to open his flies. A wave of fury surged through me and I raised my fist. 'If you don't go away I'll hit you!' He went.

It did rather spoil the morning, however. About twenty years later I was back in Sacsayhuamán and a similar thing happened. This time the optimist was a young teenager, maybe fifteen or sixteen. I remember smiling and carefully composing the sentence: 'I'm old enough to be your mother!' At which he cried 'Mama!' and threw his arms round my neck. I had to laugh and we parted on good terms.

Machu Picchu! Finally the day had arrived. I'd booked a ticket on the posh train, the *autovagón*, and the nice manager of my *hostería* said he would look after my luggage so I could spend the night away. But when the morning came it was clear that I was going nowhere. I'd spent most of the night on the loo, and throwing up *into* the loo. At around 8.30am the manager knocked on my door, worried that I'd overslept. I explained the problem. He was very solicitous, brought me coca tea, which I couldn't keep down, and kept popping in to see how I was doing. On one visit he brought another hotel guest, a man representing a pharmaceutical company, who arrived simply laden with pills and potions. I agreed to have supper with him if I was feeling better – which I was. He was such a sweet, kind man.

Machu Picchu was everything that I hoped and more. The train journey, which followed the Río Urubamba through a deep canyon with glimpses of snow-capped mountains through the glass roof, was surely the most scenic I'd ever taken, and the setting, with the ruins balanced on the one bit of flat ground between lumpy mountains and plunging valleys, was unique. Clouds settled in the dips, orchids waved their pink flowers in the breeze, and the only day trippers, a group of about ten, left after an hour's tour, leaving me, and the other three gringos I'd travelled with, alone. We had permission to spend the night in one of the ruins, which had a cosy straw-covered floor for the purpose. A full moon lit the site almost as brightly as daylight. David, a Peace Corps volunteer, and I wandered around until we were chased back into our sleeping bags by the Mad Inca who patrolled the site blowing a whistle and waving a machete to keep the evil spirits at bay.

Next day we watched the rising sun light the Inca sundial, climbed the stone staircase up Huayna Picchu, and followed a trail up to a majestic Inca archway adorned with orchids. Beyond it stretched a faint trail. 'I'm sure,' I thought to myself, 'that this path must lead to Cusco.'

Our journey from Pucallpa in Peru to Manaus in Brazil down the Ucayali and, briefly, the Amazon took fifteen days of actual river travel. Waiting around hoping for a free ride by boat or air took us twenty-six days. Ridiculous. Such is life when travelling frugally, but it somewhat soured the river experience – which was not helped by Linda catching hepatitis from Berndt, our German anthropologist travel companion, and I knew it was probably only a matter of time before I came down with it too.

Life on the river when we were actually moving, however, was constantly interesting, and is all that needs to be described here.

Our first boat, the *Huallaga*, took us from Pucallpa, the highest navigable point on the Ucayali, to Iquitos, Peru's main Amazonian port and its link to the Atlantic. We found the captain, a triangular man who looked like a frog, rocking gently in his hammock. He confirmed that he had a cabin available. It was tiny, the bunks consisted of slatted wood with straw mattresses, and there was no mosquito screening, something we only discovered the first night when we unaccountably stopped for a few hours and hundreds of excited, hungry mosquitoes swarmed in. I cocooned myself into my sheet sleeping bag which was stiflingly hot and not much help. The insects simply poked their nasty little proboscises through the thin cotton and had their meal. In the morning the bag was polka-dotted in red.

The captain, Lucho, took a fancy to us – well, to Linda – and gave us some mysterious green fruit we'd never seen before. It was absolutely delicious but there was a payback. It contained some sort of latex which performed as well as superglue, sealing our lips and fingers together. Lucho watched, chortling, for quite a while as we mimed our predicament, before releasing us with some alcohol.

I had imagined that a boat trip down a narrow tributary would be like a movie, with all sorts of wonderful wildlife queuing up to be photographed, so it was disappointing that the only terrestrial wildlife we saw the entire trip was either destined to become our dinner or unhappy pets for the other passengers. Mind you, my diary reveals that I bargained for half an hour for an Amazonian parrot, was sorely tempted by an albino squirrel monkey and was besotted by a baby kinkajou. We have come a long way in our understanding of the evils of the wildlife trade.

> Dawn on this boat sounds more like a farmyard or a zoo, with the crowing of about ten cocks, the squealing of a couple of pigs, also some ducks, turkeys, two monkeys and a parrot. This evening I was sketching while waiting my turn at Scrabble when a man came up and explained that he wants me to draw him a picture of a mermaid to have tattooed on his leg. He thought it

Above: Older brother Andrew and baby Kate with a rather impatient me, a few months before my Bournemouth adventure, 1944

Below: Val (right) and me in Greece, hitchhiking to the Middle East, 1963

Below: Driving across the USA to San Francisco, 1967

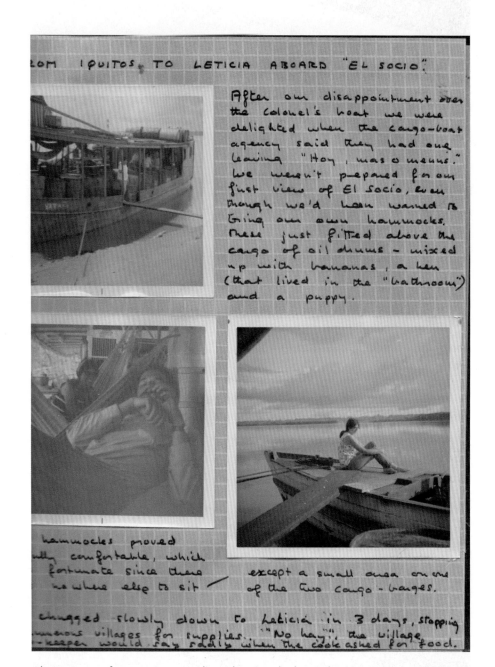

After our disappointment over the Colonel's boat we were delighted when the cargo-boat agency said they had one leaving "Hoy, mas o menos." We weren't prepared for our first view of El Socio, even though we'd been warned to bring our own hammocks. These just fitted above the cargo of oil drums – mixed up with bananas, a hen (that lived in the "bathroom") and a puppy.

hammocks proved ...lly comfortable, which ...fortunate since there ...owhere else to sit

except a small area on one of the two cargo-barges.

...chugged slowly down to Leticia in 3 days, stopping ...numerous villages for supplies. "No hay", the village ...keeper would say sadly when the cook asked for food.

Above: A page from my Amazon diary showing the boat *El Socio*, 1969

Above: 1973: Colombia's buses were particularly colourful and artistic (and of their time)

Below: A scene typical of all South American buses in the 1970s

Above: Otavalo livestock market, Ecuador

Our three weeks among the wildlife of the Galápagos Islands was one of the highlights of our South American trip. *Above:* Blue-footed booby

Below: Giant tortoise on Santa Cruz island

could move seductively with his muscles (demonstration). I was only too happy to oblige.

At dawn, shortly before our arrival at Iquitos, Berndt woke us to point out the pink river dolphins, *bufeos*, cavorting around the boat. Wonderful! At last here was some endemic wildlife. A fellow passenger told me some of the myths attached to these animals. Young girls were particularly at risk from the dolphins, which could assume the shape of a man and lure a maiden to her death. And if she had the misfortune to see a *bufeo* while having her period it might launch a sexual attack, in which case she would give birth to a baby dolphin. (My knowledge of how conception works suggests that the risk is very low.)

We stayed in Iquitos a ridiculously long time – twelve days – so once we knew for sure that we were not going to be offered a free ride on a luxury boat we were ready to take the first vessel available. Linda and I were taken aback when we first saw *El Socio*. Our transport for the next few days was a small, sturdy motor boat. Firmly roped on each side were two barges, one piled with oil drums from bow to stern, the other half-covered with oil drums. The remaining area was part-kitchen, part-sleeping space, and also contained the captain's cabin and the toilet. Boarding the boat with our luggage was a precarious undertaking, negotiating the two wobbly planks and an expanse of mud and river. We'd been told to buy hammocks for this journey and also mosquito nets, so our sleeping arrangements were actually much more comfortable than on the *Huallaga*. There were only five other passengers and we just had room to sling our hammocks side by side. We had to stay in them most of the day since there was nowhere to sit. The kitchen consisted of three Primus stoves, around which we queued for noodles cooked in river water.

We didn't venture into the toilet until nightfall. Crawling under the cook's bulky hammock, pocket torch in hand, Linda went in first.

A shriek, a squawk and the news that 'I think there's a hen in here!'. The poor bird looked utterly miserable. Not only was it going to end up as dinner one night, but the tiny space contained both the toilet and a makeshift shower so the hen was always underfoot or being soaked. It did indeed disappear one evening to relieve our monotonous diet, only to be replaced by turtles stacked on their backs, rendering the shower unusable and the toilet needing a feat of athleticism to accomplish successfully. Not that it mattered much, since we were the only women and all the men just peed over the side.

We disembarked at Leticia, at the tip of the prong of Colombia that gives it access to the Amazon and so to the Atlantic. On the other side of the river was the Brazilian town of Benjamin Constant and Peru's Ramón Castilla was a short boat trip away. For a few days we popped back and forth between the three countries before settling for a proper passenger boat to Manaus. At $20 for ten days it seemed reasonable enough and we'd been told there were proper meals. And we'd have a cabin.

The *Cidade de Manaus* was what is sometimes described as a 'bird-cage boat', with three storeys open at the sides. The hold was full of Brazil nuts, and the lower deck was home to a variety of livestock. We passengers had the top two decks. It was the first time we'd had decent food and the time passed agreeably although we struggled with the switch from Spanish to Portuguese. The boat stopped at every river settlement to take on more passengers or to do some trading, and there was always something interesting going on. In the first settlement a woman was weaving a palm thatch for her roof, plaiting the fronds together in a complicated pattern, and in another the whole village seemed to be involved in making ceramic pots. We watched them dig the clay out of the ground, squidge it up with pounded coarse charcoal, then roll dozens of snakes to create pots of all shapes and sizes using the coil method. Colour and decoration were added before baking in a firepit.

At another stop the cook strode into a field and slaughtered an ox, skinning and butchering it in situ while the rest of the herd crowded round to have a closer look. One of the bigger places, São Paulo de Olivença, was a perfect example of a rubber boom town without the wealth or tourism to maintain it after the price of rubber collapsed. It had a handsome church and colourful tiled streets, but with grass growing through the cracks and a feeling of decay everywhere – except inside the church, which had two new drums, an electric guitar and an amplifier ready for use.

Manaus, of course, is *the* rubber boom town, thriving from the 1870s through to the early decades of the twentieth century, and the sight of its lavish opera house, in the middle of the jungle – accessible only by river during the boom years – was quite extraordinary. And talking of extraordinary, a couple of days after disembarking we were invited aboard an American boat to listen to a broadcast of an event that would make history: the moon landing. It was tremendously exciting, if somewhat confusing with the jumble of languages as the local radio station translated the American commentary. When the *Eagle* landed on the moon at 4.17pm (EDT) on July 20, all the church bells in Manaus rang out. Indeed, bells rang out all over Brazil. Later that day I got into conversation with a local who spoke some Spanish (I never really got to grips with Portuguese). I told him a man had landed on the moon. 'Oh no,' he said, 'that's not possible. You only go there after you die.'

After six days in Manaus, trying fruitlessly to get a free flight, we did the sensible thing and paid for one. I had had enough of river travel, and anyway the closer we got to the mouth of the Amazon the less exciting it was likely to be. Linda flew to Rio to recover from hepatitis and I took the shorter route to Belém, then three consecutive and utterly dreadful days on a bus to Brasília and on to Ouro Preto to stay with my poet friend Elizabeth Bishop, and recharge my emotional batteries.

Linda and I met up again in Rio and continued up the coast of Brazil. She was still not well and I was on my way home, so sightseeing was becoming less exciting for both of us. I'd also run out of money and was starting to feel a bit poorly, but there was one more evening which deserves a mention because it was so very strange. Macumba, which we were invited to observe in Maceió, in the northeast of Brazil, was, our friends explained, a ceremony brought from West Africa through the slave trade. That's all we knew.

We were the only foreigners there. From the street we could hear the beat of drums and the sound of chanting. We went into the small room and stood with a group of people against the walls. The floor was strewn with rose petals, and paper chains strung from the ceiling. Two men were beating out the rhythm on drums, and a small boy joined in with a large triangle. About eight people, men and women, were shuffling round in a circle, keeping time but hardly dancing. They were dressed in red, the men with red satin jackets and caps and the women with a full blouse over long, full black-and-white skirts and a bandana on their heads. For about an hour there was just the beat of the drums and the chanting from one of the drummers. Then we saw a struggle outside the room where some men were trying to restrain a man in a trance. They eventually let him go and he entered the room in a crouched position, his hands clenched behind his back and his face screwed up. He danced convulsively the whole evening, sometimes letting out screams, and sometimes coming up to onlookers and bumping shoulders in a ritualistic way. Soon one of the women from the dancing circle started staring and jerking, eventually bending backwards to the floor, screaming and shouting in a harsh voice. Gradually the beat increased and the other women joined in, clapping and chanting, and more of the circle became involved, suddenly jerking their bodies, widening their eyes, and dancing convulsively. As time went on, one of the onlookers would suddenly leap forward, to be restrained by their friends who held their arms and head, blew into their ears and slapped their hands. This usually worked and with a great effort they would calm down.

What was it all about? I've no idea. That's how it often is with travel. You see things that make no sense whatsoever. It's one of the attractions.

The following day I took a bus to Recife and caught a plane home, arriving in England on August 26, just in time to have my hepatitis treated on the NHS.

After six months, however, I was back in Boston, or rather Cambridge. I missed my friends there, my former room-mates were keen to share an apartment again, and I'd been offered a good job in a nearby rehab centre – although only after six weeks. My financial state was precarious, and when I found I was down to my last $10 I was galvanised into action and visited the Massachusetts Employment Bureau and asked them to find me a temporary job. We decided I was so unskilled that waitressing was the only possibility and she sent me off to a sleazy place near the station. It looked so awful I walked up and down for fifteen minutes before venturing inside for my interview. The Greek proprietor said 'Start tomorrow at seven', so I did.

He put me to work behind the counter, and for the next hour the two other waitresses tripped over me, rushing here and there. They otherwise ignored me except when a customer pushed a tip my way, at which point one swooped down with 'Now *she* didn't wait on you, did she?' and pocketed the money. Actually, I thought I was doing rather well. I didn't drop anything, just slopped coffee into the saucers, which didn't seem to matter, and made audible calculations on my fingers to work out the change and stared at the till for long minutes trying to figure out which buttons to press. The other women continued to race around apparently producing food from their armpits while I tried to wrap a doughnut daintily and work out what someone meant by 'Two sunny side up, please'. After an hour the proprietor kindly, but firmly, took me to one side and told me he could see I wasn't going to fit in and was too slow. So I was fired. Total earnings: 10 cents.

It was now the spring of 1971. I was in a good job in Cambridge, had a comfortable shared apartment nearby, and an Amazonian parrot called Portnoy. Then I met George. On our first date I was surprised and delighted to learn that he not only knew about the Galápagos Islands (very few people did in those days) but had read up on the subject through his job as a librarian. This was only one of the many interests we found we had in common.

He was also an enthusiastic backpacker. No, he was an obsessive backpacker, spending three months every summer in some remote area of the US hiking around on his own carrying all his needs in a rucksack (including a dozen or so back copies of *The New York Times*). I'd done some backpacking – indeed, I'd hiked 100 miles of the 2,000-mile-long Appalachian Trail – but had sworn never to carry a backpack again. To George I was an obsessive traveller, willing to abandon my job and friends and head off somewhere exotic at the drop of a hat. He'd done some travelling but considered there was no reason to leave his home country, which, in his eyes, had the monopoly on beautiful scenery.

We knew early on in our relationship that we would travel together. But where? Compromise was needed. It took quite a bit of discussion but I think we both thought that we would eventually go to South America, including, of course, the Galapágos. I agreed to carry a backpack and even indulge in some gentle hiking if he agreed to travel the length of South America, from top to bottom.

Our plans were taking shape.

INTERLUDE
HITCHHIKING WITH GEORGE

For our first holiday together, George and I wanted to explore New England and northeast Canada. By thumb, of course. The of course had come as a bit of a shock when I first met this maverick American who didn't own a car (what? Is that possible?). I had assumed that I'd put my hitchhiking days behind me, that I had finally grown up. Not so, thank goodness. It's probably my enthusiasm for hitchhiking, as much as anything, that has given me my incorrigibly optimistic outlook. Here are just a few of the memorable people we met on that trip.

I can't remember the name of the island off the Maine coast where we had our most extraordinary encounter. We took a ferry there and planned to spend the day seeing as much as we could before returning to the mainland. A man soon stopped and we explained our open-ended plans. 'OK,' he said, 'I'll show you where I live'. He then drove us a few miles before stopping outside a white clapboard house where he got out, indicated the driver's seat and said, 'You kids go and explore. This is my house – just bring the car back when you've finished'.

Another time, another place, and an elderly man stopped for us and asked where we wanted to go. 'Well, where are *you* going?' we asked. He explained that it was up to us. He spent his days driving around looking for hitchhikers. 'Listen, I'm retired, I love driving, and I like people. My wife says that one day some young girl is gonna accuse me of rape. But look at me! Do I look *capable* of rape?' He gave a wheezy laugh. 'Now where do you folks wanna go?'

It's relatively rare to meet such exceptionally open-handed kindness, but every lift brings an opportunity to give as well as receive. George was good at this, a great conversationalist and always interested in other people's lives. Often the driver just wanted to talk; that was fine, we listened. But I remember one couple who drove in tight-lipped silence for half an hour after picking us up (we learned later that they'd argued about whether to stop for us). By the end of the day, however, we joined forces to have a lobster and wine feast in a hired cabin on the Canadian coast. 'Boy, I'm glad we stopped for you guys!' the husband said. 'We were going to drive back to Boston tonight.'

In Nova Scotia a pea-green VW Beetle stopped for us. We noticed the dog collar and learned that the driver was a Catholic priest in a remote rural community. He was talkative and interesting. After a while he said, 'Why don't you come and stay the night and help me eat up all the produce my parishioners insist on giving me?' Sure enough, the fridge was crammed full with home-grown vegetables, fruit and eggs. After our feast George asked if the priest could show us round his church. He looked a bit surprised. 'Are you sure?' We were, and of course it was fascinating. Neither of us had had the opportunity before to learn about the Catholic church service, the vestments, and all the intricacies of this faith.

Is there any better way of meeting surprising people? If so, I don't know of it. I can now truthfully say I've hitchhiked every decade of my life except the first, including, just a few weeks ago, in Germany – and thus can claim a full eight decades of thumbing lifts.

PART 2

SOUTH AMERICA 1973–74

at us in horror, & dived back in as
squawking & flapping -> he finally de
were the lesser of 2 evils & fled to his
    When we surprised a group close
they'd be overcome ~~in~~ by panic &
the water using all four 'feet' & to
stumbling on the boulders. I suppose
as painful as it looks — We tried our b
not to provoke ~~a~~ such a reaction bu
seemed inevitable.
    We went nearly 8 miles looking fo
before turning back & having rather
arduous walk with rain beating i
faces & strong wind.   We were ver
to get back to our nice peat stove & he
such luxury!

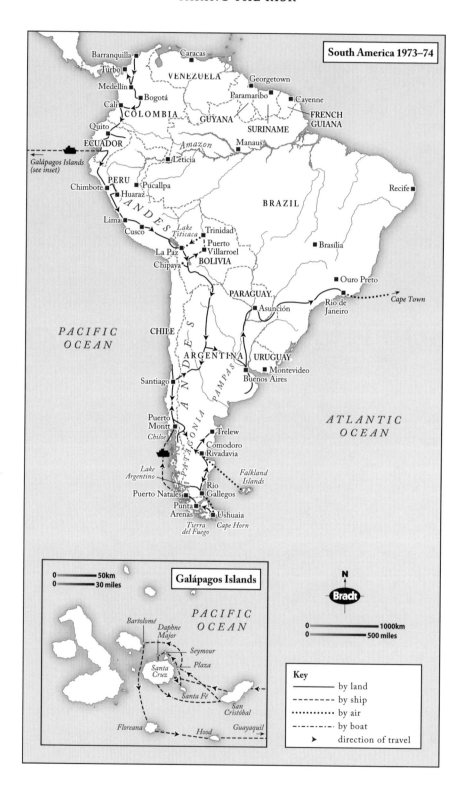

South America 1973–74

Barranquilla
Turbo
Medellín
Cali
Quito
COLOMBIA
ECUADOR

Galápagos Islands
(see inset)

Caracas
VENEZUELA
Bogotá
GUYANA

Georgetown
Paramaribo
Cayenne
SURINAME
FRENCH
GUIANA

Amazon
Manaus
Leticia

Chimbote
PERU
Pucallpa
Huaraz
Lima
Cusco
Lake Titicaca
La Paz
Chipaya
BOLIVIA

BRAZIL

Recife

Trinidad
Puerto
Villarroel
Brasília

Ouro Preto

Cape Town

PARAGUAY
Asunción
Río de
Janeiro

PACIFIC
OCEAN

CHILE
ARGENTINA
Santiago
Buenos Aires

PAMPAS

URUGUAY
Montevideo

ATLANTIC
OCEAN

Puerto
Montt
Chiloé
Trelew
Comodoro
Rivadavia

PATAGONIA

Lake
Argentino
Puerto Natales
Falkland
Islands
Río
Gallegos
Punta
Arenas
Ushuaia
Tierra
del Fuego
Cape Horn

0   50km
0   30 miles

Galápagos Islands

N

Bradt

0   1000km
0   500 miles

Bartolomé
Daphne
Major
Seymour
Santa
Cruz
Plaza
Santa Fé
San
Cristóbal
Floreana
Hood
Guayaquil

PACIFIC
OCEAN

Key
———— by land
– – – – by ship
• • • • • by air
–·–·–·– by boat
➤ direction of travel

3

THE JOURNEY BEGINS

I proposed to George on February 29 1972, thus losing my £5 bet. 'After all,' I said persuasively, 'I'm sure it will be easier to travel as Mr and Mrs Bradt and have the same name on our passports.'

It was a damned fine wedding; frugal, some might say exploitative of our friends and guests, and very American 1970s. We got married in Harvard Gardens and wrote our own vows, guests read poetry and a folk singer sang about love. The legal part was performed by a Lutheran minister who, in our pre-wedding chat, asked, 'Do you mind if I mention God?' A friend made my wedding dress, and another friend baked a magnificent cake. Our contribution was a suckling pig which turned seductively on a spit while guests tucked into a pot-luck meal with the many dishes that they themselves had supplied. My parents flew over from England and came with us on our honeymoon, touring New England in a hired car.

The best part was the wedding presents. George had done some muttering about the pointlessness of monogrammed towels when we were soon to be on our travels, so we hit on a unique plan. A list was compiled of expenses we expected to incur in South America, the first leg of what we now ambitiously assumed would be a round-the-world trip. Things like 'Hot shower – $5; bribe to get out of jail – $10; a day in the Galápagos – up to $100'. That way we raised $1,800 which, with some opportunities to earn money, lasted us eighteen months. And the givers received a reward too. Whenever we used a specific donation we wrote them a letter describing the pleasure it gave us – a hot shower after a week in the mountains, for instance, or – glory of glories – being surrounded by blue-footed boobies in the Galápagos. Whether their gift was large or small they got the full works, with the added bonus that it honed our writing skills. In this way we learned to 'paint the picture'.

A friend drove us to LL Bean, *the* store for climbers and backpackers, to get fitted out for our agreed not-much-hiking trip. But I did need a backpack, so bought the then state-of-the-art design with a light aluminium frame – good for keeping cool in tropical countries. I also purchased a sleeping bag, and a little Camping Gaz stove so we could cook our own food. A tent would be too heavy and too bulky, so I made one appropriate for the tropics out of mosquito netting with a multi-use tarpaulin for a fly. I refused to buy hiking boots; my Clarks walking shoes were fine for our sort of travel. 'We'll need some freeze-dried food,' George told me, and since he was the expert I went to wait in the car. One of my clearest visual memories of this trip was George approaching the car with a large duffle bag – really large, the kind that soldiers carry – hugged to his chest and full to the brim with freeze-dried food. He could only just walk under the weight of it. 'No, absolutely not!' I was adamant. This was about two weeks' travel budget and even divided between us, how were we going to carry it? And why? I won the argument and he returned most of it. Or some of it, at any rate.

We didn't need to compromise on our interests. In addition to our shared enthusiasm for wildlife we were also curious about ancient civilisations, and my 1969 trip to South America, travelling down the Amazon with Berndt, the German anthropologist, had ignited in me a fascination with the indigenous people of that continent. They were so different from the Spanish descendants, so self-sufficient, and so beautiful in their distinctive clothing. And their markets were a fabulous opportunity not only to see them without touristy gawping, but to buy some beautiful produce. We called the indigenous people Indians in those days, so for simplicity I have done so in the following account of our 1973 journey although I know that it is not a term we would now use.

The American system of 'drive-away cars' was brilliant. We used it a lot as an alternative to hitchhiking when we had limited time. It worked like this: wealthy Americans had big cars and two homes, often in Florida. Or they were relocating for work. Or just needed their car elsewhere but didn't want to drive it themselves. Step in 'responsible drivers over the age of twenty-one', with three referees saying they were some of the most trustworthy people you could ever hope to meet and, hey presto, you had a large, posh car to drive to your destination. The only expense was the petrol.

There was an agency in Boston and several in New York and we became accomplished drive-away customers, always looking the epitome of responsible, mature drivers when we went to the office to sign documents, and taking the car to a car wash before delivering it. Often we got a tip as well as the free ride. Miami was a popular destination for these cars and the gateway to South America, with plenty of flights to Colombia. We reserved a vehicle leaving in February 1973.

The crisp snow and monochrome chill of Boston gradually gave way to slush and then to glimmers of green as we drove south from deep midwinter to a Florida spring. We had tested all our equipment to be sure that we could carry our backpacks and any other luggage easily. Easily? My pack weighed 40lb and had no room for my clothes, which I carried in a handy little zipped suitcase. I was pleased with this arrangement since anyone who has backpacked knows the irritation of digging around for some garment in the hostile interior of their rucksack. With my little case I could find what I wanted immediately. George still had far too much freeze-dried food, but that was his problem.

The first lines in my letter home from Colombia read:

> Well, I had a fine diary started, several pages of glowing account, and had put it in the little case with my clothes. We piled all

our luggage up at the door of the hotel and went to look for a taxi and take a few pictures. When we got back the suitcase had gone, although the hotel woman swore that she had been there the whole time to keep an eye on it.

I seem to have adjusted quite quickly to the inconvenience of having only the clothes I was wearing apart from a sweater and anorak for the mountains, which were in my pack.

This morning I bought a man's shirt which is more modest than my sun-top, and I just wash clothes at night and they're dry in the morning.

I don't mention underwear but I assume I also bought some knickers… but I know I didn't have a bra. This was the '70s and women were busy burning their bras (I can't now remember why). Anyway, I wasn't wearing one under my sun-top but did have one in the case. Not an easy item to replace in rural Colombia, so I took my time. One of our early lifts was in an open truck over a very pot-holed road. We had to stand hanging on to the rail at the front and enduring the trampoline effect of flying into the air when the driver hit a particularly deep pot-hole. Well, my boobs were flying up even higher than I was and this was quite uncomfortable so George helpfully provided some support with his forearm. Then I spotted the driver's eyes in his rear-view mirror. He was certainly not looking at the road, or if he was he was selecting the best pot-holes, and he was having a very good time. He soon invited us to ride with him in the cab…

Apart from losing the suitcase, we had a rewarding and eventful time in those first few weeks, mostly in the attractive town of Medellín. I'm not sure if George had ever actually studied Spanish but he seemed to manage OK and I still had remnants from my earlier trip, but mostly we were sought out by Colombians who spoke perfect English, including Roger, a father figure in his fifties who, whenever he saw us, asked, 'When did you last eat?' and then escorted us to a restaurant whatever our answer. He said being seen with us raised his status with his acquaintances. Hard to believe, but he was certainly a kind and interesting companion. Furthermore he had a car and a chauffeur. In our quest to learn more about the Indian tribes of Colombia, we asked Roger's advice. 'The university has a very good anthropology museum. I'll drive you there this afternoon.' And so he did, saying he, or his chauffeur, would pick us up at 6.30pm. At exactly 6.30 Roger's green car arrived driven by his chauffeur. '*Buenos tardes*,' we beamed, and clambered into the back seat. '*A donde?*' he asked. 'Where do you want to go?'

'*El centro*,' and off we went. After a short while George said, 'You know, this isn't the right car or the right man.' Hmm. I haven't yet mentioned the little problem I have with prosopagnosia, or face blindness. And since neither of us was much interested in cars, all green cars looked the same. So we asked the driver to stop and asked a few pertinent questions. As we'd realised, he'd never seen us in his life so we apologised profusely and got back to the museum just as Roger drove up.

The next couple of weeks involved an abortive attempt to take a boat down the Río Atrato from the Caribbean port of Turbo (the water was too low and our attempts to buy a canoe and do it ourselves were regarded with unhelpful amusement). We made friends with a missionary, Richard, learned a lot about the Bible and quite a bit about the godless Choco tribe, and helped him remove bullets from a Choco woman's arm. Her husband had tried to kill her but was too drunk to shoot straight. We told Richard about the theft of my clothes. He was not surprised. 'I've heard that there's a school for thieves in Bogotá. Three years. A very stiff course, I believe.' At the time we laughed, but by the time we left Colombia I believed it to be true.

Travel in Colombia meant buses. All sorts of different buses with various baggage facilities.

> A man got on with four pieces of luggage, two panting sacks and two crowing bags – his dogs and his roosters – which were stowed with the rest of the luggage at the back. The dogs were very stoical and just lay in their sacks panting until a bag was dropped on them, when they emitted an anguished howl. A sentence I now know in Spanish is 'A suitcase has dropped on the dog'.

One of the dilemmas of travel faced by Westerners is that the majority of us dislike killing things. This is rarely shared in the developing world where most people are (or were) indifferent to the suffering of animals. Food is often what you can find in the forest, and animals are either useful or of no consequence. So our hunting expedition in the Antioquia region was an experience we wouldn't have missed, although it's not something I'd want to repeat.

The only 'hotel' we could find in the village where the bus dumped us was also the local cockpit and shared its human accommodation with cages of fighting cocks. Arriving after dark we didn't recognise the significance of this. At 3am the cocks started competitive crowing, and that was it. No more sleep. It didn't really matter since the hotel owner had invited us to go on a hunting expedition the following morning. It would be an early start – 4.30. We couldn't understand what was being hunted. '*Guagua*,' they told us. We knew what that meant. 'You hunt *babies*?' 'Yes, the meat is delicious.' We decided on a wait-and-see policy.

Our companions in the truck were eight men and their dogs. The houses gave way to farmland and then to forest where the road ended.

We walked through the jungle for about an hour, along a trail, before half the men split off to go through uncut jungle with the dogs. We found it hard to make progress because of the <u>incredible</u> birds. We saw toucans, macaws, parrots and numerous other colourful species we couldn't identify; more birds than I saw during my entire Amazon trip last time. The men were very good at pointing them out for us and got a big kick out of my binoculars, taking it in turns to marvel at how close everything looked.

While some of the men and dogs were hunting *guagua*, the others were preparing to go fishing. This turned out to mean dynamiting the river bed.

The technique was first to drive the fish into the chosen spot by throwing stones and swimming splashily, then the explosive – nitroglycerin, George says – was carefully packaged and weighted with a stone, then lit and thrown in. Quite a big underwater explosion and after a while stunned fish started to float to the surface.

We waited for the hunters' return with a local family, joining them in their large house. Typical of the area, built on stilts to avoid unwanted intruders and entered by climbing a notched pole, the 'house' consisted of two palm-thatched areas, one for sleeping, with mattresses on the floor protected by mosquito netting, and the other for cooking and general living. I was brought the one chair to sit on while a lavish picnic was prepared. The fishermen had brought lots of rice wrapped in banana leaves, the fish were grilled on a wood fire, cans of sardines opened, and everyone squatted in a circle to eat with their fingers. They gave George and me a bowl and a spoon, and were not in the least put out or shy at our presence.

Sometimes they talked to us, sometimes they just got on with what they needed to do, and they laughed uproariously at every feeble attempt we made at a joke in Spanish. After the meal was finished the hunters returned with a beautiful animal slung by its legs from a pole. About the size of a spaniel, and with the head of a guinea pig, it had a coat of a rich chestnut brown, with rows of white spots along its sides. I know now it was a paca, the largest jungle rodent (the even bigger capybara live in wetlands), and I have to admit that the meat, which was cooked for George and me in our hotel that evening, was the best I have ever tasted.

One *guagua* was not sufficient, and George was invited to join the next sortie with the dogs. I'd had enough killing and waited for their return, admiring the family's ingenious use of the stump of a once-enormous tree with huge buttress roots spreading across the jungle floor like fins. The area between the fins was so large that they were all put to use. One acted as a kitchen, with a fire and space for food preparation, and the others were fenced off to provide animal pens. There were turtles in one, and a large pig was contained in another while its piglets ran around hoovering up scraps of food.

More pacas arrived. George's description of the hunt made me even gladder I hadn't been there, and we returned to the hotel so tired we slept through the alarm-cocks the following morning.

The town of Dabeiba, on the way back to Medellín, was advertising a circus, so we stopped off to enjoy this event, like something right out of Fellini's *La Strada*. There were six performers, the stage was a barn with the audience standing around the perimeter, the props comprised a table, a rope and a few chairs, and the troupe's lack of professionalism provided much of the appeal. The show alternated between banter and jokes with the delighted audience and various balancing acts on a precarious pile of chairs on the table. The performers looked terrified, as were we when a fall would mean injury, and the audience were swept along with the emotion. Such fun!

We loved Colombia and stayed there six weeks, during which time we were robbed three times. If you want to learn how to travel light, go to Colombia. The next bag to disappear was on the train south from Bogotá. It was a glorious train ride, single track, narrow gauge, winding through the mountains at 8,000ft or so; the scenery was reminiscent of Wales, with bracken and foxgloves, along with grazing sheep. Then down to a hotter, drier region with banana trees brushing against the windows, multicoloured birds flitting through the trees and banks of pink and white impatiens brightening the valleys. We'd packed all the things we'd need for that journey into a small bag: camera, binoculars, and the *South American Handbook*, the only guidebook to the continent available in those days and thus treasured by all travellers. I put the bag on my feet and dozed off for about ten minutes while George moved seats to watch the scenery. During that ten minutes the bag disappeared. The train hadn't even stopped at a station but was moving slowly enough for the thief to jump off.

We did everything we could to retrieve it, searching the train, then getting off at the next station to visit the two towns where the bag could have ended up. No joy, but the police were very kind and helpful. The Colombian police had *always* been very kind and helpful.

The final robbery was different. We were on a bus (where else?) heading towards the monolithic statues at San Agustín, Colombia's most significant archaeological site. The access village was Inza – or so we thought at the time – and it was only after the bus turned off the main road that we discovered it was visiting another small town off the route and would return at 2am. Not wanting yet another night journey we asked the driver to stop, retrieved our luggage from the roof, where the baggage boy was riding, and returned to the junction to set up camp and wait for the morning bus to Inza. Then – you guessed it – we discovered that the baggage boy had helped himself to some of the few remaining items of value or usefulness that we still owned: a Swiss army knife, two other penknives, George's trinket box with gifts to give to locals, and our compass. It was the last straw, and we weren't going to take it lying down, so we planned a 2am hold-up. Over supper we decided on our strategy. I was to tell the driver what had happened while George found the boy and searched him. Surely our things would still be in his pockets. We also planned to take the security chain and padlock we carried with us which had proved singularly useless. We nurtured a plan to chain the boy to a post and walk nonchalantly away with the padlock key. Unaccustomed to playing the highway(wo)man, and much too nervous to sleep, I spent the remaining few hours rehearsing the Spanish for 'Your boy is a thief and has taken our things'. It was a gorgeous night with a full moon which popped up over the mountains like a white balloon, and we were waiting and ready at 1.30. Right on time, at 2 o'clock, we heard the bus and stepped out into the road.

A chorus of 'No room!' rang out from the sleepy passengers, and indeed the bus was packed. In my nervousness I forgot my carefully rehearsed speech but mumbled something to the driver while George grabbed a bewildered-looking youngster and started searching him. Well, you know my problem with prosopagnosia, and we hadn't really noticed what our young thief looked like. The search was fruitless. The passengers, wide awake now and completely silent, watched enthralled until the driver took charge and revved the engine, and we left the bus to an all-enveloping, never to be forgotten, roar of laughter. To cap it all, we discovered that Inza was not even the access town for San Agustín.

It was fortunate that we loved San Agustín. The anthropomorphic figures of much pre-Columbian art are always intriguing, and these were – and still are – the most fascinating in South America because of their size, their age and their relative obscurity. Carved from volcanic rock nearly two thousand years ago, these megalithic statues are now well protected in a UNESCO World Heritage Site. In 1973, however, they were just dotted about the lush Magdalena valley where trails wandered between orchid meadows and flowering shrubs over a distance of around 40 square miles. We spent days camping nearby and hired horses and a guide to see the furthest ones. Thus George got his first experience of being on a horse, having spent two years listening to me burbling about my love of riding. He made a fuss about not being able to walk the following day, but did brilliantly in the saddle, even cantering a bit because, as he said, 'This trotting business is ridiculous!' This accomplishment was important since horses were often the transport of choice on our subsequent travels.

One statue we particularly liked was a giant mouse, about six feet high, with its nose pointed to the sky and a forked tail. What a shame we had no camera to photograph it since it seems now to have disappeared. There was also a rather disturbing one, that I sketched, of a very large jaguar copulating with a very small woman.

We left the San Agustín area in great style, having got talking to an English-speaking boy, Efraím, and his parents. I must have laid it on a bit thick about our travails with buses since they invited us to ride to Popoyán with them in their car. The first time we'd sat on upholstered seats for a month or so, and through glorious and varied scenery. At the highest point we were seeing Colombia's distinctive high-altitude *páramo*, with its fluffy plants protecting themselves against the night frosts. When we arrived in Popoyán we asked Efraím to drop us off at the bus station, always the place where the cheap hotels can be found. 'Oh no, you must come back and stay with us!' It turned out that the Valencias were one of Popoyán's leading families, living in a simply beautiful modern house with a large, perfectly tended garden. We stayed there for three nights, relishing the comfort, ecstatic about having our own bathroom, and assuaging our guilt by taking them out to dinner. Efraím showed us around Popoyán, which deserved the time we gave it, being easily the most attractive town we'd seen in Colombia, all cobbled streets and white houses with overhanging roofs. No skyscrapers above and no litter below.

Craving a bit of cultural familiarity, we took the family to see the film of *Rebecca*, starring my beloved Laurence Olivier (of course I'd seen it before, but George hadn't). Fortunately they'd read the book since the reels got mixed up and the end was in the middle, which made complete rubbish of the story. But no one noticed, or if they did, they didn't mind.

And so to Ecuador.

4

ECUADOR AND THE GALÁPAGOS

The border officials at Ipiales had some trouble recording the details of my passport, which had been amended when we married and gave my name as 'Hilary Cross now Bradt'. I entered the country as Mrs Hilary Now.

We moved fairly swiftly to Quito, to my long-suffering friends the Bukovskys, so I could get my fix of riding thoroughbred horses. George, now he was no longer a saddle virgin, joined me and even managed a small jump, and we were united in our delight at wallowing in hot baths and eating lots of cake. And catching up on correspondence. In response to Mother's description of the pleasures of becoming a grandmother, I reaffirmed my lack of enthusiasm for babies and followed up with:

> Anyway, I think we've decided to have a sloth instead of a child. They're <u>gorgeous</u>! They have a sweet smile and we met one at the zoo in Medellín who lay on his back near the bars and let us scratch his tummy, beaming all the while. I tried to explain this preference to Jorge but it got complicated since the Spanish for sloth is the same as 'lazy' (as it is in English) and he thought we meant we were too lazy to have a child.

Throughout our travels we were constantly questioned about our lack of children. Just not wanting them satisfied no one so we came up with various answers. This one was the least successful.

Our attention was now firmly on the Galápagos Islands, the only place in South America that we knew we *had* to visit. After all, hadn't our relationship started with the surprise and delight of discovering that we both knew about the islands – and longed to go there? Our research found an inexpensive passenger boat which seemed to offer the ideal solution. The *Calicuchima* was a supply ship owned by the Ecuadorian navy and adapted to carry sixty passengers. It toured the most interesting islands like any Galápagos cruise. Their agent agreed to let us disembark at the easternmost island, San Cristóbal, and pick up the ship again on its next journey two weeks later, as long as we weren't fussy about having a cabin. That way we would get the opportunity for some independent travel, which was allowed in 1973, but still have transport to the more distant islands. Three weeks in the Galápagos! We could hardly contain our excitement.

Heady with the thrill of going on a cruise to the place we'd so long dreamed of visiting, we decided to take a luxury bus to Guayaquil. It allowed us five hours in the port so we could shop for essentials such as binoculars, to replace the stolen ones, and snorkelling gear. Then we heard on the news there had been a major landslide on the road leading to the coast. Jorge phoned the bus company. 'No problem!' they told him.

When the bus rolled into view it was magnificent. A sleek Mercedes Pullman Deluxe with reclining seats and plenty of leg room. The effect was rather spoiled by the fact that it was pushed into view and then pushed backwards and forwards in the bus station by volunteer male passengers until it finally deigned to start. All went well until 1am when it stopped, the engine was turned off, and all was silence apart from our fellow passengers' snores. After about an hour George and I decided to get out and see what had happened. We suspected, correctly, that the landslide was to blame, and experience had demonstrated that South Americans simply don't have the concept of being in a hurry. We walked past a long queue of stationary buses and trucks to the point where half the hillside had fallen on to the road. Some boys with fire torches guided us across a large expanse of sticky yellow mud to the other side where a bus was in the process of unloading its passengers. We understood that it would soon turn round and head back to Guayaquil and, yes, we could get on it. Our bus, we also understood, would return to Quito. It was now 3am, we had to return across the landslide to collect our luggage, and I was not in a good mood. The Ecuadorian passengers faced the challenge with their usual stoicism. Some carried quite heavy suitcases and one carried a man with his leg in plaster. Our boy guide took a wrong path and we struggled in the darkness through ankle-deep mud, finally reaching our bus to retrieve our luggage and struggle across the mud once more, then heaving the bags on to the new bus, which was now full of sleeping passengers who evidently had no plans to go anywhere. The driver had disappeared.

We finally left at 7 o'clock, and got to Guayaquil at noon, just in time for all the shops to be closed for their two-hour lunch break. So no chance to buy binoculars. But there was our ship, the *Calicuchima*; our Galápagos adventure was about to begin.

My letters home, hitherto full of vague references to 'colourful birds' or 'giant guinea pigs' took on a different, informed tone in the Galápagos. George and I had each read, and reread, the books on the islands that were available at the time. He had bought the two-volume *Galapagos: The Flow of Wildness* by Eliot Porter, and I had a well-thumbed copy of *Galapagos: Islands of Birds* by Bryan Nelson. We knew what we wanted to see.

Of course there were things we hadn't expected to see – entrancing things – before we even arrived at San Cristóbal.

> This evening we saw a really fabulous sight. Dolphins were playing in front of the ship, right by the bows, and were shining with phosphorescence so it looked as though they

were outlined in green neon. Every now and then a flying fish would be startled and zoom away leaving a green zig-zag of light. There were anything from two to six dolphins, always keeping just in front of the boat, making wavy green patterns in the water.

The word 'fabulous' is much overused these days. Not here.

During the three-day sea journey dolphins escorted us every day, anything up to fifty animals, leaping, diving and turning on their sides to look up at their audience with that dolphin smile on their faces. There is no question that they were having fun. So were we. The ship was very much more comfortable than any I had travelled on down the Amazon, though we shared a cabin with five men. The food was good and there were even a few deckchairs around. Our fellow passengers were mostly Ecuadorians, with a sprinkling of North Americans and Europeans. We chatted, played Scrabble (I was peeved to be beaten by a young Ecuadorian) and read the books which had added to the weight of our packs.

At 4am on the third day we hit San Cristóbal. Literally. The ship had run aground and there was an enjoyable feeling of chaos with the Ecuadorians running around in life jackets and the Europeans looking bewildered. It was of no consequence, we refloated at seven and were packed and ready to disembark after breakfast.

Reading my letters home I realise how unbelievably lucky we were to spend nearly three weeks here at a time when there were no restrictions on visitors. And I also know how necessary for the survival of the islands the subsequent rules were. We were just in time: in 1974, one year after our visit, a master plan was established to protect the islands and limit the impact of tourism through a set of strict rules and regulations. Uncontrolled tourism is always bad for wildlife and in a place as vulnerable as the Galápagos it would have been disastrous if allowed to continue. So we were lucky, but goodness didn't we know it, and didn't we appreciate it! In the 1980s and early '90s I was fortunate enough to return to the Galápagos six times as a tour leader and see the delight experienced by every visitor upon finding themselves so close to the islands' wildlife. I never felt that the regulations limited the enjoyment of these visits. But even forty years ago there had been a few TV programmes about the islands, hence their surging popularity, so nothing came as a total surprise. In the 1970s, however, the Galápagos were little known so despite all our reading we were unprepared for the thrill of this utterly unique experience. In over sixty years of travel that first visit remains, I think, my most entrancing wildlife encounter.

San Cristóbal was more developed than we had expected. We didn't realise there were cars on the islands, and the port had shops and a church. We took a shared taxi to the smaller town of El Progreso, and hiked up the road to a small lake where we set up camp so we could walk unencumbered to San Cristóbal's main feature, a much larger freshwater lake. While the tame and cheeky wildlife was as delightful as we had dreamed of – 'we've just watched a mockingbird remove all George's washing from the bushes', I wrote in my letter home – the friendliness of the people was an additional bonus. The locals seemed genuinely pleased to see us and offered us lifts and food at every opportunity. Very few tourists bothered to stop here, but we were determined to miss nothing. At this altitude the air was cool and the vegetation temperate not tropical. Lagoon El Junco, when we finally reached it, was misty but busy with waterbirds, but it was the smaller lake where we were camped that provided our best moment.

> At dawn the mist was lying in the valley like a white sea. As the sun came up the mist started spilling into the lake and with the sun behind us our shadows appeared on the whiteness, circled by a rainbow. Really magical!

We needed to find a boat to the next island, Santa Cruz, and as luck would have it as we walked back to the port we met a group of gringos who had arrived on a small, and very dodgy, boat, the *Don Antonio*. It nearly didn't make the crossing from Guayaquil, they had all been seasick, and the boat was so unseaworthy that it had lost its licence to carry passengers. They had to plead with the harbour master to be allowed to continue to Santa Cruz, promising not to complain whatever happened. It sounded ideal. We talked to the captain and for $5 a head were allowed to sail with them that night.

Despite, or perhaps because of, the licence business, we had an absolutely superb lobster supper on the boat. That, in itself, was worth the price we paid. The night wasn't bad at all. We were provided with hammocks; the only problem was that we had slung them in the dining room and the crew ate breakfast at 5.30am.

Santa Cruz is a much more visited island than San Cristóbal, being the headquarters of the Charles Darwin Research Station, full of scientists and researchers doing interesting work, and is also the home of the giant tortoises, the most famous Galápagos residents. We were determined to see these in the wild, not just the captive ones in the CDRS, so we asked permission to camp at the Casita – a hut in the tortoise reserve that was used by researchers – where there was fresh water.

We took a bus to the village of Bellavista, en route to Santa Rosa from where the trail to the reserve began. The road to Santa Rosa was closed for repair, however, so it was a very hot, very tiring walk. We didn't even make it all the way in one day and had to camp before we got there, using up too much of our precious water. Unless we found fresh water the following day we would only have enough for drinking, not for cooking our freeze-dried food. When we finally got to Santa Rosa we were shown the trail and set off in good spirits through a banana grove and shoulder-high elephant grass. The trail got fainter and the temperature within the oppressive vegetation was stifling. We drank our last water. Finally the trail more or less disappeared, leaving us treading cautiously over a lava field where a misstep could plunge us into an ankle-gashing hole. We had been walking all day and I started feeling a bit panicky about finding the Casita, let alone any fresh water. Or tortoises, come to that. The path, or what pretended to be a path, then ended at a barbed-wire fence and that seemed to be that.

We found no sign of a gate, though we walked up and down the fence looking for one, but there did seem to be a decent path on the other side so we pushed our packs under the wire, crawled on our bellies after them, and followed the trail in what we hoped was the right direction. We rounded a bend and there, in front of me, was a simply *enormous* tortoise! He pulled his head into his shell with a noisy hiss, but beyond him we saw two more, nonchalantly eating bananas. They ignored us, and soon the path broadened and we came to the Casita and three large barrels of fresh rainwater. Relief! We drank long and deep, gave our bodies and our clothes a wash, and set up our mosquito-net tent without its cover so we could see what was going on outside during the night. After dark, disturbed by some big-bird flutterings, we shone our torch on a short-eared owl taking a dust bath near the tent. He glared at us and continued his ablutions.

We stayed in the reserve for three nights. The days were filled with tortoise observations and spotting Darwin finches and vermilion flycatchers as well as our encounter with the Galápagos variety of tiny red fire ants which enjoyed dropping on us from branches and making our lives miserable. We preferred the other insects such as the huge, multicoloured grasshoppers, about four inches long, whose wings glittered when they flew.

What, we wondered, would two tortoises do if they met head-on along the trail? On the third day we found out.

They stood on tiptoe, stretching their heads up as high as they could, and lunged at each other for a while with their mouths open. Then the biggest suddenly lowered himself, put his head into his shell and whammed the other as hard as he could. Then he got behind it and pushed it at quite a speed, with the smaller one making an effort to outrun him. We got back to the tent to find a tortoise trying to eat it. We decided anyway it was time to break camp and start heading down to Puerto Ayora. It's strange to be sitting here, writing this letter to the familiar sound of grazing, but it's not a horse, it's a giant tortoise.

We walked back to Bellavista by moonlight, which was a lot cooler and very pleasant – so much so that the next day we hiked up to the highest place on the island, Cerro Crocker, at around 2,000ft, for the view and to see the changes in vegetation. On our way we came across a huge lava tube – a natural formation created when rope lava solidifies on the outside but the molten lava continues to force its way through. A Tube train could have passed through it, and parts had broken away to reveal the ferns and other plants growing on the damp floor. It was strange and incongruous amid the familiar bracken and grass of the hillside and probably extended for quite a way within the mountain.

We still had a week of independent travel before reboarding the *Calicuchima* so our next task was to get a group together to hire a boat to see the small, nearby islands we wouldn't be visiting on our cruise. The Galápagos in the 1970s was not only a wildlife haven but also a hippie haven because of the empty beaches and cheap rooms. We'd met a pair of American hippies on and off since crossing into Ecuador. They had told us they were going to the Galápagos because, 'Like, man, you can sleep on the beach there and catch fish with a bit of banana peel, and when you feel like lobster you just put your hand in the sea and grab one.' Well, we met them on San Cristóbal, finding them somewhat chastened having collected a pile of wood to cook all the fish they expected to catch, and then failing to catch any. We met them again in Santa Cruz in a much worse state, after being lost without water in the baking hot arid zone for two days. Most of the trees in this band of vegetation have spines – acacia, thorn scrub and cacti – making passage through them treacherous, and they were lucky to have survived. They explained that they had set out for a beach, Tortuga Bay, where they intended to camp, and headed into the bushes to answer a call of nature. They had failed to find their way out to the trail again, getting more and more lost as panic set in. They dumped their packs to make the struggle easier and after a very thirsty and unpleasant night, managed to get back to the trail. They asked us to accompany them while they looked for their packs, and since we anyway wanted to visit what was reputed to be the prettiest beach on Santa Cruz, we agreed. They never found their packs, but we were able to guide them back to the trail by shouting, and then shared our supper with them on the beach because they had no food.

We were not going to invite them to join our planned boat trip.

There were other, more compatible, gringos on the island, including Heather who had been there for several months working on a research project (George called her the 'tick lady' because she was always hung with bags like giant ticks), and three French men who were good company and had a sensible attitude to the wildlife. The six of us managed to find a small boat willing to visit our chosen islands. We had to provide the food but the boatmen would catch fish to supplement our supplies. First we would take a day trip to Barrington (better known as Santa Fé) then a three-day trip to Plaza, Seymour and Daphne Major.

I sometimes wonder if this place is real! Here we are sitting on a beach on Barrington Island, surrounded by basking or frolicking sea lions, with two Galápagos hawks watching us from a rock. The sea lions are as friendly and inquisitive as puppies and play in a similar way. They like to grab at sticks and throw them around, and they loved swimming with us, gambolling around in the water and leaping out like dolphins. We spent most of the day watching them frolic in the sea then haul themselves back on the sand for a snooze. The little ones feed from their mothers until she swats them away with a flipper, when they tumble around together or play chasing games. They have an extraordinary range of noises: barks, belches, wheezes, retching sounds and a bleat like a lamb. The only thing against them is the smell. Their shit smells absolutely dreadful and it takes an effort of will to remain in a sea-lion-crowded area.

Our little boat was pretty basic, but cheap. Only one person could sleep under cover, the rest of us had to make do with the deck, and there was a bucket behind a curtain for the loo. It didn't matter, our co-passengers were a jolly bunch – although agreeing with three French men about what food to bring on a three-day trip was exhausting. We settled on eighty bread rolls (that must have emptied the Puerto Ayora bakery), some sardines and lots of chocolate.

As we approached Plaza our boat was accompanied by a joyous group of sea lions, and as we scrambled on to land a dozen or so huge land iguanas came racing towards us looking for handouts. They were about three feet long, yellowish, and very ugly, with rows of spines along their backs and smug smiles. Understandably, since they were also *very* fat. Obese.

We learned that they have been fed titbits by tourists for the past few years and surely this must be prohibited or they will just pop.

They liked bananas and yellow cactus flowers, and made a beeline for George's yellow socks, which must have resulted in some disappointment.

Over on the other side of the island were black marine iguanas, even uglier than the land variety, but minding their own business and not expecting handouts since they feed exclusively on the algae that grows on the seabed. We also saw swallowtail gulls with their chicks. Beautiful birds with a red ring around their large eyes and an appealing way of suddenly staring at their feet as though wondering whether they needed a pedicure. Up above, squabbling frigate birds fought for an eel. The victor would be forced to drop it, then it would be grabbed mid-air, only to be dropped again. And so on, until they all missed it and it fell to the ground to be retrieved by George and thrown up to the nearest frigate who managed to keep hold of it.

Walking back to the boat we saw dozens of scarlet and sky-blue Sally Lightfoot crabs, a delightful name for this nimble and exceptionally pretty crustacean. Scores of them posed against the black lava, watching us with their purple stalk-eyes.

Seymour island was absolutely covered in nests belonging to frigate birds, both magnificent frigate birds and the – to us – very similar great frigate birds. These make a practice of attacking boobies in mid-flight to force them to regurgitate their catch, which seems terribly unfair, given that the boobies do all the work, but they are also house burglars, swooping in to grab a few twigs from a neighbour's nest if its owner is absent. We learned early to approach nests slowly so the incubating birds were not scared into flight, risking both their eggs which, we'd read, sometimes just got flicked off the shallow nest, or precious twigs. We were hoping to see the absurd display of the male trying to attract a mate – extraordinary what some females find sexy – with his crimson balloon of a throat sac fully inflated, his beak pointing hopefully skyward, and his wings shivering seductively. We did see one doing the full works, but as we didn't have binoculars he was really too far away for us to get the full effect.

The other courting display we were longing to see, because we'd read so much about it, was the mating dance of the blue-footed booby. We'd spotted a few of these birds standing demurely on white guano-splashed rocks which showed off their astonishingly blue feet, but none was displaying, so our afternoon visit to Daphne Major, the best place for boobies in the Galápagos, promised to be a high spot. High spot doesn't come close to it. The few hours we spent here is what pushed the Galápagos into my 'best ever' wildlife experience.

Daphne is simply a conical volcano rising abruptly from the sea. Long extinct, it has two deep adjoining craters with flat sandy floors where, we knew, there would be blue-footed boobies. Landing on the side of the volcano was tricky; we had to leap off on to rocks where a faint trail led up the steep sides. Progress to the top was slow, not because it was difficult, but because we were distracted by masses of very dapper masked boobies (now called Nazca boobies), dressed in pristine black and white with glaring yellow eyes and a bright yellow bill surrounded by a black mask. It was apparently too early for any breeding activity; they just stood around looking handsome. When we reached the edge of the crater and looked down we gasped. The crater floor was simply covered with blue-footed boobies, barely a yard separating them, and even from that distance we could see that there was a lot of dancing going on.

We climbed down into the crater and for the next two hours just sat quietly observing, and giggling with delight at their antics.

> The boobies were much too busy with affairs of importance to take any notice of us. And they were all doing the mating dance. You need to understand that boobies look funny enough just standing around doing nothing. They are a nice soft brown

colour with comical spiky feathers on their heads and necks and pale yellow eyes which seem to be stuck on to the top of their beaks. And their feet! Sky blue, turquoise blue, dark blue – every shade of blue – and webbed between all four toes, so very prominent. In their displaying they make great use of these feet, strutting around their territory lifting them exaggeratedly high like Russian soldiers, and tucking their beaks into their chests. When they come into land they salute their mate by lifting their feet forward on their white breasts so their spouse can admire the beautiful colour. Courtship is even more elaborate. They face each other, flick their wings forward in an anatomically impossible position, point their bills at the sky and whistle seductively. We watched a pair do this repeatedly. Oh, and they do 'symbolic nest building'. Very symbolic, since their nest is just a scrape in the sand but after a bit of goose-stepping one will pick up a twig or straw and with a great show of generosity pass it to his mate who will lay it reverently beside her 'nest'.

Our mini-cruise was coming to an end and we were sad. Yes, we still had the rest of the tour with the *Calicuchima*, but this had been extra special. We'd chosen our companions well and our islands brilliantly. They had given us unbeatable memories, and we later worked out that it had cost us $5 per day for the two of us including meals. Good meals; we never opened those tins of sardines. As we headed back to Santa Cruz we had a final bit of excitement. Every day the crew (I say crew but I think there were only two of them) caught fish to supplement our bread rolls. This time I was watching as they reeled in a large tuna, around three or four feet long. Just as they were about to reach for it to pull it on board, an *enormous* shark leapt out of the water, chomped the fish, and disappeared, leaving us with the head and about six inches of very surprised-looking tuna. Nevertheless, that and the small fish that George managed to catch provided enough for a celebratory evening meal at Heather's, supplemented by a vast quantity of potatoes that we bought for our new French friends.

On April 22, fifteen days after landing in San Cristóbal, we reboarded the *Calicuchima*. This time we were the only gringos apart from one Australian girl. The rest of the passengers were charming and very polite Ecuadorian students on a rather special field trip. There were no cabins available, so we slept on deck in hammocks which swung wildly in the swell, giving us strange dreams. As is completely normal in South America our desire for sleep seemed not only frivolous but completely unnecessary so we were regularly kept awake by the crew having shouted conversations over our recumbent bodies or the students holding noisy deck parties until the small hours.

After a repeat visit to Plaza we arrived at Bartolomé.

We understood that we had three hours to explore this strange island so set off on our own. It consists almost entirely of lava: squirls and mounds like melted chocolate, along with tubes and spikes, caves and tunnels. A few cacti provided the only green. We had to walk carefully so as not to break through the crust. Near the sea were some crazy lava pools with emerald green fish swimming around. After exactly three hours we returned to the ship to find everyone gnashing their teeth in fury since we had misunderstood the instruction and were supposed to be back at 3 o'clock so were an hour late, thus missing the next small island.

Bad.

The rather larger island of Floreana made up for this disappointment.

Now, just imagine seeing a penguin on the same island as flamingos! The penguin was sitting nonchalantly on a rock and the flamingos were standing around in a lagoon, some way distant but still pinkly beautiful, and fancy seeing them in their natural habitat, not in a zoo. We walked to a white-sand beach intending to have a swim but there were several sharks cruising in the shallows, so we changed our minds. We'd seen what they could do to a tuna.

Our final visit was to Hood island, much anticipated since I had read about its speciality in *Islands of Birds*: the waved albatross.

They are absolutely beautiful, squatting motionless like plastic bathtub ducks. They have huge bright yellow beaks and a rather stern look in their large black eyes. We had read about their fascinating courtship 'dance' but I think we were a bit too early for this, unfortunately. But we watched their comings and goings. They have a lot of trouble taking off, and either had to trip and stumble to the edge of the cliff to catch a thermal or run along a disused road trying to get lift off, and sometimes falling flat on their faces in the process. So much to watch! And there were also a subspecies of marine iguana, much prettier than the usual charcoal black. On this island they come in reds and greens and are almost attractive. Our tour finished at a blowhole which gushed up like a geyser and provided a backdrop for a group of blue-footed boobies.

And that was it. On April 29 we landed back in Guayaquil, ready to resume our journey through Ecuador and replete with memories to last a lifetime. The generous donors at our wedding who had made this possible each received a long letter of description and thanks.

❖ ❖ ❖ ❖

Ecuador is one of the smaller countries in South America (a bone of contention – it used to be larger, and they blame Peru) but they are proud of their Amazon region, the Oriente. This seemed to have some of the most accessible rainforest we were likely to find, and maybe we would manage the river trip that had been my goal since the Amazon had failed to show me much wildlife. Also, and importantly, we'd managed to replace our binoculars, so could properly look at birds.

Alas, it was not to be. It rained incessantly and there were no boats available to take us deep into the rainforest. After eighteen days we gave up and started back towards Quito, hoping to catch a ride. As we trudged up the road, a man came running behind us, out of breath, and calling out, 'Come with me. I have something to show you!' We followed him to his house and with a flourish he said, 'This is Juanita and you must buy her!' Juanita was a gorgeous, half-grown peccary. She had lovely thick bristles almost as stiff as porcupine quills, and a mobile pink nose. And when she saw us she rolled on her back in the expectation of having her tummy tickled. Her owner, encouraged by my enthusiasm, added to his sales pitch.

'She'll follow you around like a dog. No problem.'

'Well, I think it would be a little inconvenient… buses, you know.'

'No problem, I'll sell you a sack as well to put her in so you can just carry her over your shoulder!'

'It really would be quite difficult. We already have a lot of luggage…'

'You could take her on the aeroplane with you!'

We finally managed to convince him that we really couldn't buy Juanita, so he picked us some papayas to show there was no hard feelings and we continued on our way. Poor fellow, I'm quite sure he couldn't bring himself to kill and eat his pet, which was surely what everyone was urging him to do.

From Quito we took a bus to Cuenca.

Our first surprise was when the driver handed us some soda-pop and sandwiches just before arrival. Even more surprising was to be serenaded off the bus, for our luggage to be serenaded off the top of the bus, and to find the whole bus station transformed into a shrine. Someone explained that it was the birthday of the patron saint of that bus company – Our Lady of Sorrows (how appropriate). There she was near the ticket counter, looking gloomy and surrounded by candles and lilies, with rows of solemn people looking as though they were at a wake. Then they started sending off coloured tissue-paper balloons which sailed off into the night powered by a small fire inside. These were followed by fireworks and finally a huge coloured-paper and bamboo moon rocket, two storeys high, which was dragged out and all the Catherine wheels and other fireworks adorning it were set off and everything was a whirling mass of lights. Glasses of the local liquor were handed to us and everyone toasted the bus company, shook hands and left. Just a sprinkling of people were watching this extraordinary display and we were the only foreigners. Wouldn't have missed it for the world.

We were on the point of leaving Ecuador and celebrated in a better than usual restaurant.

At dinner in Cuenca last night we met a roomful of gringos. Word has got around that this restaurant serves the best vegetarian food in South America and it is very good – although I have my eye on the roast guinea pigs I saw outside a shop yesterday. Anyway, one of the gringos told us of a four-day hike to Machu Picchu which sounds absolutely fantastic. We'll certainly do it when we get to Peru.

So that's where we headed next.

INTERLUDE
THE FROG LADY

We went to Ecuador's Oriente determined to see wildlife, but it never happened. We resorted to the lie that we were zoology students and *needed* to study the local fauna, and it still didn't happen. Finally someone suggested we go to Muñozlandia, by the Río Aguarico. '*Hay muchos animales, insectos, aves... todos.*' My diary entry for May 14 paints a gloomy picture:

> It poured all night and all day and it's still hard at it at dusk today. The bus didn't turn up but we found a truck selling Coca-Cola, which took an age since he stopped at every house to ask if they wanted to buy Cola. Finally we arrived at a crossroad with a sign for Muñozlandia. We walked the mile there, still in the rain, and arrived at this place which is a huge disappointment. Maybe once upon a time it really was something, but now it's a run-down, dilapidated place with a few huts for visitors and some dejected-looking reptiles in broken-down cages. And they charge the earth – at least twice as much as we usually pay for accommodation and food. So we'll just stay here tonight because it's too damned wet to walk anywhere else, and hope to God it's stopped raining tomorrow so we can look at birds more comfortably. There's only one other person here – a zoologist studying frogs. We hope we'll meet her tonight and perhaps she'll be interesting.

Things looked up as soon as we met the 'frog lady'. She was a proper herpetologist, enough so that she was thrilled at all the rain. Just the right conditions for frog collecting, so she was heading out into the rain after dinner.

'May we come?'

'OK, as long as you don't get in the way.'

We had a fantastic time. It had simply never occurred to us that hunting animals at night with a torch was so much more rewarding than a daytime search, at least when it came to small creatures and invertebrates. We were entranced. We saw numerous insects, mainly grasshoppers of all shapes and sizes, praying mantises and a beautiful leaf insect, about four inches long and doing a perfect imitation of a dead leaf. And of course the frogs. All those ventriloquist 'peep peep' sounds which we could never track down to a frog were like radar to this expert.

She found dozens of frogs: tree frogs, poison dart frogs, big croaking monsters and delicate little green fellows with huge bug eyes and sticky fingers. She showed us how to hold them so they could be examined before popping them into a plastic bag. We hardly noticed how wet we were.

Next day Marty showed us her collection so far. There were pea-green frogs with red tummies, gold ones with brown spots and yellow ones which turn red at night. She told us that one of the poison dart frogs is a particularly good parent. The eggs are laid and fertilised on the ground, and when they hatch he – or she – straddles the tadpoles and they climb on to his back to be carried safely to water.

That evening was a turning point. Next day Sr Muñoz himself arrived, said we'd been overcharged and halved the rate, and the sun shone. The road, as we walked back to the crossroads, was splashy with puddles and simply covered in butterflies including blue morphos. We'd never seen so many beautiful varieties.

Fifty years later an internet search helped me find the 'frog lady'. Marty Crump is now a distinguished academic with a number of books to her name. An evening's generosity on her part gave us the standout memory of our time in mainland Ecuador.

5

PERU

It was now June, more than three months since we'd left Miami, and the beginning of the dry season in the central Andes. We followed the same route along the coastal Pan-American Highway as I'd taken in 1969 but turned left at Chimbote towards the Cordillera Blanca, 'The Switzerland of Peru'. Chimbote stank of fishmeal, but offered some splendid fish meals – which was a good thing since we were stuck there a couple of days waiting for transport into the Andes.

A crowded open truck took us into the mountains along a tortuous road which was once a railway line. It had been completely destroyed in a devastating earthquake three years earlier; the rails had been ripped up and lay about the place like spaghetti. We proceeded at walking pace, which allowed us to admire the extraordinary scenery: huge, bare multicoloured mountains in shades of red, brown and yellow with not a touch of green – the Cordillera Negra, which lies parallel to the 'white range' of the Cordillera Blanca but receives no precipitation.

At ten that evening, in darkness and four hours late, our driver told us we had arrived at our destination so we scrambled down with our packs. We had no idea where we were. There were just four houses in this 'village' so we settled down to sleep in the porch of one of them. Next morning, at dawn, the family emerged and gazed at their unexpected guests in astonishment. '*Buenos dias,*' we said sheepishly, emerging from our sleeping bags. We bought two oranges from them and walked a couple of miles up the road to a proper village where we ate a hearty breakfast watched by fascinated locals. A number of free-range guinea pigs scuttled around the kitchen area. Another truck took us to some thermal baths where we were able to get clean at last. We had learned by now that these sturdy open trucks were the public transport of the Andes, and charged the same as buses.

Our private bath was huge and deep – and warm. Nights at this altitude were very cold, and there didn't seem to be much oxygen in the air. Even a short walk uphill left us breathless. We pitched our tent on the soft, lush grass by the baths and slept well until woken in the early morning by footsteps and chattering. The Quechua people were off to market dressed in their best. The women wore several embroidered skirts, all layered on top of each other, embroidered blouses trimmed with lace and high-crowned straw hats with tassels. The babies on their backs were swaddled, biblical style, stiff as a rod, with their little hands sticking out from the binding like starfish. They looked like wooden dolls. Their mothers looked rather doll-like too, so stiff were they with clothes.

The Callejón de Huaylas follows the Río Santa between the cordilleras Blanca and Negra and the views from our open-topped truck as we drove towards Huaraz were breathtaking. Our fellow passengers were gently amused at our delight, but pleased to point out the highest mountain in Peru, Huascarán, its snow-covered double peaks shining in the morning sun. One man, a folk singer, told us his story. He had lived in Yungay, which had been completely buried in the mudslide that followed the earthquake. Two days before the quake he had left, with his wife, to visit relatives. So they were unharmed, but lost their home, and all his wife's family perished beneath the mud. Now he toured the region with his group, raising money with his songs about the disaster.

The Hotel Monterrey turned out to be a mountaineering centre. A group of Canadians was staying here and they told us about their plans to climb a 6,000m peak (nearly 20,000ft). No one seemed to have thought of walking *between* mountains, which was George's preferred course of action. I had no course of action. Yes, we had already done some long hikes, including some that involved overnight camping, but most were combined with hitchhiking and were a means to an end rather than for enjoyment. So when, later, I found George gazing at a huge topographical wall map, published in Germany in the 1930s, I was cautious in my enthusiasm. He had spotted a trail running from the village of Olleros, not far from Huaraz, across the Cordillera to the town of Chavín, famous for its archaeological ruins. We had planned to go there anyway, but the road took a much longer route. Would that trail still exist? 'Sure,' one of the Canadians reassured us. 'The local people will use it to get to the villages across the Cordillera. If it existed in the 1930s it will be there now. Nothing much has changed.'

George was thrilled, I was dubious. It seemed suspiciously like serious backpacking, which I had sworn I was done with. And it would be very cold. And without a map we would have to rely on our compass and locals to keep us on the path – assuming it even existed. And the pass was nearly 4,700m – about 15,500ft in my more familiar measurements. The highest I would ever have been.

Olleros was off the main route and it took ages to find transport there. Once in the village we were urged to return to the road when we asked directions to Chavín. So steered by compass rather than locals, we set out along a good trail in high spirits. This was going to work! The sun was hot and the scenery ever-changing, with snow-covered peaks peeping over the lower grassy foothills. The locals stared at us in astonishment. One told us he'd never seen a gringo here before; we were clearly pioneers, and we liked that. The night was very cold. We wore everything we had, including woolly hats, and crisped around in the frost the following morning scraping the ice off our gear. The path towards the pass was still clear, but the uphill plod, with heavy packs, left us breathless. Somehow, we followed the wrong path and in the late afternoon found ourselves in a meadow with grazing cows and a burned-down shepherd's hut where we decided to pause and review our options. We could see where we needed to go – there was the trail towards the pass over to our left, and there was a brook and a large expanse of very wet bog to cross before we could get there. We agreed to put it off until the following day and make ourselves cosy in the hut with plenty of hay for bedding and our tarpaulin for a roof.

I'm not sure it was the right decision. There seemed no alternative the next morning but to take our shoes off (yes, only George had boots, I still had my Clarks lace-ups) and wade through the bogs, breaking the ice on the peaty puddles, and across the freezing stream. By the time we reached the trail I was weeping from the pain in my feet. But our footgear was dry, and the sun shone, and the way up was clear.

Since Olleros, the trail had shown signs of ancient paving, probably pre-Columbian, possibly Inca. It added an extra interest to the walk, along with the gorgeous scenery. By the time I'd gasped my way to the top of the pass and surveyed the scene of snow peaks and green cultivated foothills far below, I think I'd had my Damascene conversion. From then on I no longer looked at mountain backpacking as something to avoid, but something to seek out.

We didn't reach Chavín that day. The route was much longer than we expected and the locals clearly scared of us. Women ran into their huts, dragging their screaming children, and the men just stared, rarely returning our greetings. The final night was spent in an intact shepherd's hut, with a roof and a hay bed. I felt like Goldilocks, expecting its owner to creep in during the night, so waking up to find a man squatting by the entrance, whistling a little tune, was disconcerting but not unexpected. No, it wasn't his hut, but he wanted to talk. George made him a cup of tea and he told his story. Four years previously the government had pushed through a programme of agrarian reform to give the peasants more control over their land. Before that he had worked for a *patrón*, and life was very hard, but now he was part of a rural cooperative and free.

And happy. His father had died when he was very young, but his elder brother had made sure that he had been to school, which is probably why he spoke good, clear Spanish.

Chavín (eventually) lived up to expectations.

> We found a guide who unlocked some doors and led us inside some of the chambers. We had our torches so could admire the extraordinary stone stelae, probably carved to guard against evil spirits. Most were a sort of hybrid between a human and a jaguar, with nice fierce expressions, and there was also a bear. They were reminiscent of the San Agustín ones in Colombia, but others were unique with abstract designs morphing into an animal or human face, and one lovely Medusa-type woman with snake hair.

By mid-June 1973 we were city dwellers in Lima, and I had found myself a job! My friend Jorge in Quito had a sister, Rosa, whom I'd stayed with on my earlier trip. I look back at these prolonged stays with gnawing guilt, but at the time we really did feel welcome. Or at least our hosts were skilled at making us feel welcome. Rosa spoke fluent English, her husband Lucho only Spanish, but he was so interesting – he'd been a political prisoner for many years – that our language skills improved just listening to him. It was Rosa who told me that the Portuguese Ambassador was looking for someone to teach his small children, aged three and four, English. I borrowed some respectable clothes and went for an interview. The job involved spending a few hours each morning with the girls, playing games which included such useful English phrases as 'And you do the hokey-cokey and you turn around – that's what it's all about!' George and I had ambitious plans to stay in Lima for six months, earn lots of money – because surely George could also find a job – rent a cheap place to live, enjoy the food and culture of this vibrant capital and the many friends that we had made, and arrive in the *Cono Sur*, the extreme south of the continent, in time for the austral summer. Well, it didn't work out. George couldn't find a job, my earnings were lower than I'd realised, and it all seemed impractical. So after a couple of weeks I handed in my notice and we headed for Cusco.

The Inca capital felt very different from when I was there four years earlier. It was now infested with rather rude French tourists. My letters home talk ominously of the fifteen thousand French who had invaded Peru – I don't know where I got that figure from – but we had met none in the north, apart from our enjoyable companions in the Galápagos, so Cusco seemed to be the magnet. They had transformed the city. It still smelt of urine, since the French were never too bothered by this (think Parisian *pissoirs*), but they do like eating so there were lots of new restaurants and new *hostales* with new prices. We had three goals. I wanted to show George the wonderful Inca sites around the town, we had to find out how to do the walk to Machu Picchu we'd heard about in Cuenca, and we wanted to make another trip to the jungle in yet another attempt at a proper river journey.

First the river journey. My letter home grandly stated that we were going to Atalaya by truck, then down the Río Manu (the Manu National Park had yet to be established) to Manu itself, from where we would take a boat down the Río Madre de Dios to Puerto Maldonado and the road back to Cusco, making a jungle circuit. The reality was that we were gone for two weeks but during that time spent only five days actually travelling, either walking or sitting on a canoe. For the rest of the time we were waiting for boats which never came or an aeroplane (having given up on the boats) which also never came, before grumpily retracing our steps. In a way this didn't really matter because we did see plenty of the rainforest fauna, which was our main reason for going there, but a proper river journey would remain only a hope. My main memory of this trip is being very cold. Who would imagine that this would be a problem in the Amazonian jungle? I also remember sitting for a day in a jungle lodge-cum-shop-cum-restaurant embroidering a butterfly on to one of George's shirts while he and a couple of other gringos who had tagged along with us went in search of boats in the pouring rain. Every now and then the woman who ran the place would scan the trail for their return, sigh, and say, '*Ah, los locos pobres!*' (The poor crazy ones.)

Of course there were highlights and memorable incidents. There always are. I remember with a smile the little café where I was surprised to see a row of tortoises ranged along a shelf in the kitchen. Not tortoises, I saw on closer inspection, but tortoise shells. I asked the woman why they were there but didn't understand the answer. So she picked up a shell and out popped a guinea pig. The same with the others. Tonight's dinner.

There was also Paucartambo, a village on our route to the jungle. We ensured that we timed our arrival with their annual fiesta, which was well known to be unusual. And so it was.

> There was a raised platform where dancers in very fancy costumes and masks were hopping around. Some represented white men, and some black men, *negritos*, but none as far as we could see were Indians except perhaps the very endearing group with costumes made from Spanish moss and animal-skin masks which could have been forest spirits. We never had a clue what anything represented. Mostly they danced around on the platform but sometimes there would be a procession led by musicians with flutes, drums and a harp-type thing. The fiesta was in honour of the Virgen del Carmen, and before she was paraded round there was a strange ceremony in front of

the church. Two men dressed in white knitted masks and hung with the skins of baby llamas circled round each other carrying whips. Then they started lashing at each other on their bare legs, first slowly then faster and faster, working up to a frenzy. It must have been incredibly painful but there was no reaction at all in their faces. Finally, during the most frantic part, a man dressed as a woman with a black stocking mask over his face, 'parted' them and they went off with their arms around each other while another pair took their place. The virgin was very pretty when she emerged from the church on a high plinth and surrounded by paper flowers and plastic cherubs. Pretty vulgar, actually, but revered by the locals so there was much bead clicking and muttered prayers. She was paraded round the town, preceded by musicians and followed by a peevish-looking llama hung about with gifts of fruit and vegetables.

Later we found a large hall full of dancers and as soon as I showed my face I was whisked off to dance, getting very hot in my long underwear which I had needed for the chill Cusco morning. The following day they were still at it, looking rather the worse for wear, as we continued into the jungle.

Back in Cusco it was time to plan our hike to Machu Picchu, the trek we had been told about in Ecuador. An American in our hotel showed us a rather faint, photocopied, handwritten description, complete with drawings, created by a Swedish hiker. I can't remember where we got hold of a copy – perhaps from the tourist office, perhaps from another traveller. The walk was called 'Km 88 to Machu Picchu'.

We expected the trek to take four or five days, so spent a morning shopping for Knorr soup, bread and cheese and other goodies, our stock of American freeze dried food having been finally used up. We took notebooks, too. Whenever we told other keen hikers about our Cordillera Blanca walk they were interested to know the details, and the idea that we could write magazine articles, or even a little book, on the trails we were discovering took hold, fuelled by my new enthusiasm for mountain walking.

Four years earlier I had taken the posh *autovagón* to Machu Picchu. This time we needed to squeeze our way on to the 'Indian train', which stopped at Km 88.

> By the time we left Cusco people were stacked up along the aisles. The lady on the bench opposite me was buying produce to sell at her village at the end of the line. Each time the train stopped at a station she'd stand on my feet in order to lean out of the window to bargain with the Indians below. They were selling all manner of things and she was buying them all. At one station she bought a live hen and then found it wouldn't fit through the bars of the window, despite much squeezing and squawking. Finally the vendor managed to push it through a gap at the top. When it was time for us to get out it was quite a challenge to extricate ourselves from the pile of potatoes, onions and cabbages which occupied all available space.

The first day filled us with excitement. This was a beautiful walk, gently uphill, with a gorgeous snow peak making its appearance at intervals ahead of us. We slept in an empty hut at the only village en route and continued up a much steeper and less distinct path to camp near the top of the pass. It's now known as 'Dead Woman's Pass' but we were ignorant of all such names, even those of the Inca ruins we were seeing. Maybe that made them more interesting. Even the rain couldn't dampen our spirits, just reinforcing the ethereal beauty of the cloudforest where every tree seemed to be painted green and festooned with Spanish moss, while pink bromeliads thrust their spikes towards the sky. We were frequently lost, and kept careful details on the correct route for our still-to-be-written book, noting that so many people had taken the wrong paths that they were now as worn as the correct ones – more worn, in fact, because of the additional wear caused by hikers retracing their steps. In my letter/journal, written each evening on the trail, I bemoaned the weather:

> … cloudy and drizzly, and for hours we walked through ankle-deep bog and mud. I think it's <u>always</u> wet here and that's part of the beauty. Finally, after passing many viewpoints hidden in mist, we rounded a bend, the clouds rolled back, and there was the valley bathed in sunlight and <u>beautiful</u>. A little later we rounded another bend and there was Machu Picchu across the valley!

Since that hike in 1973 I've done the Inca Trail several times, in considerable comfort as part of a well-supported group, and that first view of faraway Machu Picchu always brings a tingle of recognition and happiness. But none like this first realisation that we really *could* walk to Machu Picchu, just as I had imagined four years earlier.

> Now the sun was shining we decided it was much too nice to press on to Machu Picchu so took a turn off to some ruins called Weeny Wy… something, where we spent the night. The ruins were not as spectacular as Machu Picchu, of course, but lovely and <u>personal</u>, with flowers all over the place and some of the stones almost disappearing beneath ferns and mosses.

We continued to make our leisurely way to Machu Picchu, pausing at the Gate of the Sun for me to recall that morning four years ago when I had stood at the same spot, looked back along a faint path, and said to myself, 'I bet this trail leads to Cusco.' And so it did – or at least to Km 88.

We weren't done yet with our explorations.

> Rather than tamely camp at the official campsite we hid our packs in the bushes and after the ruins were closed we climbed up to the summit of Huayna Picchu, the sugarloaf mountain backing all those famous photos. You climb up narrow Inca steps to reach the top where I had previously admired the view. We thought sunrise would be pretty good from there, and we'd heard that there was a cave one could sleep in but it was occupied by a rather evil-looking Englishman who told us proudly that he had enough food for a week, although why anyone would want to spend a week living in a cave on a mountaintop... We found the only flat place outside and put out our sleeping bags. A few hours later it started to rain and didn't let up until dawn. We had a plastic sheet over us but puddles of water collected in strategic places and trickled on to our bodies so we got rather wet. But at dawn the clouds rolled away and we had a gorgeous sunrise with the distant snow-covered mountains all pink and then like orange satin. And in the valley below us, puffs of cloud and the light constantly changing.

Now, a word about our irresponsibility and that of other hikers. As in the Galápagos, where unregulated tourism would have been a disaster for the wildlife, the same is true for the ruins of Machu Picchu. The year 1973 was, I suspect, the first that the Inca Trail was truly discovered. Our book, published in 1974, was certainly the first to describe it in print. We were conscientious in urging readers not to drop litter and to be careful when making fires – and refrained from mentioning our own indiscretions. We'd seen for ourselves that hiking needed to be regulated. The biggest problem in later years, when the route became popular, was the lack of toilet facilities, with human excrement piled everywhere, and litter. Lots of litter. Hikers – and sometimes porters – lit fires next to the ruins, cracking the stones. The South American Explorers' Club was instrumental in organising trail clean-ups, and when I last walked it, in the 1990s, I welcomed the changes which had resulted in a clean, protected trail.

Our final indulgence was a hot bath. Hearing that the village of Aguas Calientes, a mile or so down the railway track, lived up to its name of 'hot water', we decided to camp there for the night. There was a full moon and we had a marvellous dip.

> If you can imagine swimming nude in the moonlight, but in hot-bath temperature, you'll get the idea. It was fabulous!

Before leaving the subject of Machu Picchu and our book – these days known as the Little Yellow Book – a word about Ron Fear. People who still have a copy of that first edition ask me about the dedication. 'This book is dedicated to the memory of Ron Fear. After encouraging us to write this book Ron was killed on the Urubamba River in August 1973.' We had met this American adventurer and his party near Machu Picchu, shared a campfire, toasted marshmallows, and discussed our mutual plans. They were insistent that we should, indeed, write a guidebook about our backpacking trips because no one, but no one, knew about the original pre-Columbian trails that ran through the Andes, and the new popularity of the Inca Way to Machu Picchu showed the need. We listened, fascinated, to his group's plans to take the train to the station beyond Machu Picchu, Quillabamba, where the Río Urubamba broadens and becomes navigable, and raft down to Pucallpa, where Linda and I had started our Amazon journey four years earlier.

The group were well prepared and very experienced. We were particularly impressed by Ron, an exceptionally nice guy, who had rafted extensively in Canada and Alaska, had led mountain-climbing expeditions in Nepal and acted as mountain guide and PR to one of the largest suppliers of climbing equipment. In other words he had the personality and experience for this adventure. So we were profoundly shocked to meet some Americans a few days later who had just returned from taking part in a search party for a group that went missing on the Urubamba. They had found fragments of the raft but no bodies. We realised this was Ron's party and pieced together the story, which was confirmed by his girlfriend who we met again in Cusco. It was agonisingly simple. When his party missed the train to Quillabamba, Ron had become very upset, completely lost his cool, and said that he and one other chap were going to put in to the river by the Machu Picchu station and would meet the rest of the group in Quillabamba. Apparently the locals urged them not to go, told them it was too dangerous, but Ron's mind was made up. They set off and probably were killed within minutes. Just round the bend was a huge waterfall that no raft could survive intact. We'll never know why such an experienced man would take that risk, but have often wondered if it boiled down to something as simple as his name. If you are called Fear perhaps you spend your life proving it wrong.

'Now, how can a sleeping bag detach itself from my backpack, climb over the little rail on the bus roof, and jump off to disappear forever?'

This was the most disastrous of all our many robberies because now we were committed to high-altitude trekking a down sleeping bag was essential. Actually, we didn't know if it really had been stolen because there was no baggage boy riding on top this time, but it seemed the only plausible suggestion. Experience had told us what to do in these circumstances. After we discovered the loss in

Cusco, we took an open truck back to Urubamba to see if we could spot it beside the road, and I leapt off at each police checkpoint to ask if it had been handed in. It hadn't. The police in Urubamba threw themselves into the challenge and corralled the driver when he returned with the bus and marched us all to the police station. I explained what had happened, and the police said menacingly that it was the bus company's responsibility to keep passengers' luggage safe. When he heard the value of this *bolsita*, or 'little bag', the driver looked close to tears and we felt very sorry for him. We told him about insurance and assured him that American insurance companies were very rich, and everyone brightened up. The police gave us an impressive document, covered in red stamps and signatures for the insurance company, and we all parted good friends.

It was time to move on to Bolivia. I was excited to be heading for a new country with, we hoped, more trails to explore for the backpacking guide we were now committed to writing, but worried about how I would keep warm at night.

6

BOLIVIA

It had snowed over the Altiplano and the Aymara women who live in this harsh, high-altitude environment were having a marvellous time. They had rolled huge snowballs, which lay around the grasslands along with occasional snowmen or snow-llamas. Their creators sat resting in the snow, blobs of red and black against the white. We smiled at this obvious relief from their day-to-day drudgery as we drove towards the border and on to La Paz. The sun shone and Lake Titicaca was Mediterranean blue, surrounded by the white-flecked shore and backed by jagged snow mountains.

La Paz, one of the highest capitals in the world, sits in a bowl surrounded by mountains. We arrived at El Alto above the city after dark and we gasped at the sudden sight of the twinkling lights of the capital far below us. We knew already that we were going to love this place.

The tourist office was helpful but somewhat mystified. 'A Jesus cross? Near La Paz? That's probably the Cristo Redentor at La Cumbre. No, we don't know of any walks around there.'

'We were told we could go on foot from there down to Coroico.'

'No, that wouldn't be possible. But we could find you a tour of the Yungas region.'

As always, we were encouraged by this negative advice. La Paz was as popular with French tourists as Cusco and we wanted to feel alone. It had been a bit of a long shot anyway, inspired by a conversation with a backpacking American, who said that they had been told about this trail by a member of the Costa Rican National Orchestra while they were touring Ecuador. 'They said to find a big Jesus cross on a hill outside La Paz and follow his left hand. This would point the way to an Inca trail to Coroico in the tropical region. Mind you, they were very drunk at the time so we never followed it up.'

La Paz was high and cold; La Cumbre, at around 15,500ft, was very high and very cold. Indeed it was snowing hard when we got stiffly out of the truck. I had no sleeping bag for this trek, only a Peruvian poncho, and visualised us tramping around in the snow looking fruitlessly for a path before spending the night in a snow cave, dying, quite slowly, of hypothermia. I had also left my sunglasses behind and was suffering from snow blindness. Or what I diagnosed as snow blindness. I wasn't a very agreeable companion.

We climbed up to the statue of Jesus and, indeed, with his left arm he was helpfully pointing to rows of footsteps and llama tracks leading to two small lakes, half hidden in the snow, and then a scree slope up to a ridge. Any effort at that altitude made us breathless, more so in deep snow, but we were confident that we were on the right track, literally. It took about an hour to reach the top of the ridge but once we did the grey cloud of my mood lifted as we surveyed the scene. Half of Bolivia seemed to stretch below us, mostly green, not white, with a few puffy clouds settling in the deep valleys. Even more encouraging, where the snow had melted there was clearly a trail, partly paved, leading seductively down into the trees.

It was just a question of following this track as it led downhill, gradually taking on an Inca, or maybe pre-Inca, aspect: stone-paved and descending in a series of switchbacks, reinforced at the curves and with channels cut into the stone for drainage. Then the clouds blew in and it started to rain and my gloom descended again. I needed all the clothing I had to sleep in, and my anorak was already soaked. When we reached a farm with no let-up in the rain we asked a woman who was sitting in her doorway spinning if we could shelter in one of their huts for a while. She showed us into a storehouse about a foot deep in potatoes with sheepskins rolled up around the sides. It was so cosy we enquired whether it might be possible to sleep there. No problem. So after sharing our soup with her and her husband we scooped out two depressions in the potatoes, covered them in sheepskins, and had a really snug night.

That was the last cold night. Once we were below the treeline there were the usual colourful birds, fluttering butterflies, and lots of wayside flowers. Tiny children passed us in sole charge of huge oxen, and herds of llamas, decorated with coloured ear tassels and bibs, skittered by with their loads of potatoes and other produce bound for La Cumbre where trucks were waiting to transport their goods to La Paz.

Progress on the third day was slow because of all the wild strawberries growing by the trail. We seemed to be the only people who knew these were edible and we stuffed ourselves. The trail was now very narrow, but still clear. Bracken and flowering shrubs brushed our legs and it was hard to remember that we had ever been cold. Towards the end of that day the houses changed: corrugated iron instead of thatch, and some windows were glazed. Clearly we were approaching civilisation. Our narrow path became a track and the track became a road. A shop advertised cold beer so we sat outside, toasting our success, and registering that we had descended from the heights of La Cumbre to a little over 4,000ft – an altitude loss of more than 10,000ft. We now had an excellent Bolivian hike for our book.

A truck carrying sacks of coffee beans stopped for us and took us to Coroico which turned out to be a good 30 miles further on. Here we rested, ate enormous meals and quantities of oranges, and enjoyed being thoroughly warm for the first time in several weeks.

The dirt road from the Yungas to La Cumbre and La Paz is now, melodramatically, known as the 'Death Road' and has become a macabre tourist attraction in itself. In 1973, hardened travellers that we were, we hardly noticed the several waterfalls splashing over the road and drenching us, the sheer drop to one side and the cliff on the other, barely a truck's width apart, or the numerous wayside crosses commemorating those who had plunged to their death.

> It's very strange. Here we are in the jungle again, but instead of the usual delays and broken promises everything is going smoothly. So smoothly, in fact, that we've just had to look at the map to find out which river we are floating down.

We'd started making enquiries in Cochabamba, where we'd retreated from La Paz to get away from the tourist hordes. George also managed to buy a used camera:

> … from an exceptionally dishonest-looking man who runs a second-hand shop full of dilapidated saddles and bridles, old typewriters and broken furniture. But it seems to work.

With the help of an enthusiastic local girl who insisted we joined her family for lunch (her father owned a trucking company) we completed our plans for a river trip, learning that indeed the small riverside town of Trinidad was the best destination because that's where most boats delivered their cargo. We should be able to pick up some sort of vessel at Puerto Villarroel, she told us, adding that a landslide was blocking the road so no cargo could get through. Anyway, father mentioned as an afterthought, the cargo-boatmen were on strike. However, those not on strike and living the far side of the landslide were transporting local gravel downriver for the new Trinidad airport, so these barges were our best bet. We were lucky. We found the *Louis Albert* loaded and ready to leave, talked to the captain and settled the price, and hopped aboard. This was the Río Ichilo, which joins the Mamore, which meets the Madeira, which flows into the Amazon at Manaus. So we were officially on a tributary of the Amazon (which is a relief, since that's what I've been telling people for fifty years). And we were the only passengers.

We slept on the only available area of deck, behind the steering wheel and under the roof, just large enough to fit our mosquito-netting tent (a mercy: when we stopped at night the insects poured in joyfully looking for human flesh). The only disadvantage was having to get up at 5.30am each day when the area was needed by the helmsman (if that's the right name for the man who steers the boat). We floated downriver for a week, and days settled into a happy routine. After our dawn awakening the cook would hand us a mug of strong, sweet black coffee. We would retrieve our binoculars from the captain and watch the birds and other wildlife wake up while the sun – and there was sun this time – rose through the mists as a perfect red disc. The Ichilo was narrow, our progress slow, and we finally saw that long-sought-after wildlife. A flock of blue and yellow macaws flew overhead on our first morning, banking so that the sun caught their buttercup-yellow breasts. They were followed by scarlet macaws and then a toucan. Once a small alligator slid down the bank into the water, and, as the river widened into the Mamore, we were joined by river dolphins. There were always herons and storks, including the spectacularly ugly jabiru stork. Once we disturbed a family of capybara; the adult climbed the bank easily but the youngsters kept slipping back, eliciting 'aaahs' from their audience.

Breakfast was at 8am, a huge meal of banana mash mixed with corn, onions and whatever was left over from supper. We would then dangle our feet in the water and watch the riverbank for birds and animals, waiting for the captain to snatch up our binoculars in his daily quest for meat. When we approached a riverside house he would scan it to see if they had a carcass hanging outside. If so he'd unhook the dugout canoe which we towed behind us, and paddle out to strike a bargain. We enjoyed quite a variety: peccary was the most common, but we also had smoked turtle and quantities of turtle eggs which are something of an acquired taste but we learned to enjoy them. When boiled the shell remains soft and the 'white' glutinous, but the yolk firms up into a cakey texture. The trick was to half peel one then squeeze it into your mouth with a satisfying pop.

After lunch it was siesta time. We strung up our hammocks in the shady dining room, and did most of our writing there. We had a book to write, remember, and this was the ideal time to do it. We took alternate chapters, then swapped them for review and criticism. Not always harmonious, but it got done – it would be a slim volume, describing just three long-distance trails and two walks.

As the day got cooler, the wildlife stirred again and we would continue with our nature watching. In some ways it was the best time of day with parrots and macaws heading home to their roosts shouting at each other, and the herons busy with their fishing. At dusk the pilot would find a steep bank over deep water, swing the boat around so it faced upriver, and a crewman would scramble up the bank to tie it to a tree. Supper was a light meal, sometimes just soup, and afterwards we might fit in a game of Scrabble until the mosquitoes arrived, then set up our tent for an early night.

Trinidad was hot, dusty and expensive. And isolated. The only practical way out was by river or the weekly plane, so we were stuck there for a few days. George put this time to good use and found, surprisingly, a typing school where they agreed, even more surprisingly, to let him come when there were no classes and use one of their typewriters to transcribe our book. I couldn't type so spent my time wandering round town eating ice cream.

The typing school was closed at weekends so we decided to see the surrounding countryside. Very dull, actually, flat cattle-grazing pampas spattered with termite mounds. Our two days away would have been a bit of a disappointment had our truck not been stopped by a man shouting that he had '*Huevos de pillú*' to sell. We had no idea what a *pillú* was, but the other passengers did and were very excited, as was the driver. They turned out to be the enormous eggs of the rhea, South America's version of the ostrich. We bought one and later asked a restaurant to cook it for us. Somewhat like a hen's egg but richer, it made a huge and very tasty omelette – and was enough for about six people (we shared it with other customers).

With time in hand we jumped in a jeep prepared to go wherever it was going. The small town we ended up in would have been quite dull had they not been celebrating a little fiesta. A greasy pole had been erected, hung with gifts and flags. Before anyone attempted to climb it, a group of children wearing bull masks and with bells on their legs danced round it to the accompaniment of drums and flutes. Then a boy attempted to climb the pole but slid down, unable to reach the top. A bigger boy made a big show of preparing himself, flexing his muscles and so on, and made it to the top to much applause. He draped himself in a flag and threw down the gifts to the crowd below. These included a can of tuna fish, a bra, a pair of shoes and a packet of cream crackers. Once safely down he was piped into the little church to be blessed.

Returning to Trinidad we saw several rheas, the birds which had generously given up their egg for our omelette. I would think the parent bird might have been quite relieved. He has the misfortune to be a rarity in the animal kingdom in that the male has all the parental responsibility, mating with several females who each lay a clutch of eggs then say, 'OK, your job now, I'm off to have fun!' He collects all 'his' eggs together, incubates them and takes care of the numerous chicks.

Back in La Paz, shivering in the chill after the sticky heat of Trinidad, we wanted to take a look at Lake Titicaca which we'd only seen from the bus. First, though, we needed to go to the post office and mail our precious typescript to George's mother in Boston.

We hadn't intended to stop at Achacachi but our progress was blocked by an exuberant fiesta, something we had discovered that Bolivia does better than anywhere else in South America. We dumped our stuff in a hotel and went to watch. A 'brass' band (though the instruments were silver) led the dancers round the plaza, making a lot of splendid noise, helped by men in their best suits carrying wooden monkeys on a handle that made a ratchet sound when turned. They were followed by dancing villagers, mostly women with women, and men with men. I was soon snatched up by two giggling, bowler-hatted women, while George was grabbed by a man unfortunately too drunk to stand up so his session was shorter. After a break, when we slipped off to have lunch, the dancers reappeared in magnificent costumes, probably representing highly stylised *conquistadores* with masses of blond hemp hair attached to gringo masks with blue goggle eyes made from light bulbs; one was smoking a pipe. A few had helmets or crowns and they all wore high plumed headdresses. The rest of their costume was made of cardboard, fantastically decorated with silver and gold, or embroidered with birds, beasts and flowers. There were armadillos and alligators too, and a rather endearing insect, species unknown.

> As soon as we appeared again we were engulfed, and George soon disappeared dancing down the street hand-in-hand with a white bear. When they reappeared after their stint around the plaza, George was thoroughly in the swing of things which apparently involved hitting people on the head with a banana. On seeing me the bear decided it was my turn and off we went, hand-in-hand and occasionally doing pirouettes. Every now and then someone would dance up with a jug of aguardiente (the local firewater) and a little glass. The requirement was to down it in one gulp but fortunately it was also the custom to donate some to Mother Earth who did rather well out of me

that day. Everyone seemed genuinely delighted to see us. Just when I was on the verge of exhaustion we reached a square which was apparently the official rest place, the men took off part of their costumes and we were passed glasses of beer and plates of food. Everyone wanted to talk to us, but with Spanish their second language and a high degree of inebriation we didn't understand very much.

We hid in our hotel for a while and watched from the balcony as the straggling dancers came past, the drunk men being held up by their women or falling down if they had no human support.

When it got too cold to stay in our room any longer we rejoined the dancers, drank some more, and George did his funny-man act. This delighted everyone, especially the señora serving the drinks who had to hug me in her mirth.

Finally, inevitably, everyone was too drunk to enjoy themselves and the women resorted to the Bolivian woman's favourite recreation when the worse for wear – crying and hitting each other. We retreated to our hotel.

Back in La Paz we planned one more excursion from the capital before heading south for Argentina. I bought a rather grungy sleeping bag from a home-going American and we journeyed first to bleak, chilly Oruro, then west towards the Chilean border. We'd read in the *South American Handbook*: 'Rugged tourists or anthropologists can try going to Chipaya'. So we did.

The village of Chipaya is truly isolated. Even getting to the nearest town, from where we knew we would have to walk for 16 miles, involved a twelve-hour truck ride across rubble-strewn salt flats dotted with depressed-looking shrubs, and a permanent biting wind. We were lucky to be picked up by a group of oil prospectors who took pity on us as we trudged along the straight, featureless track, and took us to Chipaya where we were formally greeted by the mayor and paid an entrance fee of $10. He led us to a thatched hut with an raised adobe bed covered with sheepskins. It was all very organised, and pretending to be anthropologists seemed an embarrassing, and probably unwise, deception.

Chipaya has been isolated for so long that its customs, clothing and language are unique. The clothing came straight from the sheep which scavenged around the village and provided meat and wool, so the striped poncho and men's trousers were in natural shades of brown and white. The coarsely woven black dresses of the women must have been very scratchy. Both men and women had random blanket pins in their clothes, whether for decoration or because they might be useful, we never knew. Most men wore large caps somewhat in the shape of their strange houses, which were more like African huts than anything else we'd seen in South America: round with a conical roof. Women and girls wore their long hair in rows of tiny plaits, which were then combined into two large braids. Missionaries had made an effort to convert these people and there was a nice little white church. The religious message was somewhat spoilt, however, since the people worshipped the tower as a phallic symbol. We also saw evidence of animal sacrifice in front of the church: a flat, bloodstained stone.

Our four days in the village settled into a routine. First greet the women and children clustered round our door ready to see what the visitors looked like this morning and to finger George's blond beard; then buy bread straight from the clay oven heated with dried dung from llamas or sheep. At some point George would have his little ritual with an elderly villager, or *mi abuelo* (my grandfather) as he called him. This grizzled old fellow was unsteady on his feet and never seemed quite sure where his short legs would take him. When he spotted George he would give a little squeak of delight and wobble towards him for their ceremonial greeting: first a handshake, then a kiss, and finally a bear hug. He would then start talking – or rather chanting – slowly at first, building up to a crescendo, then dropping down to pianissimo. George would carefully follow the same pattern, in English, telling him what we'd done that day or were planning to do, revving up to the climax then slowing down to the almost whispered finale. That prompted the next phase. The two men gazed seriously at each other, and then chanted in unison, not always words, sometimes just different sounds. Finally a cordial handshake and that was it for the day. A respectful crowd had always gathered at that point. Who knows what they made of it.

There was always something new to see as we strolled around the village. We were curious about a young woman inside her courtyard, holding the wall with both hands and swaying, twisting, from side to side. Very strange! Her beaming smile indicated that it would be fine to take a closer look. She was standing with both feet in a large hollowed-out stone bowl, grinding the local grain with her feet. Women always went barefoot (only men wore sandals, made from car tyres) so I suppose her feet were as tough as a stone pestle.

Another time we came across a woman squatting on the ground, quietly breastfeeding a lamb.

We got quite a bit of information from the two Spanish-speaking schoolteachers who had been sent here by the government for a year as a sort of national-service requirement. While we sat chatting to them in the schoolyard, some girls cautiously approached, giggling, and I soon felt my long hair being gathered up in nimble, experienced fingers. At the end of half an hour or so I had six thin plaits on each side. I was hugely proud of them and kept them for the rest of our stay.

The schoolteachers told us that Chipaya would be holding a fiesta in a few days' time so, after our wonderful experience at Achacachi, we were keen to stick around for this. It was mid-afternoon before we heard music, and it all seemed to be happening at the far end of the village, an area we hadn't ventured into before. We sat on a wall and watched for a while. The men wore clusters of animal bones from their belts and circled round a sort of altar made from cactus wood, wheat sheaves and poles topped by a silver disc. Every now and then a man would break off and kiss the structure. It was a dour event, very different from the exuberant fiesta on the Altiplano. A few musicians played drums, pan pipes and a *charango* (a rather lovely stringed instrument with an armadillo shell as a soundbox) and some women were dancing. The men, mostly drunk on stove alcohol, were keen to talk to us, showering us with saliva green from the coca leaves they were chewing. We were both pulled into a dancing circle of grim-faced villagers, but it soon turned nasty when a woman started pulling me around and hitting me. I decided perhaps this wasn't like Achacachi. Four angry men appeared asking for money and wanted to see our documents. We tried to explain that we had already paid and that Santiago, the mayor, had checked our documents, but this didn't work. Finally we fled, chased by the men with raised fists.

The schoolteachers explained. The village was divided, socially, into two halves. 'Our' side, where we had rented the hut and been checked in by the mayor, was accustomed to gringos. It's where the anthropologists stayed. The far side, which was celebrating the fiesta, was separate and saw few outsiders so was naturally suspicious of them. It was a sobering discovery – the last thing we had wanted to do was offend anyone.

We left the next day. Our visit to Chipaya cured us of our desire, which we had held throughout South America, to 'visit Indians'. I think this notion stemmed from my stay at San Cristóbal de las

Casas, in Mexico, where the local tribes were accustomed to being studied, were proud of their heritage, and integrated into local affairs. We were out of line in Chipaya. We contributed nothing except the money that went to the mayor and probably got no further. Villagers were constantly trying to sell us things that we didn't want to buy and were accustomed to being paid by anthropologists for information about their lives and culture. We were no use to them. We took some interesting photos but never paid for the privilege. From the point of view of being good, sensitive travellers it was a rather shoddy episode, but of course as a personal experience it was exceptional and I wouldn't have missed it for the world.

And there was one more, very different, Indian experience that we didn't want to miss: the weekly market in Tarabuco. Indian markets provided the opportunity for a meaningful encounter because there was usually something we wanted to buy. We'd seen photos of the Tarabuco people's extraordinarily elaborate and unusual costumes, and the people themselves showed every sign of being self-confident and proud of their distinctiveness. Our bus passed streams of them on their way to the market, in full costume and playing their *charangos* as they walked. In my letter home I describe their costume in detail, along with illustrations.

> Both men and women wear an amazing helmet-shaped hat made out of suede and decorated by various tassels and baubles. When the women aren't wearing the helmets they have even more elaborate headgear: a sort of winged sombrero, completely covered by pearl buttons, silver baubles, and coloured yarns so they look like a Christmas tree. The men wear three-quarter-length very baggy trousers woven from coarse wool, and held up by a wide, tooled leather belt with pockets and decorated with silver, and a little shoulder-poncho under their large, and gorgeously coloured and striped, poncho with woollen fringes.

The women wear a skirt of dark green or navy blue, with a black 'apron' covering it with intricate designs woven into the lower part. Absolutely gorgeous!

No wonder they looked so proud as they walked to market.

We had the whole day in Tarabuco before our onward transport left and were wondering what to do when a whole bunch of costumed people, followed by a band, burst out of a building and went dancing off down the street. We'd stumbled across yet another fiesta! Here the costumes were obviously home-made and full of character. There were some particularly handsome lions and tigers, as well as the usual *conquistadores* and devils. They paraded round the town for a while before ending up in a corral where a sort of bullfight took place. Very sort of. Bulls were led into the arena and had money tied to their horns before being let loose. The aim was obviously for the village lads to bravely retrieve the money from the ferocious bulls. The trouble was the bulls were much keener on going home than being fierce, but since the exit was blocked they made a show of rolling their eyes and pawing the ground. If they so much as looked in the toreador's direction he fled, but while the bulls' backs were turned a certain amount of poncho flapping took place. A vessel full of *chicha* stood in the centre and as the lads got drunker they became braver and also less nimble so two even managed to get knocked over, to the applause of the crowd. We didn't see any succeed in retrieving the money.

It was mid-October, and we needed to keep moving if we were to get the best weather in the far south. We'd been in Bolivia for nearly two months and it was our favourite country so far. The scenery, the fiestas, the friendliness and above all the traditional way of life apparently untouched by outside influences far exceeded our expectations. Perhaps it was a good thing that our penultimate bit of transport was one of the most uncomfortable yet.

Nearly 44 hours, including a sleepless night since the seats didn't push back and our knee room was six inches. And the state of the road was such that the bus lurched and bounced like the bucking bronco painted on its side. When we did nod off our foreheads received a direct hit from the wooden back of the seat in front of us.

Interlude
The Little Yellow Book

Has any successful company had a more inauspicious start? Or to put it another way, if you need proof that the information matters more than appearance in a travel guide, it's here.

Our first guidebook, published in 1974 and only fifty-four pages long, was riddled with spelling mistakes – one on almost every page. Maybe it was inevitable. George is dyslexic but can type; I can spell but couldn't type. His mother, Sally, who had the dubious pleasure of properly typing up the wonky text that George mailed to her in Boston, was a busy woman who maybe didn't proofread her work that carefully. And where place names were concerned, and Spanish words, she had to assume we'd got them right.

Backpacking along Ancient Ways in Peru and Bolivia rather grandly carried the subtitle, on the title page: *Three Hikes for Experts/Two Walks for Beginners*. There are no maps, no index, and the illustrations that I had lovingly supplied were rather clumsily outlined by a friend to make them easier to reproduce. In appearance, to be honest, it's an embarrassment. The text, however, is surprisingly good: detailed and based on knowledge of what a backpacker needs, so the trail directions are supplemented by advice on transport and lodgings. There's even a recipe for granola (which could be made at the gringo hotel in Cusco) on the last page. On the back cover is the price: $1.95 including postage. And it fitted easily into a pocket.

One of my well-thumbed copies of that first edition has a typed message signed by George stapled inside. 'TRAVELLERS... There are errors in "Backpacking..." Although only two are at all confusing. We apologise to our readers. Being 7,000 miles away from Boston and out of contact due to our flexible itinerary, we were unable to proofread hence the following ERRATA: The description "Getting from Cusco to Chincheros", page 42, should appear in its logical place on page 44. "Getting from Cusco to La Paz" on page 43 escaped from its natural place between pages 46 & 47. Okay? The map is accurate for Peru and Bolivia, the crucial area. But you may have noticed that the surrounding areas are "inoperative". Indeed. Ecuador had become Equador and Argentina morphed into 'Para', which presumably was supposed to represent Paraguay.

Sally had a thousand copies printed in Boston, and sent review copies to a few backpacking journals. They were also on sale at the Harvard Coop, a popular general store in Cambridge. I recorded that the production cost was £250 and I seem to remember that our profit, once they had all been sold – or given away – was about $200. We were well pleased.

7

WESTERN ARGENTINA AND CHILE

It was an unusual choice. The bus to Jujuy from the Argentine border town would have taken four hours, the train took ten, but we'd had enough of road transport for a while, even though we noted with some astonishment that there were paved roads in Argentina (Bolivia had only two stretches of tarmac road in the whole country). My first letter home on this leg of our journey was peppered with exclamation marks.

> Tarred roads! Loo seats! Hot water! Not just hot water but it comes out of a tap!

Apart from in private houses and a very few fancy hotels, this was the first time we'd seen this miracle in all of South America.

> Normally there's a nasty little contraption above the shower head which heats the water, very inadequately just before it comes out, and sometimes involves joining two sparking bits of wire together.
>
> Argentina seems ridiculously prosperous after Bolivia, and Jujuy feels like Oxford Street on a Saturday morning, with posh shops and far too many people crowding the pavement, pushing humble backpackers off the side. George is causing waves of laughter because of his shorts. I showed him the passage in the Handbook which says, bluntly, 'Shorts are not worn', but he took no notice. The accent here is very different from the countries further north so we are struggling to understand what anyone says. Indeed, we have a lot of adjustments to make.

We fairly sped through the monotonous landscape toward the Andes. We were eager to reach our goal, Tierra del Fuego, before the end of summer, and our map showed a good road running south through Chile, so that seemed our obvious route. The road ended at Puerto Montt where we would re-enter Argentina. Yes, we had it all planned. Then we heard the news.

'What do you mean, a coup?' We were enjoying a glass of red wine (cheaper than beer) in a Cordoba bar with an American expat. We had been only too successful in removing ourselves from tourist haunts and the news grapevine.

'In Chile? So Allende's gone?'

We had no idea, and it seemed that we needed to adjust our plans. The picture this chap painted of Chile was a worrying one. The president was dead, a brutal military regime was in power, there was a curfew and people breaking it were shot. Surely our style of travel would be too risky. The coup had taken place on September 11 (yes, it is sometimes referred to as 'the other 9/11'), and it was now early November, so perhaps things would have settled down. Or perhaps not. We would have been quite happy to skip Chile and keep to the eastern side of the Andes, but there was no main road running south, just minor ones wandering in all directions. It would take us ages, but still... perhaps we had no choice.

We decided to continue to Mendoza, the other side of the Andes from Santiago, and hope to get some up-to-date news there.

We loved Mendoza. It was in a beautiful situation in the foothills of the Andes and the centre of the wine industry. Had we not discovered that we could take a train to Santiago on the narrow-gauge Trans-Andean railway we might have given up on Chile, but this sounded too enjoyable to miss. Yes, we would take the risk, and just travel south as fast as we could – by public transport.

When we went to the station to buy our tickets we found a large crowd gathered, many carrying flowers. Were they expecting some celebrity, we asked. No, it was the body of an Argentinian shot by the army in Chile.

'Um… do you think we'll be safe in Chile?'

'Perhaps that is a question to ask in Chile,' the stationmaster responded dryly.

The train journey was gorgeous, passing between snow-covered mountains and weird rock formations and through a long tunnel. We emerged to spring in the western Andes, looking down into a verdant valley with roses proliferating by the track. We found a hotel near the station and planned to spend two days in the city before speeding south. Having changed some dollars to Chilean escudos in Mendoza, we expected the cost of living and travelling to be the same as in Argentina, so were prepared for some hardship.

The next instalment of my diary/letters explodes with superlatives and explains why we ended up spending a week in the capital. It turned out that one of Pinochet's first actions had been to devalue the currency by one hundred per cent, a change not fully reflected on the Argentine side of the border, and we suddenly found ourselves in a highly sophisticated and ridiculously cheap city. We went a bit wild. There was wine, there were strawberries, there were delicious fish dinners, and terrific museums and art galleries to visit. And if the buildings were mostly architecturally uninspiring, the parks and plazas were ablaze with carefully tended flowers, manicured lawns, and a grand variety of trees. It was more like a European city than any we had encountered so far, and we were ready for a taste of a familiar culture.

There were, however, plenty of signs of the coup – bullet holes, piles of sandbags and propaganda posters – though everyone, even the army, were pleasant and friendly. We were perfectly happy to obey the 10pm curfew and behave with propriety. The posters were clearly aimed at the middle classes, the housewives who had demonstrated against the shortages during the latter part of the Allende regime, banging their pots and pans in a nightly noisy march through the city. One poster showed a pile of weapons with the claim that these were 'owned by extremists who planned to kill your son because he didn't think like them'. And another that made us particularly anxious: a row of hippie types with the caption that they were 'foreign extremists dedicated to killing and assassination'. That night I gave George a hair and beard trim and he cut my long hair.

My letter home breaks off mid sentence:

> Well, gulp, had to interrupt there and throw ourselves melodramatically to the floor owing to a burst of gunfire near the hotel. After turning out the light we watched the scene through binoculars. There were lots of military men milling around a body. A man walked towards them with his hands up but we don't know what happened to him. Don't worry, we wouldn't <u>dream</u> of going out after curfew.

It was time to buy a few clothes; we were too embarrassingly, and perhaps dangerously, scruffy. After asking us what we thought of Chile, to which we gave cautiously non-committal answers, the shopkeeper told us how happy they all were now that Allende had gone. She was furious at what she said was the foreign press's biased view of her country. She repeated several times, 'Now we are happy!' and a woman emerged from the back of the shop to say the same thing. The following day we were stopped in the street by a woman asking where we were from and reiterating that the last few months had been absolute hell, queueing for hours for staples such as sugar. 'Please tell your friends and families at home,' she urged.

> Tomorrow we're going to do something so decadent, I'm embarrassed to tell you what it is. George's father gave us an American Express card before we left to use in an emergency.

Well, he wrote recently and said that for George's birthday present we could buy something and charge it to the card. Trouble is, there's nothing you can buy and charge in South America, they just don't have that sort of shop, so we're staying one night in a posh hotel and charging it. I think it's a marvellous idea! I've been rather sad at the thought that I'd probably never stay in a posh hotel for the rest of my life (because I married a Maverick not a Success) and now I can. We will have breakfast in bed and stay in our own private hot bath for an hour. I can hardly wait! I hope they won't turn us away when they see our backpacks.

The hotel lived up to expectations. I stayed in the bath long enough to get pink and wrinkly and took particular delight in choosing what I wanted for breakfast and hanging the list on the door. I spend a page of my letter describing in mouth-watering detail our dinner the night before, complete with cocktail, then wine, and a dessert.

One item on the menu was translated as 'A small locust'. I know there are shortages in Chile but this is ridiculous.

The charge on the American Express card for dinner, bed and breakfast for two was less than $19.

It was nearly time to leave Santiago for the train ride to Concepción and beyond, and we were having a final catch-up of newspapers in the British Library. Noticing what we were reading, a young woman came and sat by us. Pointing to our copies of the *Guardian* and *Observer*, she said, with some venom, 'No one who hasn't lived in Santiago during the last three years has any right to report on Chile. Your papers are so biased. I had to give up eating bread for three months because I couldn't queue for hours because of getting to work.' She clicked my pen on and off in her agitation and continued, 'Everything was The Party. If you weren't in you were out.

And you must remember,' she continued, 'that Allende only got thirty-six per cent of the vote in 1970. I voted for him myself because I thought it was time for a change.' We told her that we had heard the same story from other people, but then described the shooting outside our hotel and the difficulty of finding out the truth from a censored press. She shrugged and just said, 'It's so much better now.'

When we got to the station, there was our *Rapido* train, sleek and gleaming, smart as a Rolls-Royce: soft seats, air conditioning, meals served. We glided past vineyards, pastures full of grazing cows and frolicking foals, rows of Lombardy poplars lining the fields. The English-looking landscape was incongruously backed by the Andes, snow-covered and jagged, and at one point we saw a perfectly conical volcano wearing a little cap of smoke. And the flowers! Fields of purple flowers, yellow blooms, carpets of poppies and hedges of roses. And that's the thing. No one really wants to read about happy holidays, and Chile was proving to be a wonderful holiday from the rigours of Real Travel. So for now I shall leave it there.

However, I do want to recall here some of the fascinating conversations we had as we journeyed back and forth between Argentina and Chile in the spring of 1973 and in the autumn of 1974 – even though it means jumping forward more than a year in the narrative – because these encounters highlight the importance of discarding preconceptions and experiencing first-hand a country or regime which we are taught by our media is evil.

Our several visits to Chile, and the people we met there, had a profound effect on me. Up until then I had been willing to follow the travellers' convention of boycotting countries with a dubious human-rights record. After Chile I knew that how a country is governed is not the whole picture, it is what an open-minded traveller can learn from observation and conversation that matters. This understanding influenced my decision to publish some controversial guidebooks years down the line: titles like Burma, Iraq, Iran and North Korea.

The person we remember best, because we spent several days with him, was Alberto. He picked us up in the rain as we travelled north again in March 1994 after our sojourn in the *Cono Sur* ('southern cone', the cone-shaped south of the continent). During the long drive and while staying at his farm we learned his story. Alberto spoke fluent English and had clearly been the sort of rich landowner that Allende had been so keen to get rid of in order to redistribute his land among the workers. An admirable objective, but…

One day Alberto returned to his farm and found roadblocks and armed men. He was told to leave at once, and could not even collect any valuables. Of his five workers only two agreed to sign the expropriation paper and join the Communist Party. The other three were jobless for three years, managing on their own small plots of land. They were told repeatedly that their *patrón* would not return, but they never gave up hope. The 'interveners' moved into the house with a group of outsiders who knew nothing about farming.

The new farm manager soon retired to Europe, becoming the sort of absentee landlord that Allende was trying to get rid of. His five workers were anyway being paid less by this new chap than by Alberto, and were not used to working without direction. 'I was told that I was paternalistic,' said Alberto sadly. 'Well, perhaps that's true, but it seemed OK at the time.'

A large number of sheep were slaughtered for fiestas, and no crops were sown. Because so little money was coming in, wages were low and the workers started to sell off anything they could on the black market. A man was employed full-time to make sure Alberto didn't come back, dynamiting the airstrip and patrolling the lake in case he tried to sneak in by boat. Which he did once, but was shot at. Alberto's seven Anglo-Arab horses, valuable riding animals, were slaughtered for meat. 'And as you know, horses are nice people.' A homeless family for whom he had provided land and organised loans so they could set up a pig business, sold their animals, then the shed roof, then the rest of the shed for immediate profit.

The interveners left when the coup took place and Alberto returned three days later to be greeted joyfully by his original workers. He found fifteen labourers and felt obliged to keep most of them and provide new projects for them. There was plenty to do. No animals had survived the intervention, and very little machinery. His complex irrigation system had not been maintained and was abandoned, and he found five discarded motorboats with rusty engines. Each time a motor broke down for lack of oil they had simply bought another boat. Alberto had been anxious to get his sailing boat back, but found it had been towed into the middle of a field and left to decay.

Alberto's story was corroborated by his workers with whom we often chatted, especially the manager, Sixto, a delightful elderly man although his Spanish was almost unintelligible. Alberto said that city dwellers in Chile would have difficulty understanding his rural vocabulary. He had his own phrases, calling bees 'nice little birds', for example. Apart from Sixto, who was comfortable talking to us, we never succeeded in bridging the class barrier with the other workers. Once, when Alberto was away all day, we invited them in for tea. Their embarrassment at sitting down with us was painful, and none of our attempts to break the ice were successful.

Later on in our journey through Chile we were picked up by a fluent English-speaker (his mother was British) who was the local representative of CORFO, Chile's government-run agricultural technical advisory board. He took us to visit a farm and described how it had been taken over by the workers during Allende's time. 'We did everything we could to help. We bought all the stock and machinery from the owner and lent them back to the workers. They only had it for a year but during that time production dropped to ten per cent of the previous year. Chile's an agricultural economy. Those sorts of losses just weren't sustainable.'

Another delightful – and poignant – encounter took place in southern Chile in Villarica.

> We'd been recommended a hotel and since it would be our first for two weeks we thought we could live it up a little. We asked directions from an old gentleman taking an evening stroll. He responded in impeccable English, with no trace of an accent, and turned out to be that fast-disappearing breed, an Anglo-Chilean.

Mr Shand told us he was born in Chile, to English parents, and like his perfect, unaccented English (unless you count 'posh' as an accent) his manner was reminiscent of the nineteenth century. He asked us wistfully if we needed any books, and taking up the hint that he wanted to talk we arranged to go to his house the following day. Mr Shand was waiting for us, his wispy grey hair carefully combed, and a pile of books ready for us which we didn't have room for. It was obvious that what he really wanted to do was chat, so we invited him for a picnic. He was so buoyed at the idea that he practically danced along to the wine shop to buy some bubbly – our treat, since he'd told us earlier that he'd had to cut out wine a few months ago because it was too expensive. He explained, without a trace of self-pity, that he managed on the equivalent of £6 a month, supplementing it by teaching English.

Once we had settled down in the park with our fresh bread and cheese and popped open the bubbly, he told us about what he referred to as the terror of the last days of Allende. As the situation grew more volatile he was convinced that the government would kill off all non-communists, and on the day of the coup he had heard Allende's broadcast on a neighbour's radio, urging all the comrades to go out on to the streets and fight. The neighbours then turned it off, so he missed the following announcement, that the military had taken over the radio station. Thinking his hour had come, he'd put a large stone in his pocket and gone outside to 'meet the enemy'. Here his voice broke. 'Instead I found excited groups of people in the street, laughing and talking. They told me about the coup.' The atmosphere he described sounded almost like VE Day in London. Several times as he talked he had to pause because his eyes filled with tears. It was the first time he'd talked about his experiences to 'English people', and, 'I'm so relieved. Your press has misrepresented Chile for so long'. (It was now six months since the coup.)

Before we left, to more tears, he told us about his early life, riding around Chile on horseback visiting isolated farms to sell shares for the paper mill that his parents owned. He reflected on his heroes, Churchill and Nelson, and repeated how happy he was to speak English again. It was a memorable encounter.

Chile was not the first country to embrace a tyrant believing him to be a saviour. And it won't be the last.

Our spring journey – in November 1973 – south ended in the Lake District where we pottered between Chile and Argentina, enjoying some of the most beautiful scenery to be found anywhere. George bought some fishing tackle and a permit and optimistically marooned us with our tent by a lake teeming with trout. Because of those fish dinners we were going to enjoy we only packed a few Knorr soups. After three days George was in a thoroughly bad temper, we'd lost a lot of hooks and lures to wily trout, and we were pretty hungry.

Months later we were pushing through snowdrifts in our attempt to enjoy some mountain hiking around Bariloche, Argentina, before winter closed in. We timed it wrong, gave up and camped in a place with the marvellous name of Hua Hum where someone told us that the best hot bath in the world was to be found in the natural hot springs a half-day's walk away. They may have sniffed out our need.

We walked for hours through meadows and forests before spotting steam rising through the long grass. This was what we had come for. Walking upstream we soon came to a bamboo forest where the stream had been dammed to create a perfect bath. We could lie back and gaze at a ceiling of bamboo fronds. It was the furthest we'd ever walked for a hot bath, but absolutely worth it.

Later still, we were not sure how we would get to the frontier from our camping spot in the Argentine Lake District. As we got chatting to some military types standing by a jeep, we were pleased to recognise Chilean accents and happy to accept their offer to take us to the border. This frontier was obviously little used and perhaps they had never checked foreigners through before. The young Argentine official hoped to cover up his uncertainty with little flourishes, but his nervousness couldn't be hidden. At one point, with one of his biggest flourishes, he opened a drawer in, we guessed, the hopes of finding an instruction book on how to check out foreigners, failed in this mission and closed it with yet another flourish. He spent a long time gazing at the page of my passport which asked that I be admitted to his country without let or hindrance, and then tried to unstick the passport renewal page. He wrote out all our details on a separate piece of paper so he could copy it out properly later. Finally he stamped us through with such a flourish, and with so many dippings of the stamp in ink, that it was just a blur. And motioned us across the border. With a flourish.

The Chileans were more relaxed but still not quite sure what to do. They typed up a large sheet of paper that included such useful details as my address in London (I invented one) and finished with a description of us and the requirement to report to Interpol on our third day. I was rather offended that they described George as *de aspecto deportivo* (of sporty appearance) on account of his shorts, and carrying a backpack, while I was only described as accompanying my husband.

INTERLUDE
A WEEK IN WALES

Perhaps I just couldn't wait for my injection of Britishness, but before we took our Christmas flight to the Falklands it became imperative that we visit Trelew's Welsh Tea Shop.

The Chubut Valley is, weirdly, the centre of a Welsh-speaking community descended from the brave souls who arrived in 1865 looking for a place where their culture and language would be safe from English interference. Patagonia was not a bad choice, since there was no one around to interfere except for a few Indians. The Argentine government, quick to see the benefit of having hard-working immigrants in this underpopulated region, gave them some land, and the community eventually flourished, to be augmented from time to time by more Welsh speakers.

We did not flourish in Trelew – at least not at first. The Welsh Tea Shop was the real thing, with real tea with milk and cake, and a real Welsh lady running it, but she was pretty frosty and the cost was exorbitant. We skipped lunch so we could have a decent meal in the evening but were treated like filthy hippies (most unfair – we were exceptionally clean) and told we couldn't sit near their mural of a Welsh landscape in case we damaged it, and to leave our backpacks by the door. Then we were charged for food we hadn't eaten, and shouted at. Not nice. So we were both in an exceptionally bad mood when we walked around town looking for a half-completed building we could sleep in and arguing, I suspect, rather loudly. A small man shot out of a bar and, in a strong Welsh accent, said, 'I heard you speaking English. Please come and stay in my house – I'm fed up with the bloody Spanish!' We accepted.

Phil's wife Laura greeted us in Spanish but I soon became completely lost as they continued to talk, despite my increasing confidence in understanding Argentine Spanish. Then Phil explained, 'We can only communicate in Welsh. Laura's English is lousy as is my Spanish.' They had met at university in Wales, and Phil had returned with Laura to help out on her family farm. She invited us to visit the farm the following day and we readily agreed.

The family history was as interesting as the fertile and well-tended farm and the town of Gaiman with its original Welsh chapel. Laura's grandfather had arrived at the turn of the century, sent there for his health and to assist three sisters who were distant relatives. Two had recently been widowed and they 'needed a man' on the farm. A classical scholar, so surely way out of his comfort zone on this windswept piece of nowhere, he nevertheless accepted the role of farm manager and married the youngest sister.

'Come and see Grandfather's library,' said Laura, after we'd looked round the farm, and charged off through the undergrowth. She led us to a two-room adobe building, with a little turret at the top. Inside, stacked up on the floor and along the shelves, were about a thousand books: mostly classics in, Laura told us, forty-two different languages, 'although he only spoke fifteen'. He would order books from all over the world, and once a week Laura's mother would be sent to Gaiman with the horse and cart to collect the latest shipment, while he watched for her return through binoculars. That's what the little turret was for.

In a corner of the room was a bed, just rough planks covered in rags, and in the adjacent room were piles of newspapers. 'Grandfather had this built some way from the house,' Laura said, 'to get away from "all those women".' In his mid-eighties he started to go blind, so taught himself Braille in both English and Welsh. He died at the age of eighty-seven.

Laura's mother was equally impressive. She was very much her father's daughter, and despite having only two years of schooling, was a well-read intellectual. She told us that as a child she would get up at 4.30am to study before going out to milk the cows.

She had also married an outsider (Welsh, but not from Wales) who used to spend Christmas with them because he was on his own. So inevitably he stayed to manage the farm, and now Phil was doing the same.

The strength of the family ties to their land was striking and typical of the Welsh community in the Chubut Valley. I am confident that the Welsh language will continue to thrive in this little corner of Patagonia.

8

THE FALKLAND ISLANDS

Picking up the chronological story again, it was now December 1973 and we had grand plans on where to spend Christmas: the Falkland Islands.

We had always hoped to include the Falkland Islands in our itinerary, but as December approached this took on an urgency. Even George felt a bit homesick for the English language and a familiar culture. Thus we were thrilled to discover that the Argentine air force operated twice-weekly flights from the southern town of Comodoro Rivadavia, more or less due east of the Lake District where we were pottering around trying to catch trout. Our plan was to stay a week, eat a British Christmas dinner and see a few penguins.

Until the early 1970s the Falklands were truly isolated, only accessible by a monthly supply ship, but in 1973, as part of its bid to win hearts and minds in its long-standing sovereignty claim, Argentina built a temporary airstrip on a peninsula jutting out into the sea. So our timing was perfect – the islands had only been accessible to tourists for a few months, the flights full of excited Argentines on day trips to buy duty-free British goods and take a look at the Malvinas. The air service also enabled seriously ill islanders to be flown to hospital in Buenos Aires for free treatment.

The airport terminal in Stanley was surely the smallest in the world – a Nissen hut with portraits of the Queen and Prince Philip hanging above the desk. I knew that this place was going to be irresistibly different from South America; what we didn't know was how different it would be to my home country, like stepping back thirty years or so.

We were given a lift into town and set about finding somewhere to stay since the one hotel, the Upland Goose, was beyond our means.

Our search ended with us drinking tea in a cosy kitchen, listening to the following one-sided telephone conversation: 'All they want is bed and breakfast... They seem very nice, they're sitting right here stroking the cat... No, they're not very big... I don't think so – you're not Jehovah's Witnesses, are you? All right, I'll send them along.' And along we went to meet 84-year-old Mrs Williams who eyed us dubiously and said she'd put us up for a week – it turned out to be a month, on and off – 'As long as I keep going.' And keep going she did, cooking us enormous breakfasts on her peat stove – including on one occasion a huge penguin-egg omelette – to the steady accompaniment of mutters and grumbles. She was impervious to our offers to help ('I'm not having you messin' around in my kitchen, neither') and to our delighted reports of our new discoveries. 'Penguins, penguins, that's all I ever hear from you two. One day you'll come in flappin' like one!'

Our first few days were taken up with exploring Stanley and drooling over the British goodies in the shops. I stocked up with enough Crosse & Blackwell's steamed puddings to last for months. Although it claims to be the world's most southerly capital, Stanley was really just a small town, albeit it one with a cathedral. The houses were mostly white with different coloured corrugated iron roofs, all with glass conservatories for flower- and vegetable-growing. Outside there were more vegetable beds and an almost obligatory mass of lupins. There were no trees except for half a dozen conifers in the 'governor's forest' by Government House. During one of my early explorations I was reduced to tears of happiness to find Andrex toilet paper in the spotless public loo. If this seems a bit over the top, try spending a year wiping your bum on small squares of newspaper or torn-out pages of children's school exercise books.

We were the only outsiders and soon everyone knew who we were; we were invited out to lunch almost every day. This was the chance to learn what the islanders thought about the sovereignty claim from Argentina. 'I think Britain is going to give up on us,' said one man reflectively. 'Britain refuses to invest any money here. You know it was the Argentine government that built the airstrip and they also supply us with oil. And scholarships for bright children. So who knows...' A proper airport had been promised but no one believed it would actually be built. We felt that the 'Keep the Falklands British' posters everywhere were as much a plea to the British government as a warning to the Argentines.

An oft-told story, and one we always enjoyed, concerned the Great Hijacking of 1966. An Argentine plane, which just happened to have the Governor of Tierra del Fuego on board – the Malvinas, according to the Argentine claim, would have come under his jurisdiction – was seized by hijackers with the intention of 'liberating the islands'. They landed on the racecourse and sank into the boggy ground. Islanders who lived nearby ran out to help, assuming the plane was in trouble and had crash-landed, and were taken hostage. The Falklands Defence League – the islands' version of Dad's Army, though perhaps not as competent – was roused, and gathered as many guns as they could find. They approached cautiously, forming an outer circle with their guns facing forward towards the hijackers who faced outwards with their guns. The passengers and hostages sat in the stricken plane. Everyone was very jumpy, and our narrators all agreed that it was a miracle that no shots were fired, particularly by the Defence League who were rather excited at this unexpected turn of events. 'Whenever there's a crisis in the Falklands someone bakes a cake, so the women were running backwards and forwards with trays of tea and cakes for everyone, including the bandits.' Eventually they gave themselves up. I think the hijackers were locked in the town jail at night but were free to wander around during the day and the crew and passengers were put up by local families – including the governor, who was reported to take great pleasure in pointing out Government House with the comment, 'So that's my other house'.

After a couple of weeks a boat came from Argentina to pick everyone up, and the plane was stripped of its fittings until it was light enough to extract itself from the bog and take off again. Many families we visited owned bits of the plane as souvenirs and quite a few spoke fondly of their own personal 'Argy' who had stayed with them for the duration.

Having had our plans for a proper Christmas dinner dashed when we discovered that the restaurant at the Upland Goose was fully booked, we were rescued by a British geologist who invited us to join his family for their traditional festive picnic. On the morning of Christmas Day we took a long walk to work up an appetite, returning to our lodgings to change out of our hiking clothes. We found Mrs Williams muttering in her kitchen, enveloped in delicious cooking smells, and explained what we were doing. 'Aren't you staying for dinner then? I've got it all ready for you!' There was nothing for it but to eat two traditional Falkland Christmas dinners: spring lamb with all the trimmings in Mrs Williams's dining room, and roast upland goose and all the trimmings sitting propped up against a Land Rover, both followed by Christmas pudding and brandy butter. We were so full we were barely able to breathe. It was the only time in my life that anyone has had cause to comment on my small appetite. Afterwards I wondered if I would live, let alone be fit enough to take part in the next day's Boxing Day Races.

Everyone comes to Stanley for the Boxing Day Races, we were told and as visitors we were encouraged to take part. Horse races alternated with foot races, and the bookies did a thriving business. There were no roads in the 'camp' (the local term for the countryside, derived from the Spanish *campo*), just tracks, and the farmers arrived from all over the outlying settlements on or in whatever transport was available: horseback, motorbike or Land Rover. Originally the horse races were just for the shepherds' ponies, but some thoroughbreds had been imported, making for a diverse, and somewhat unfair, field.

There were no thoroughbreds in the foot races – anyone could enter the sack race, the three-legged race or, given the right credentials, the over-sixties handicap. We entered the three-legged race and came last.

We'd been in Stanley nearly a week and had yet to see many penguins. We needed to book Micky Clarke to take us to Kidney Island for the rockhoppers and to plan our visit to Volunteer Point for the king penguins. To get permission to visit the latter we needed to have our request read out over the radio. Not everyone had a phone but they were all avid radio listeners, with some popular BBC programmes broadcast after 8pm and local news or announcements at other times. To make a phone call you cranked a handle a few times until the operator answered. If you didn't know the number you just asked for the person by name. Sometimes the operator would say, 'Oh, John's just popped over to the Smiths, I'll put you through to their house, shall I?'

Micky was booked for December 30 – we would see in the new year on an uninhabited island where there was a shack for visitors – but first we would spend a couple of days with the gentoos at Port Harriet. The eight-mile walk there was full of interest because for once we knew what we were seeing. We'd done our homework in Stanley and could now recognise diddle-dee, a shrub similar to heather, and the pretty pink and white flowers of scurvy grass, so called because the leaves are packed with vitamin C. With our binoculars we could differentiate between kelp geese (beautiful, pure white ganders; don't taste good) and the understandably more nervous upland geese that compete with sheep for grazing – and are tasty, as we had discovered at Christmas. We knew johnny rook was the local name for the striated caracara and snotty-nose was the pigeon-like sheathbill. But it was the penguins we had come to see and my heart still lifts at the memory of realising that those 'gulls' on the beach were actually gentoos.

We spent two days just watching them. The rookery was a dense mass of penguins incubating eggs or feeding young chicks. They took no notice of us at all unless we came very close, when they would step back on to someone else's territory to be biffed and pecked. We learned to be careful and sit quietly at the optimum distance. A startled bird, we discovered, sometimes knocked its chick off the nest where it would be attacked most painfully by its neighbours, being pulled here and there by a flipper, shrieking all the while.

The adults are medium-sized with the usual black back and white breast, but sporting a classy white bow on the top of their heads. Their beaks are bright orange and their feet range from yellow to red, but mostly orange. They are very noisy, since the arrival of their mate results in an 'ecstatic display' where they stick their beak to the sky and make a sound like a sheep trying to bray.

Our favourite spectacle was the sight of a line of penguins heading for the sea while another line returned to the rookery.

It looks exactly like a family reunion, with both groups rushing towards each other with outstretched arms, only to step aside at the last moment and continue on their way. On the approach to the beach there's a pile of boulders to negotiate. Sometimes they misjudge the hop and fall flat on their faces. Once on the beach they gather in groups to reflect on life before the urge to get in the water becomes too strong and they run into the surf. Once in deep water they're fantastic, their fastest and most effective swimming is by 'porpoising' – leaping out of the water at regular intervals so they can breathe without losing momentum. This way they can keep up a steady 15mph and reach speeds of 39mph.

After a while we realised there were other types of penguin on the beach. There were Magellanic penguins – known locally as Jackass penguins – which always struck us as a bit silly. They nest in burrows, for one thing, which doesn't seem proper for a penguin, and have a crazy way of lurking at the entrance of their burrow looking at you out of first one eye then the other, weaving their heads from side to side. And their call is just like the bray of a donkey. Finally, they run on all fours, using their flippers as an extra set of legs. Effective but undignified. Talking of dignified, we were thrilled to see a lone king penguin on the edge of the gentoo rookery. He was stately but a bit sad being so far from his friends who we hoped to see in a couple of weeks' time. He walked in a more upright manner than the gentoos, on the back of his feet like a head waiter with corns.

On December 30 we were dropped on Kidney Island with the instruction that in an emergency we were to set fire to the tussock grass and the lighthouse keeper would summon help. Not sure if that was reassuring or worrying. We thought we knew about tussock grass – hadn't we hopped over clumps of it in Scotland? – but nothing prepared us for the Falklands' variety, which covered the whole island. Imagine a very chunky palm tree, six or seven feet high, with its trunk consisting of tangled roots held together by mud, and a luxuriant canopy of stiff, sharp-edged leaves which were happy to draw blood if you grabbed them for balance. Penguins had made pathways and tunnels through and around the 'stem' parts but at our waist height was a tangle of foliage which we either had to force our way through or crouch down to penguin stature and shuffle through. The traffic of hundreds of webbed feet, along with rain and guano, meant that the glutinous mud was sometimes ankle-deep so we didn't want to crawl on our hands and knees. Then there was the problem of the penguin logjams. We were often so concentrated on moving forward that we didn't notice the pile-up of penguins behind us. When we stepped aside they would sprint past, glaring at us, and sometimes aiming a peck at our shins, sensibly protected by borrowed wellington boots.

We quickly learned to make only one sortie to the penguin cliff each day, bringing lunch and waterproofs with us. We settled ourselves down on a rock, and watched. It was never dull and the time flew by.

Back at the hut three short-eared owls were clearly thrilled to have something interesting to look at after what had been a long, bleak period of inactivity. Their lives were immeasurably brightened by our presence and it wasn't enough just to monitor our emergence each morning for our penguin watch. They took it in turns to take long low flights so they could peer through the windows and check on our cooking or Scrabble game.

But back to the penguins. On the first day we just watched the activity on the clifftop rookery. The rockhoppers are the smallest of the five species in the Falklands, feisty little birds with yellow eyebrows fanning out into plumes which look as though they've been secured in place with a hairpin. They nested cheek by jowl with the very handsome king shags, although the latter sit smugly on top of mud chimneys, old tussock roots, so are out of pecking range of the penguins. Plenty of squabbling goes on, however, if they get close to each other – they reacted as though they were the same species. We were sure that the penguin chicks must have believed that they would be able to fly once they were grown up and that their parents hadn't the heart to tell them about that rock face.

That rock face. It was about 100ft high and so steep it would have been a challenge to an experienced human climber. A stormy, rainy day had kept us in the hut until evening when we walked around the rocky coast to get a better view of just what the return from the sea means to a little rockhopper. The surf was bashing against the rocks at the base of the cliff, with the white spray speckled with upside-down penguins that had mistimed their landing. They had to get

Above: Mount Huascarán, Peru's highest mountain

Below: Armadillos in conversation at a Bolivian fiesta, 1973

Below: An unusual dance partner in Achacachi, Bolivia

Above: Young girl in Chipaya, Bolivia, 1973

Above: Chipayan woman grinding grain with her feet

Below: Chipayan woman breastfeeding a lamb

Above: Third-generation Welsh-speaking brothers in Chubut, Patagonia

Below: A gift from fishermen in Punta Arenas, Chile

Below: The *bonde* that took us up to Santa Teresa in Rio de Janeiro

Above: Stanley's 'temporary' airport, the Falkland Islands, 1973

Above: Boxing Day Races in Stanley

Below: Tackling the tussock grass on Kidney Island

Below: Rockhopper penguin cuddle

it just right to catch a wave and fling themselves out at exactly the right time to land on the first ledge. If they didn't immediately start rock-hopping upwards they would be washed off by the next wave and have to start all over again. And just imagine. Penguins only have one set of feet, admittedly supplied with long, sharp nails, but no fingers to hang on by, just flippers, which were OK for balance but useless for grip. So it would be hop-hop-hop, slide, whoops... big slide down on to the ledge and... hop-hop-hop, just avoid getting washed off again, whoops, grab rock with beak, hop-hop-hop. Phew, reached a ledge well above the highest wave. Stop and preen and admire the view. Then remember you have Responsibilities. So hop-hop-hop, slide... etc. The ecstatic display with which the chick-guarder greets his or her spouse is entirely deserved. Beaks to the sky, flippers spread, and a melodious and triumphant trumpet call.

Among the rockhoppers were a few pairs of macaroni penguins, the dandies of the penguin world, with unruly golden plumes. They looked smug and superior, and demonstrated a rather more elaborate ecstatic display just to show off.

Amid all this parental activity, the babies were less than admirable. So fat they were pear-shaped, they sat around with half-shut eyes waiting for the next meal or sprawled on their grotesque bellies with their legs stretched out behind them. And they were sticky. I picked one up and regretted it (serves me right). Penguins and shags have a dramatic method of defecation, leaning forward to shoot a stream of evil-smelling shit some two feet away. It usually hit another bird or a chick. The adults went in the sea often enough to keep sleek and clean, but not so the chicks. Yuk.

Our planned two-day hike to Volunteer Point, the only breeding site for king penguins in the archipelago, turned into four days because we couldn't say no to the Falklands hospitality. After each night's stay at one of the settlements we'd barely started walking before we'd see a Land Rover bouncing towards us with an invitation to stay at the next settlement. These sheep stations consisted of the Big House, where the manager lived, and a few shepherd's cottages along with the Cookhouse where meals were taken. Self-sufficiency was essential in the roadless camp. A cow was kept for fresh milk (which was unobtainable in Stanley) and a few chickens for eggs, which helped relieve the monotony of '365 meat', mutton, eaten every day. Vegetables grew well, despite the constant wind, and peat was a reliable source of fuel for cooking and heat.

There was no doubt that the highlight of the day on every settlement – and in Stanley – was the radio doctor. Smoko, the midmorning break, was timed so that each family could settle round the radio to listen in to their neighbours' symptoms and speculate on the cause and likely outcome. A medicine chest kept at the Big House dealt with most ailments, and there was a cottage hospital in Stanley. Islanders with serious conditions were sent to Argentina.

Education was not rated highly by the Kelpers (people born in the Falklands). Who needed it? Their skill in shearing a sheep and baling up the wool in record time was far more valuable than the three Rs. Children were taught by a volunteer teacher (often a VSO from Britain) who left them with a pile of homework before moving on to the next settlement, but it seemed that it was within the station manager's rights to refuse to accommodate a teacher. We stayed in one settlement where the seven-year-old couldn't read, but was skilled in all the farm work he was expected to do. We ourselves tried to gain some skills but without much success. Milking a cow proved more difficult than expected, and we could only watch in admiration as sheep were sheared at lightning speed and the wool graded and baled. Those people worked *hard*. I'd never seen such effortful work undertaken with such cheerfulness. Nor, come to that, so many cakes and cream consumed as a reward.

We tried to make ourselves useful but in fact it was our entertainment value – especially George's jokes – which were the most appreciated. As one family explained, after we crept up to our room at 1am after a film show, a recital from a variety of musical instruments, and a couple of games of cards and Chinese chequers, 'We get tired of looking at each other so usually go to bed rather early.'

After all that unexpected hospitality, Volunteer Point, when we finally reached it, could almost have been an anticlimax, but king penguins and elephant seals can never disappoint. There was a comfortable shack for visitors, with a huge pile of peat so we could keep cosy in the squalls that swept across the peninsula, and from where we could admire those gorgeous penguins who surely knew how beautiful they were. The ones incubating eggs on their feet could only look at us disdainfully, but the bachelor group found us seriously interesting, undertaking a careful inspection and then walking back to their group doing an 'advertisement walk', a ridiculously exaggerated strut with wagging head. What the males of the animal kingdom get up to in order to attract a mate never failed to entertain us.

The elephant seals were the opposite of dignified. They were grotesque, smelly, and infinitely entertaining. These days we are all familiar with these animals from television but this was the first time George and I had seen them and we were naturally entranced. They were so huge, so ugly, and so vocal with their range of burps, rumbles, snores and roars. Mostly they lay around snoring in a phlegmy, bubbly sort of way, but if we got too close they would raise their heads, roll their eyes, and belch at us. The halitosis alone was enough to remind us to keep our distance. We discovered that when relaxed, the enormous bulls could retract their noses to look almost normal, but faced with a rival they would release it to hang down ready to vibrate menacingly when they opened their red mouths wide for an enraged roar. With further provocation they would rear up and wallop each other, with their flab wobbling in waves down their sides.

They were capable, however, of one very dainty manoeuvre. When they wanted to scratch an itch, and they had plenty of itches to scratch, they would do it very precisely with one fingernail. It made us realise that under that paddle of webbed digits, they had the same muscles and bones in their hands as we do. It was the same with their back flippers. These were surprisingly dexterous. They had three obvious toes on each side, and could delicately scratch the opposite flipper with a nail or fan them out and press them together like praying hands. Or twine them around each other as if they were wringing their hands. Or feet. Intriguing.

It was time to leave the Falklands. We'd stayed a month, not a week, met some wonderful people, and had a proper holiday at a thrilling wildlife spot comparable to the Galápagos. As we wandered round Stanley saying goodbye, we were accosted: 'I've been looking for you for ten days. We want you two to be interviewed for *Visitors' Book* on the radio.' So we trooped across to 'Broadcasting House', so to speak (just a Nissen hut, I seem to remember), and had an enjoyable conversation in which we described some of our adventures in South America. Remembering a similar conversation in one of the settlements where our host said, 'I've never seen a donkey but I hear they are nice animals', we thought even our more mundane experiences must seem very exotic. But in no way superior to the gentle rhythm of life in this distant corner of Britain.

9

THE SOUTHERN CONE

Distances in the spindly *Cono Sur* were small, and our goal, Tierra del Fuego, tantalisingly near, but it would still take us a while.

In Argentina we were *mochileros*, backpackers, part of a recognised tribe who were as despised as they were welcomed. In the northern countries of South America we generally used buses or trucks for transport because they were plentiful and cheap. Here in Argentina the public transport was scarce and often pricey. Indeed, everything was expensive, so to keep within our budget we needed to hitchhike.

The wait beside the dusty Patagonian roads could seem endless. We might sit there all day before giving up and finding alternative transport (sometimes it worked out more cheaply to fly because we wouldn't be paying for meals and accommodation). Six or seven hours' wait was not unusual, and it was not unknown for drivers to speed past yelling insults. I remember when one rolled down his window to shout, 'I'm not stopping for you because you're dirty!'

Without hitchhiking, however, I doubt if we would have met the doctor and his wife who took us to their house to show us their collection of prehistoric artefacts that they had acquired over the years: stone arrowheads arranged in order of sophistication, a set of *bolas* – three stone balls attached to cord and used by the Indians to trip a fleeing animal – and enough pieces of petrified wood to create a very beautiful fireplace, which they made by pushing the fragments into cement. The doctor's impressive collection of fossils included snails, fruit, pine cones and rather beautiful curved things which might have been the claws of a prehistoric animal.

Talking of fossils, we later met the director of an important natural history museum, and he told us of his frustration over lack of government funding for palaeontology. 'I get phone calls all the time from builders or other diggers. They say, "I've found a fossilised bone. Can you come and look?" And all I can say is, "Keep on digging." That's why so much of this stuff is in private collections.' As was the special treasure shown us proudly by the man who found it: half of a human pelvic girdle, with a stone arrowhead embedded in the seat bone. The bone had grown up around the arrow so that it was almost hidden. 'I was told by a doctor that it would have taken about twelve years to grow like this,' he told us. 'And he would not have been able to sit down.' We winced in sympathy.

We had one essential bit of sightseeing to do before continuing to Tierra del Fuego: Lake Argentino and the Perito Moreno Glacier. We'd seen photos but nothing prepares you for the experience of seeing, and hearing, a glacier doing its thing. People talk about 'glacial slowness' but from our two viewpoints from the cliffs above and a little peninsula of land jutting into the lake, there was constant activity. Perito Moreno is a tongue of ice which slips from its birthplace in the mountains down a gulley and into Lake Argentino. The pressure behind ensures that chunks of ice break off and tumble into the lake to become icebergs.

I never imagined that a glacier could look like that. It meets the water in a vertical cliff about 300ft high. We watched it from above and then climbed down to the lake where there was just a narrow strip of ice-filled water separating us from the glacier. While we watched whole sides of the ice cliff broke away and toppled into the water in slow motion, making a huge boom like a skyscraper being demolished. As it bobbed up to the surface the enormous wave caused other icebergs to roll and turn, revealing other sides in their sculptured forms. And these forms are remarkable! Angles, curves, perfect lines, and beautiful colours. One iceberg from a particularly spectacular fall was a pure sapphire blue, while others were all shades of blue from delicate duck-egg to dark turquoise to almost purple. And the cliffs were a myriad of shapes and colours – again, all shades of blue, and emerald green, with caves and holes and turrets and pinnacles all leaning precariously and waiting to fall. And the noises! Sharp gunshot bangs, rumbling booms like thunder, creakings, crunchings... Honestly, it's the most spectacular natural thing we've seen on this trip.

Continuing south to the utterly dreary and expensive coastal town of Río Gallegos, where two cups of coffee used up most of our daily budget, the backpackers' support group came to our rescue. Having left our packs in the post office while we investigated our sleeping options (unsuccessfully), we returned to find a note tucked under the flap telling us that if we wanted somewhere to sleep we should go to the school near the plaza where we could get permission to doss down in one of the classrooms. It was signed 'Another mochilero'.

The classrooms resembled one of those post-disaster scenes you see on TV, with groups of people sprawled in sleeping bags all over the floor. The atmosphere, however, was convivial and multinational as tales were told and warnings and advice given. We learned that in Ushuaia, where we were heading, the place to stay was the Gymnasium.

As indeed it was. We found it beautifully organised for backpackers, were checked in by the warden and shown where we could sleep. The place was heated, had good loos and hot showers, and tables and chairs as well as space on the floor to put our sleeping bags.

That evening I took a shower. It seemed excessively public, even for a gymnasium shower room. A little troupe of six children came in and were so enthralled at the sight they lined up in front of me for a better view. The older girl pulled up a chair so she could properly enjoy the entertainment. There were plenty of questions: 'Are you a woman or a man?' each asked in turn, apparently unsatisfied by the answer given to the previous questioner. 'Are you taking a shower?' And then 'Why are you in the men's room?' A revealing question. The door had said *Varones*, which I assumed was a deep-south version of *Señoras*. Watching me dress was even more interesting. My clothes were passed round for examination and discussion before I was allowed to put them on. Finally when I managed to get dressed I was followed upstairs by all six who announced that they wanted to meet the other *mochileros*. To my relief they were kicked out by the warden who said it was no place for children.

For us Ushuaia was a long-anticipated, and significant, destination before we entered Chile again at Punta Arenas and headed back north. We were not the only visitors attracted to its 'Most southerly town in South America' status. It was going all out for tourism, hence welcoming even backpackers, and there were plenty of brochures advising us what to do in the region. After the flat, dry pampas, the green, mountainous landscape was a joy, and we bought several bottles of celebratory wine. We'd travelled overland the length of South America, so were pretty pleased with ourselves, although we'd cheated by flying to Ushuaia from Río Gallegos because it was cheaper than the bus. It made a lovely change to see the landscape from above, rather than out of a dirty bus window.

> We started off over desert-like pampas, absolutely flat and devoid of feature except for the river valleys with their green borders. Because it's so flat the rivers meander all over the place like unravelled knitting. After a while small hills appeared, and then little clumps of trees looking like patches of moss, then larger mountains 'til we were going over snow-covered peaks and thickly forested valleys.

The two days we spent camping in the Tierra del Fuego National Park were mainly given over to foraging for wild food and eating enormous and exceptionally delicious meals. The temperate climate with frequent rain produced some splendid field mushrooms and bushes laden with calafate berries. These are somewhat like bilberries but with a sharper taste, and we found that the best way to enjoy them was to stew them in a little water and then strain the juice through our mosquito netting. This gave us a yummy concentrate which could be mixed with water as a drink or poured over morning porridge. The culinary highlight was the abundance of mussels which revealed themselves at low tide along the Beagle Channel. We collected huge quantities and cooked them in a little of the white wine that we had brought with us, garnished with wild garlic. The remainder made a splendid chowder.

Our next goal was to cross the Magellan Strait into Chile and Punta Arenas, where we could afford a hotel after two weeks of sleeping on floors or in our tent.

> We are feeling positively euphoric having found a lovely hotel for $4. Breakfast in bed – and such a beautiful bed! Crab for supper and more celebratory Chilean wine. Punta Arenas, after all, is the most southerly city in South America.

A note at the bottom of my letter, commenting on the fact that mail prices had gone up a thousand per cent, reminds me of a tale told by a traveller in Allende's Chile when inflation was such that the stamp printers could not keep up with appropriate denominations. Mailing a letter to Britain required all the available space on the envelope for the multitude of stamps – and sometimes there wasn't enough room. This chap had made his own envelope, specifically to the right dimensions to fit all the stamps needed for a specific weight for Great Britain. He proudly brought it to the post office and covered the front with stamps, leaving a small square for the address. 'I'm sorry, Señor,' sighed the clerk after weighing it, 'but with all those stamps I'm afraid your letter is now too heavy. You need more stamps.'

We spent three days in Punta Arenas trying to get tickets for a boat – any boat – going north. It was, I'd read, 'a marvellous trip, going through all the fjords and canals of the southern Chilean coast'. If we could get to Puerto Montt this way we could speed up to Santiago, cross the Andes, and be in Buenos Aires in no time. Autumn was approaching and we needed to chase the fine weather. When tickets finally went on sale we queued for three hours without success and decided to give up, at least for the time being, since we had one last hiking trip to do before the winter arrived and the mountains became off limits. That trek was in the National Park of Torres del Paine, now famous as having arguably the most spectacular mountain scenery in South America, but in 1974 little known. We hadn't heard of it, anyway, until we saw photos in Punta Arenas. We were planning a two-day hike to a glacier. There were *refugios* to stay in on the way, and we were warned to take lots of warm clothes and waterproofs, since the weather is famously bad, and to bring enough food to allow us to hole up in one of the refuges were there to be a storm.

> I know I must stop saying 'this is the best scenery ever' but Paine really is the most spectacular. The mountains look as though they were designed by Georges Braque, all pale-coloured lines and angles, with crumbly-looking black rock on top. Look like a fruit cake in a tin.

All this, and absolutely unbelievable weather. For the four days we were walking it was hot, sunny and windless. Almost too hot for sunbathing, although since we had the place to ourselves I indulged in some nudism. It was even free of mosquitoes since they wouldn't survive in the normal conditions. We walked slowly, binoculars at the ready to spot guanacos and pausing to pick the berries from the calafate bushes that lined the trail. The path took us round turquoise lakes, along gulleys lined with foxgloves, and up and down headlands, with the distinctive Paine mountains changing shape as we viewed them from different angles and reflected in the still waters of the lakes. Every now and then there would be a rumble like thunder as a glacier slipped. We walked through forests of southern beech where woodpeckers with bright red crests hammered at the trees and owls stared at us from tree stumps. New white, knobby mountains revealed themselves from the top of every hill. To crown it all, as we approached the second refuge we found two enormous puffballs to augment our dinner.

The *refugios* were anything but basic. The second one had a stove and two beds as well as a table and chairs. We decided to stay for at least two nights. We were carrying too much food anyway, so there was no point in hurrying, and there was the glacier to investigate about a mile away. Like Perito Moreno, this one slid down a trough between mountains to land in a lake, but this time it went right to the shore, and that meant we could walk on it and explore the ice caves.

You can't <u>imagine</u> what it's like inside an ice cave! So beautiful it brought tears to my eyes. The ice is sculpted into rounded forms. In some places it was quite transparent and looked like the sky, blue with 'clouds' of white bubbles. Some places it's dark blue, others it's the palest of blues, but the shapes predominate. It's as though Henry Moore had been let loose here with a chisel to suggest human forms.

The next day, after breakfast of porridge with calafate juice, we headed back to the first refuge. The weather was still hot, cloudless and without a breath of wind. We had left some thinly sliced puffball to dry in the sun, and we found a perfect snack wating for us, crisp and tasty. The next day we collected two more giant puffballs, weighing at least a pound each, to dry for future use in Puerto Natales. The family that picked us up at the park entrance stared at our booty in horror. '*Venenoso!*' they insisted when we said we were going to eat them.

Puerto Natales was swarming with soldiers carrying machine guns, but as always they greeted us with great courtesy at the checkpoint and gave us lunch – a very good lunch – in the Mess. Back in Punta Arenas we landed up in student accommodation. I can't remember how, but it was free and there were kitchen facilities. The six students were delightful and included Pablo, a political prisoner who had been released on grounds of ill health. I suspect mental health. One evening he insisted on singing us a series of communist songs – we were sure the doors would be kicked open and we'd be arrested. We repaid the hospitality of the students by cooking some good meals and baking cakes, but our stay ended after four days when their supervisor made an unexpected visit and told us to leave.

Getting tickets for a boat to Puerto Montt became a preoccupation. Each morning we would check with the agent, and finally we were successful. There was plenty to do in Punta Arenas while we waited for the ship's departure. One day we went to the port and were given an enormous spider crab by some fishermen: bright red, spidery, with legs about a foot long. We cooked it in the student kitchen as a special treat. And we paid a visit to the British Club which was utterly wonderful. Decaying furniture occupied by decaying old men. The ancient leather armchairs were covered with fragments from the ornate ceiling, while the portraits on the wall were of Winston Churchill and Queen Victoria – and of course of the Queen. Old sporting prints lined the corridor, along with black-and-white prints of fighting ships. It had a good library where we could improve our knowledge of the region.

Finally it was time to board our ship to begin our cruise to Chiloe island, just south of Puerto Montt. How wonderful not to have to think or move for five days – *and* see some of Chile's very best scenery. We'd read the brochures. The ship would pass close to the shore, nudging past forest-covered islands, sneaking a look at the Chilean fjords and close to glaciers sweeping majestically down to the ocean with the snow-capped Andes as a backdrop. On a practical level it was also the easiest way to travel north, and the cheapest, so we were greatly pleased to have managed to purchase tickets.

Chilean families crowded the boarding area, heading north for the winter, and we were pushed up the gangplank by the surge of humanity and down into the ship's hold where an official exchanged our passports for two regulation blankets. 'Men to the left, women to the right,' he snapped. Bunks were in tiers three high, with about sixty beds in each cavernous room. I watched, sadly, as George disappeared into his child-free accommodation. My section was packed and each woman seemed to have at least two babies. Between the two bunk rooms was the dining room, with two long trestle tables – supposedly one for men and one for women, though we ignored this. We were served three meals a day, identical except for the colour: white sludge for breakfast, yellow for lunch and brown for dinner. For variety the sludge was sometimes green and once it was grey. It was, however, usually accompanied by soup and a hunk of bread.

This didn't seem to be working out quite as expected. The hold was very cold. Our breath came in clouds and we wore all our warm clothes. The first evening the captain came to sit by us to practise his English and chummily put his arm round me. To deflect him we asked to be shown our route on the detailed map we'd managed to purchase. He put on two pairs of glasses, pursed his lips, and drew an imaginative line north. I described the result in my letter home.

It's going to be a fascinating cruise. We make a large number of portages over various islands and peninsulas, then meander inland and over the cordillera glaciers to stop uncertainly somewhere near Mt Fitzroy. At that point the line gives up so I assume we're just there for the view before backtracking to the sea. Another bout of portages brings us to the northern border of the map. I'll send you the map so you can see for yourself. I think perhaps the captain was a bit drunk.

The first night was pretty bad. I had grabbed the top bunk for a bit of privacy and only slept for a few minutes at a time since a bright light shone in my eyes and the child in the bunk below cried unceasingly. Next morning George and I greeted each other blearily and went on deck to look at the stupendous view. Nothing, just fog and drizzle. A bit of excitement when we later stopped at the misnamed Puerto Eden, where a small community of indigenous people survived by selling food and artefacts to the passing ships. It was pouring with rain and the bedraggled traders looked appropriately desperate. We bought some smoked mussels and found a spot on deck out of the rain where we could enjoy them.

The mist and drizzle persisted. Each day we'd clamber on to the deck with our binoculars, hoping to see something, anything, and each day we were disappointed. On the fourth day the crew spent the afternoon collapsing the trestle tables and lashing them together. We were approaching the infamous stretch of open water known as the Golfo de Penas, or gulf of troubles. When I asked about dinner they just laughed, assuring me that no one would want dinner. They were right. I retired to my bunk with an appropriate receptacle to endure a wakeful night filled with the sound of sixty women and children being seasick, plus the accentuated wailing of the babies, punctuated by loud bangs as the collapsed trestle tables slid across the floor and crashed against the walls.

Emerging into calm once more, we were served tripe for lunch and disembarked, euphorically, at Castro on the island of Chiloe, just south of Puerto Montt. The sun shone for the first time in five days, the mist dispersed, and we headed for a hotel to begin our recovery.

Our encounters on the route north from Puerto Montt to Santiago in 1974 are described in Chapter 7. Chased by deteriorating weather, we crossed the Andes to Mendoza, travelled speedily east and were soon established in an apartment in Buenos Aires. Through one of those extraordinary pieces of luck which came our way more often than we deserved, we had been picked up by a young man, Eloy, who had recently got married but was keeping on his bachelor place (we didn't like to ask why). He invited us to stay there, free of charge.

After the deep south, the sophistication of Buenos Aires astonished us. We felt like grubby country cousins amid these beautifully dressed, elegant citizens of all backgrounds. I knew one person in the city, 'Dr John', with whom I'd worked in Boston. We'd exchanged letters and he'd sent me a warm invitation to visit him, so after a week of settling in we took him up on this. He gave us a wonderful evening out, with a lavish meal and plenty of wine. On the way back George asked him to stop the car and was violently sick in the gutter. I assumed he was drunk and was less than sympathetic, but Dr John looked at him carefully. 'You have hepatitis,' he said.

That night George's temperature rose to 40°C. I needed to rethink our plans for the next month or two.

INTERLUDE
WICKED!

I've noticed that when I'm reminiscing about my life on the road, it is the accounts of irresponsible travel that catch the listener's or reader's attention rather than their opposite. So as long as you bear in mind that I am now a respectable citizen who's curtsied to the Queen, so wouldn't dream of misbehaving – and trust that our motive was always to find a way to see the wonders of the world – I'll tell you how George and I sometimes managed to afford to hire cars.

Our first experiment was in Big Bend National Park in Texas, a million acres of desert and mountain enclosed by the mighty Rio Grande. We were exploring the western USA in 1972 and the only way to see this spectacular place was by car. Hiring a car was affordable – just – but we had to pay extra for every mile beyond the first hundred, and just driving to the park and back would take up most of that allowance. At our campsite just inside the park, we hatched a cunning plan. If the milometer went inexorably up as we drove forward, surely it would go down if we drove in reverse? And it worked, but only for the small numbers. Back down from 159 to 150 was fine, but there it stuck. So we spent the day on the empty roads driving forward for nine miles, then doing a three-point turn and driving backwards for nine miles.

We had the same problem in Patagonia. We arrived at the wildlife hotspot of Peninsula Valdés, thrilled at the prospect of seeing penguins and elephant seals, and positioned ourselves at the turn-off to the peninsula with our smiles and thumbs at the ready, waiting for a lift. Five hours later we were still there; Patagonia had come to us, the gritty dust lodging in our hair, nostrils, lungs and clothes. We gave up and hired a car in Trelew. Horribly expensive, even worse than Texas for a clapped-out vehicle which, when we got a puncture, turned out to have no jack. And here, too, there was an additional charge per kilometre. But while reversing on the broad roads of Big Bend had been a doddle, the narrow gravel tracks of Argentina were a different matter. Suddenly there was a loud kerplonk! We got out and surveyed the situation in dismay. I'd reversed over a cattle grid without seeing that most of the bars were missing. The car was resting on its chassis over the hole with its rear wheels still turning pathetically.

There was nothing for it but to wait for help. A cheerful family arrived, including several strapping young men, and together they lifted the car out of the hole. They stayed to wave us on our way, so they thought, back to Trelew. We had to drive for quite a distance until they were out of sight and we could turn round and head back, forwards, towards the peninsula.

10

BUENOS AIRES AND ON TO RIO

I sometimes think that when travelling our bodies hold off getting ill until the right moment. Or perhaps it's just hepatitis. My liver waited until I was back in England and George's chose the best time and place in over a year. Any other time would have been a major problem because hepatitis, as we know, needs a prolonged period of rest.

Eloy treated the news with remarkable calmness, and wouldn't hear of us moving out or even paying for our unintentionally prolonged stay. And what a fascinating place Buenos Aires was to spend this enforced stay, particularly in the 1970s when it was all about Juan Perón. This immensely popular, charismatic and economically disastrous president had been kicked out by the military in 1955 and gone into exile, but returned to be re-elected in June 1973. When we arrived, ten months later, he was in failing health and his supporters had split into two factions, with periodic outbursts of violence. Most of their demonstrations, however, seemed to involve driving around the city with their cars draped in the Argentine flag, chanting, 'Perón! Perón! Perón!' We left just before he died in July 1974.

Such leftist political fervour was of little interest to the people we got to know best in Buenos Aires (BA). They could be divided into three groups: Argentine upper class, the young middle-class friends of Eloy, and then the Anglo-Argentines. Each group was fascinatingly different in their culture and interests, and all were wonderfully hospitable and generous – a standout trait of Argentines.

Our dinner (before George got ill) with Dr John's aunt, whom we had met in the Lake District, was memorable. She had given us her address on the second floor of a large, colonial building. We were concerned because she hadn't told us the apartment number and we knew from experience that residents were coy about revealing their names on the doorbell. We needn't have worried: she lived on the *whole* of the second floor. The door was opened by a uniformed maid and we were ushered into a reception room where a few carefully selected guests were introduced to us. It felt like a scene from Jane Austen, except for our clothes, which were clean but very crumpled and shabby.

Dinner was served by two maids – one for the food and one for the wine – wearing white gloves. We gasped when we saw what we'd be eating. Something in aspic, the best steak, a wide selection of delicately prepared vegetables, and all the condiments you could imagine.

> The dining room table was as big as the one in *Rebecca*. By shouting you could just make yourself heard by the person next to you. I was in such a tizzy at the sight of the food that I started conveying a quivering mass of aspic towards my plate, unaware of the snow-white fine-linen napkin still lying there. A maid darted forward and removed it so inconspicuously that I was only aware of the incident later when George told me.

In total contrast was the *asado* that Eloy invited us to. George was too ill to go so I went alone, which I learned later was considered very improper. Wives didn't attend social events without their husbands. An a*sado* is an Argentine speciality and we had learned about their enthusiasm for eating huge quantities of barbecued beef within an hour or two of entering the country. You come across it everywhere – road workers stop their digging to set up a fire and arrange chunks of beef on a grill, while at a serious event like a fiesta, a whole side of a cow will be attached to a sort of metal crucifix slanted over the fire to be cooked very slowly, and very deliciously.

The *asado* was hosted by friends of Eloy, and I learned that it was a regular Saturday evening event. The house was full of people: two grown-up children with their spouses and kids, along with a couple of siblings. Eloy had explained to me that most Argentine men live with their parents until they get married, and then visit either set of parents every Saturday night. And he'd also mentioned, quite unnecessarily, that all Argentines love to tell jokes. As if we hadn't noticed! It made social events very tiring because of the constant laughter and the effort it took to understand the ribaldry. Even our pathetic jokes would have everyone rolling about with mirth, although without funny-man George I didn't do so well. Meanwhile the meat, cooked outside, came and went with regularity. Even if I couldn't follow much of what was going on, I loved the conviviality and closeness of this family. Nothing seemed forced, they just enjoyed each other's company. A lot. Towards the end of the meal the mother, who had spent three months in Australia with a daughter, brought out some treasures that she thought might interest me. One was a page from a newspaper advertising all the lovely slash-cost goodies at the supermarket that week, and another was an estate agent's page showing all the boring suburban houses for sale. I hope I showed sufficient delighted interest. She had also been to New Zealand, but described it as, '*No hay nada*' ('There's nothing there'), just boring old mountains.

Eloy had asked me to bring the slides I'd had developed from the earlier part of our trip, so I showed them after supper. I soon realised that this was a mistake, but plugged on doggedly. My audience were too polite to show their boredom, but I tried to whizz through the landscapes which held no interest, likewise the wildlife photos. The Bolivian Indians entertained them – they found them funny. I selfishly subjected them to the movies I had taken in the

Falklands because they had a projector and I was dying to see them myself. Although mystified that anyone would take six reels of film of penguins, they did enjoy their antics, because penguins *are* funny and of course things that would make us simply smile made them guffaw with laughter.

There's a saying in South America: 'Argentines are Italians who speak Spanish and think they're British'. It seemed very accurate to us. Many are indeed of Italian descent, and they share the poise and elegance of that nation, particularly the young men. And the British influence is everywhere, with the extraordinary phenomenon of the Anglo-Argentines still inhabiting their own private world. During the Victorian times Argentina was where British adventurers went to make their fortune. They built the railways, set up banks, owned huge expanses of land, and seldom deigned to mix with the natives, preferring the company of their own kind. We met quite a few Anglo-Argentines, sometimes third generation, who barely spoke Spanish. They intrigued us.

Shortly after we'd crossed into the country from Chile, we met a woman on the boat going across Lake Lácar who addressed me in such an English Home Counties accent that I asked her how long she had lived in Argentina. 'Oh, I was born here – Mummy and Daddy had a farm on the pampas.' She had no trace of a Spanish accent or manner. She told us that while she was growing up she was forbidden even to talk to the Argentine children on nearby farms, only to those of the other British farmers. Her husband was equally British, though also born in Argentina, and their children had untranslatable British names. She told me that when Prince Philip visited the Hurlingham (British) Club in Buenos Aires he said, 'Goodness, you people are more English than my wife!'

So when we met Charles Hardy in the Royal Bank of Canada, we were not so surprised to learn that he, too, was Argentine despite seeming so British. This unfortunate young man had been sent to deal with George who was trying to exchange some dollars. I can't remember what the problem was but I do remember that George was getting quite belligerent. Charles started each sentence with, 'It's the bank's policy to…', which didn't go down well. After about fifteen minutes of discussion he asked, 'Would you like to join me for a drink after work?' We did, and the friendship has lasted fifty years.

When it was clear that I would be spending a few weeks in BA waiting for George to recover, Charles said his mother would like to invite me to Sunday lunch. This sounded a splendid idea and I accepted with alacrity.

> He kept telling me how dreadfully boring it would be which made me full of happy anticipation since events that other people find boring I often find the most entertaining. And vice versa. He lives in a suburb called Hurlingham and you don't need to know Spanish to realise that this isn't exactly a gaucho name. Their road was indistinguishable from a nice residential area in Croydon. English houses set back in English gardens with English front doors.

His mother greeted me warmly, racing downstairs in her tweeds and calling me 'dear'. Sunday lunch was just what it should be – a joint of beef and roast potatoes, accompanied by apologies for the absence of Yorkshire pudding and horseradish sauce. 'I'm *so* sorry Hilary, dear, what *will* you think of us!'

After lunch Charles took me to see the Hurlingham Club, which occupied most of that suburb: a huge country-style house, golf course, tennis and squash courts, polo fields… and so on. Lots of elegant blonde women wandering about speaking English. Inside the clubhouse elderly gentlemen were sitting around reading old copies of *The Field* and *The Daily Telegraph*. I was entranced. Charles said if I thought that was British I should have stayed in a British estancia. There it was still obligatory to dress for dinner (yes, dinner jacket) and parties of just the right people would go down to the beach for a picnic, accompanied by a uniformed maid to serve them, followed by a game of tennis (in whites, of course).

Mrs Hardy invited me back the following weekend to show George's slides. After the debacle of the Argentine family's response I was full of foreboding, especially when quite a sizeable group had been assembled. But of course I needn't have worried. We were on exactly the same wavelength and they were all genuinely interested, especially in the natural history.

Poor George. Writing about all this gallivanting while he stayed ill in bed, I'm inclined to agree with his assertion that I didn't treat him well. At the time I thought I was the model of a caring wife, trundling off to Harrods (yes, there was a branch in BA, although under Argentine ownership) to buy the Roquefort cheese which he was craving. To aid his recovery I instigated a regime of Progressive Resistance Exercise, graded from peeling potatoes to chopping carrots. And even more caringly, I got a job teaching English so I could keep him in Roquefort cheese and chocolate digestive biscuits. It started at a place called Toil and Chat. They paid very poorly but it was ideal since they provided a manual to follow for each lesson, so you didn't need any experience. The students were nice and didn't seem to notice that I wasn't a real teacher, so I took on more work – conversation classes – at an institute that really did pay well, progressing to some individual work with a man who was soon going to England to university. He asked if I'd teach his children, too, so I went to his house each day.

I was now earning decent money and George was gradually improving, helped no doubt by the arrival of a package: four copies of *Backpacking along Ancient Ways in Peru and Bolivia*. I don't recall whether we noticed, or minded, all the misprints. We were just thrilled to have the book in our hands and were not shy about showing it off. One day someone turned up at the apartment having heard that we gave English lessons so George took him on, and soon had a regular stream of people coming to the house for their English sessions. In that way, without having to move, he was able to earn some money.

It was time to move on. After two months in BA George's blood test showed that he was clear of hepatitis (though no alcohol for six months) and we still had quite a bit of South America to explore. And promises to keep. A friend from Boston was going to join us at the Iguazú falls and I had a job lined up in Cape Town in November. We wanted to see the Spanish missions in Paraguay, and then there was Brazil.

I don't remember where we met Nick and Romy, a British couple who were teaching English in Rio de Janeiro, but we ended up sharing their apartment high on a hill in Santa Teresa. We rode up and down on the *bonde*, the yellow tram, and we both found rewarding English-teaching jobs in the city. Life became very pleasant. Nick and Romy were excellent company and seemed genuinely to enjoy having us there, the sassy maid, Gloria, was a delight and even did our laundry ('All your clothes will be Persil-white when Gloria's finished with them – whatever colour they were originally,' said Romy), and the apartment block had a swimming pool. Once I spotted a business meeting taking place there – in the pool. Each plump businessman was bobbing around in a white styrofoam ring, and in front of him was another little white styrofoam ring holding his wine glass. Copacabana beach was a tram ride away, and we were earning enough to eat well and start saving for South Africa. The only problem was the language. Oh, the trauma of abandoning the Spanish that we'd become comfortable with for Portuguese, which was just impossible. We did try, and it was similar enough to Spanish that we could read it fairly well, but speaking and understanding? No! Actually George just spoke Spanish a little more vehemently, which sometimes worked, and I kept silent but smiled a lot. It was a shame not to be able to communicate because we loved the Brazilians. They were so exuberant, so multiracial, so positive about life.

One absolute essential when it came to teaching English, we found, was to learn the names and fortunes of the city's football clubs, along with their star players. Before I headed off to my Monday conversation class I would check the weekend results so I could rejoice or commiserate appropriately. Sometimes the conversation went in mysterious ways. I remember one discussion, appropriately illustrated, where I tried to explain what happens in a vasectomy (no, I can't remember how the topic arose).

Despite all this enjoyment and comfort George and I were at loggerheads. I had to be in Cape Town at the beginning of November. The job I had lined up was one I really wanted, working in a hospital specialising in spinal injuries. My OT acquaintance who was leaving had filled me in with the details and I was pretty confident that it would be both interesting and rewarding. George had landed a really super teaching job in Rio which paid very well and he was loath to leave it for an uncertain future in South Africa. We went for a long, long walk along a sandy beach and thrashed out all the possibilities. Eventually we agreed that I would go alone to Cape Town and he would follow as soon as he could.

Interlude
A day in May in BA

I had plenty of time to describe unusual events in my letters home. Here is one of them.

A few days after we'd received our copies of the Little Yellow Book Eloy mentioned that he was going to talk to a friend of his who had connections with TV because, he said, 'you might as well go on TV'. Well, why not? The producer was apparently willing to chat to us so Eloy drove us to the TV studio. George was supposed to be bedridden but there is nothing like the promise of publicity to heal an ailing liver so we set forth in our grungy clothes (producers expect hitchhikers to look grungy). We waited an hour and finally he came, looked at us vaguely, and said, 'Oh yes, you'd better follow that man'. That Man took us to an ill-tempered girl who snapped out a few questions and wrote out a sort of resumé and then That Man said 'Follow me' again, and to our absolute horror we found ourselves inside the TV studio, and not only inside, but being motioned towards two brilliantly lit shiny chairs surrounded by cameras. We looked round in desperation, saying 'Not now', and pointing at our clothes, but were told 'Yes now' and that was it. George actually was looking quite dapper, although somewhat yellow, since the scorch mark on his shirt is at the back and his hiking boots were hidden. I, on the other hand, was wearing my grubby man's shirt and a cardigan I'd just fished out of six months' storage from which it had emerged unaccountably covered in feathers and six-month-old blobs of food. Well, it couldn't be helped.

At this point I should explain about the TV programme. If you judge Argentine TV by UK or even US standards, you might think it quite an honour to appear, but afternoon (women's) TV in this country is very mundane. The programme on which we were due to appear drags on for three hours each day with a steady flow of nothingness punctuated by exclamations of '*Ah, que linda!*' which means 'How beautiful' but in Argentina is used for anything – food, floor polish, a journey through South America... The bulk of the programme is supposedly taken up with interesting people with something to say or show. And when they can't find any interesting people they settle on boring ones. So there we were, being interviewed by a plastic young man in tan make-up. We didn't need make-up since I was naturally tanned and George was a fetching golden yellow.

I kept trying to look at myself on the little screen and speak fluent Spanish at the same time. Fortunately our interviewer spoke English but in the mistaken belief that the viewers would get more out of a wobbly Spanish conversation we plugged on doggedly, with me trying to explain what OT was (I can't even explain it in English) and George talking a little about our trip. We didn't say much. Mostly it was a plug for our book, which the presenter held up for the camera like a new type of nasal spray and explained its contents in glowing terms. I'm not sure how many Argentine matrons would want to backpack in Peru and Bolivia with an English guidebook, but never mind.

At one point backstage I made George sit on a plastic table on account of his supposedly bedridden status, and the thing collapsed with a huge crash, producing anguished groans from the cameramen and director who would blench if anyone so much as <u>whispered</u> when the cameras were rolling. A Japanese woman who'd been demonstrating flower arranging (*ah, que linda!*) must have taken us for producers (reasonably assuming only a producer could look so scruffy) and did a myriad little bows and smiles and handshakes.

So finally, after making a second appearance (where I'd hoped to bring up the subject of the Falklands, perhaps fortunately without success), we left.

We thought that was that, but apparently more people watch that TV programme than you might suppose. When I went to the local shop the following day the boy said, 'Tee hee, television, ha ha' or something equally revealing. Then when I went to call on Sra Escurra, Dr John's aunt, she said, 'Now I was *very* cross with George when I saw him on TV yesterday, he's supposed to be in bed.' And when I was browsing in a shop sale a couple started nudging each other and pointing at me. With my usual paranoia I assumed it was anti-gringo stuff but then she said, 'Weren't you on TV yesterday? I recognised your voice.' And then she chatted amiably, telling everyone else in the shop about it. And later (yes, even more) I was making a phone call in a restaurant (the nearest public phone) and a group of boys came up and asked if I was indeed the *mochilera* on the box yesterday. Such fun. It was a shame that George wasn't up and around; it would have doubled the exposure.

I was suitably deflated, however, a day or so later, when I was sitting in on classes at an English institute with a mind to teaching. A woman said sharply, 'We've met before!' to which I self-effacingly responded, 'Well, I do a little television work, you know,' but she ignored this and decided it must have been Greece in January.

PART 3

AFRICA 1976

Africa 1976

Mediterranean Sea

TUNISIA
Tripoli

LIBYA

EGYPT

Cairo
Luxor
Aswan

S A H A R A

Nile

Red Sea

see main map

N
Bradt

0 ———————— 1000km
0 ———————— 500 miles

NIGER

CHAD

Khartoum
Gedaref
Metema
Simien Mountains

SUDAN

DJIBOUTI
Djibouti

NIGERIA
N'djamena

Socotra

Addis Ababa
Bale Mountains

ETHIOPIA

SOMALIA

CENTRAL AFRICAN REPUBLIC

CAMEROON
Yaoundé
Bangui

Lake Turkana

Mogadishu

GABON
CONGO

ZAIRE

UGANDA
Kampala
Kasese
Goma
Lake Victoria
RWANDA
Kigali
Bujumbura
BURUNDI
Kigoma

KENYA

Nairobi
Arusha
Lamu

Mombasa

INDIAN OCEAN

Brazzaville
Kinshasa

Tabora
Dodoma

Zanzibar
Dar es Salaam

TANZANIA

Luanda

Lake Tanganyika

ANGOLA

Lake Malawi

MALAWI
Lilongwe

Diego Suarez
Sambava

ZAMBIA
Lusaka
Blantyre

SOUTH-WEST AFRICA
Windhoek

Victoria Falls
Salisbury

BOTSWANA

RHODESIA

MOZAMBIQUE

Majunga

Tananarive

MADAGASCAR

SWAZILAND
Mbabane

Bloemfontein
Maseru
LESOTHO

SOUTH AFRICA
Cape Town

Key
——— by land
········· by air
–·–·– by boat
➤ direction of travel
Country and place names as in 1976

148

11

SOUTH AFRICA

It wasn't the first time I'd said to myself 'I really must stop doing this!', but it was the most heartfelt. How many times had I upped sticks and moved to a new country, to a new job and an alien culture? And on my own. Four times at least, and it was always hard, but never as hard as finding myself in the Nurses' Home at Conradie Hospital in Cape Town, in a new job for which I was unprepared, and without George who had stayed behind in Brazil.

It goes without saying that South Africa in the mid-1970s, with apartheid entrenched, was about as different as I could have found after multiracial, fun-loving Brazil. What does go with saying, however, is what a remarkably good hospital Conradie was, supporting my contention that it never pays, as a visitor, to make blanket assumptions about systems or governments. Conradie was closed down soon after apartheid ended in 1994.

The hospital mainly treated spinal cord injuries, taking in patients from all over the Cape Province, a huge area roughly the size of England, as well as the 'Bantu Homelands' of Transkei and Ciskei. Patients from the remote areas were flown in by small plane. The vast majority of them, about ninety per cent, were non-Whites. (Under apartheid's dehumanising classifications, the population was divided into and labelled as 'White' or 'European' and 'non-White' – a category that encompassed black (Bantu) people and 'Coloureds', a term that included mixed-race people, Indians and Malays.) Their high incidence of injury was unsurprising when their lives were so much more dangerous than that of Whites. We occupational therapists worked mostly with the quadriplegics – patients who had some degree of paralysis from the neck down – and whereas Whites damaged their cervical spines playing rugby or diving into shallow water, non-

Whites had sacks of cement dropped on them, fell from donkey carts or were hit by cars. Or were shot by the police. Physiotherapists took care of the rehabilitation of paraplegics, which spared us having to confront perhaps the most distressing injury of all – those cases when damage to the spinal cord was deliberately inflicted with a sharpened bicycle spoke stabbed between two vertebrae at exactly the right level to knock out sexual function. Gang warfare in the townships was rife.

Even when the muscles in their fingers were paralysed, many patients were able to move their arms and extend – bend back – their wrists. With so few White patients, most of the OTs worked exclusively with non-Whites, focusing on teaching them to use a flexor-hinge splint in order to harness that wrist movement into a strong and useful pinch grip. Once they had graduated from traction in bed to a wheelchair, my job was to work with them through activities such as games and crafts to strengthen their wrist muscles and get them so accustomed to the splints that it became second nature to use them for everyday activities. We were fortunate to have a technician on the premises who custom-made the splints and who was a skilful problem solver. One of my favourite patients was Ian, a musician (he played – or used to play – the trombone), whose complicated injury meant that although his right hand could be fitted with the usual splint, he was unable to extend his left wrist and had limited movement in that arm. Jack, the technician, created a device that was operated electronically by a shrug of Ian's shoulder, a movement that closed his fingers. With practice he was able to open a box of matches, extract a match and light a cigarette. No wonder I was proud of him!

In Conradie, at least, South Africa's claims that non-Whites were 'separate but equal' seemed in some ways to be true. I think they really did get equal treatment here. The irony was that they were discharged home, with their new wheelchair and splints, to a township or Homeland where the conditions were so hopelessly inadequate, and the aftercare so limited, that many were readmitted with bedsores or worse in a matter of months.

Working here threw me into the absurdity of apartheid almost from the start. Once I had moved out of the Nurses' Home I had to travel to the hospital, each morning catching the train from the Whites-only section of the station, sitting in an almost empty first-class carriage while the non-Whites crammed themselves into third class. Then I crossed the railway line on the Whites-only bridge, while the other passengers streamed across a separate one. The hospital had separate wards for non-Whites and 'Europeans', with staff of the same racial category looking after each group – except there were no black doctors. Only the physios and OTs treated all races. There were separate rooms for Whites and non-Whites, and we had to use separate cutlery for each (I was reprimanded for using 'White' cutlery and crockery for the wrong type of patient). My patients were brought to the department by a black porter, Archie; White patients were transported to their separate department by a White porter. Once I was asked to work with a White artist, teaching him to paint with the brush held in his mouth. I had to ask him if he minded being in my department with the non-White patients; I didn't ask them if they minded him being there.

Archie was a very bright entrepreneur, always looking for ways to make money. One time I heard his shout of 'Apples for sale!' long before a wheelchair arrived piled high with boxes of apples. The patient's head was only just visible.

So that was Conradie. My OT career lasted for fifteen years on and off, and I never had a more rewarding job.

Meanwhile, back to finding myself in the Nurses' Home. No one spoke to me and I was very lonely. My OT colleagues were all Afrikaans-speaking, so I was isolated from the conversation unless they remembered to speak English. A month later, however, another OT arrived, a German girl who felt as lost as I did. Christmas loomed, everyone was making cheery plans for the break, and Monika and I decided to climb Table Mountain on Christmas Day. It didn't start well. The Nurses' Home warden had assumed that everyone had left and locked the main door so Monika and I climbed out of a window. It's a tough hike to the top of the mountain, but spectacularly beautiful, starting in the Kirstenbosch botanical gardens, aflame with protea, and scrambling up the steep, rocky Skeleton Gorge. The café at the top was open for a celebratory drink, we took the cable car down and had Christmas dinner in town. My time in South Africa was going to be all right.

Time passed. I found a houseshare in Rondebosch, became accustomed to having a maid, and more confident in my work. I learned a few sentences in Afrikaans, and in the click-language of Xhosa, and immersed myself in activities. I gave a talk on my travels in Peru and Bolivia to the appreciative Mountain Club, and sold a few copies of the Little Yellow Book which Sally had sent me. I joined the Ramblers, the Wildlife Society and the Film Society, and learned how to do batik, screen-printing and natural dyeing to provide a range of colours for my new loom. And I took sculpture classes. After six months George arrived, rather anticlimactically by plane, having tried to get a crewing job on a yacht or – surely optimistically – on a shrimping vessel.

It was a hugely enjoyable year, I'm somewhat ashamed to say. The usual diversions of TV and a serious daily newspaper were absent, and with hundreds of new species of birds to recognise, splendid walking country and some new friends, it was a hedonistic life given over to enjoyment. I worked from 8.30am to 4pm, which gave me long evenings to get stuck into whatever creative activity was my current passion. George found work in the book section of Stuttafords, Cape Town's department store, where he lurked in the cookery section copying down recipes to experiment with in the evenings.

Membership of the Wildlife Society brought a life-changing event. I attended a talk on 'Collecting animals in Madagascar'. It's unthinkable now that in the 1970s expeditions still went to wildlife hotspots to collect animals for zoos, though of course that's what Gerald Durrell did and wrote about so entertainingly, so we thought nothing of it. The talk was a complete eye-opener. I knew nothing about Madagascar, lemurs barely came into my consciousness, and as for other endemic marvels such as giant chameleons, I hadn't known that they existed. I was enthralled. Madagascar was added to our planned itinerary for when we headed north on the next leg of what we still imagined would be a round-the-world adventure.

If Madagascar has the world's largest chameleons, South Africa has one of the smallest, the charming dwarf chameleon. I was told that they were sometimes found in gardens and met someone who kept a chameleon as a pet. She would take it on her finger to the local butcher's where there were plenty of flies for its breakfast. I wanted one. The hospital was set in spacious grounds tended by Jakob the gardener. I asked him if he would look out for a chameleon for me and a few days later he appeared with the most gorgeous little chameleon on a stick. I was overjoyed and christened him Jakob. He spent the rest of that day in a display cabinet which showcased the different splints we provided and it was only natural that when Archie arrived with my first patient I would show off my new possession. I didn't expect his reaction: a blood-curdling scream. That was when I learned that in many black African cultures the chameleon is a creature to be feared. The gardener, being Coloured, had no such phobia.

Now my eye was trained to spot chameleons, I found a girlfriend for Jakob in the hydrangeas outside the house, but love was not on the cards. Henrietta spent most of her time wearing the dark colours of rejection and Jakob didn't force the matter. The Mad Rapist, however, practised no such niceties. His tenure in the cage was short – when we saw that nuanced foreplay was not in his repertoire we hastily released him but he had already impregnated Henrietta. Alas, we left Cape Town before the babies were born, but her new owner sent photos of the three tiny offspring (unlike most chameleons, dwarf chameleons give birth to live young rather than laying eggs). Maternal care is not a strong point with chameleons and they had to be removed to a separate cage before Ma or Pa absent-mindedly ate them.

It was time to start saving up seriously for our journey north. Having travelled South America top to toe, we wanted to reverse this and travel Africa toe to top. I made us a new, more spacious tent, and even bought some hand-made boots for the equivalent of £30, my trusty Clarks lace-ups having worn out after several hundred miles. Our latest enthusiasm was mushroom hunting – well, not strictly our latest, as it was knowledge we'd acquired in New England and unlike other species in the natural world, fungi are pretty much the same everywhere. We discovered that the very tasty saffron milk cap grew in abundance in a nearby national forest so for a couple of months we made weekend forays to collect them. It was a great money saver. Sunday and Monday's dinner would be fresh mushrooms on toast, Tuesday's a tasty mushroom stew and the rather tired fungi that formed the bulk of Wednesday's curry could be stretched to last two days. It ended rather abruptly when a warden threatened to arrest us for collecting fruits of the forest in a protected area and confiscated our booty.

There were extravagances. Of course there were, we were in Africa for the first time. We hiked the Otter Trail, one of the best long-distance trails in any country and possibly the only one where a tide table is needed – it entails crossing the estuary of the Bloukrans River. Even at low tide, and with our backpacks on our heads, the water swirled around our waists. And of course we had to visit a game park to see our first African animals, though without a car our choice was limited. We chose a foot safari in Umfolozi.

'If I shout "trees",' Chris, our ranger, explained, 'you climb the nearest tree. What if it's a thorn tree? Believe me, if a rhino is charging, you'll climb it. And if I say "Lion!" you freeze, then walk slowly backwards away from it. No screaming please or I might have to shoot it, which would be a pity. If a buffalo charges I will have no option but to shoot it. This is the most dangerous animal in Umfolozi.'

We were already prepared for the worst, having signed an impressive form devised by the Natal Parks Board relieving them of all responsibility should we die from an attack by any member of the animal kingdom, a snakebite, cobra venom in the eyes, drowning, lightning, a vehicle collision… and a few others that I forget.

We'd only been walking for about an hour when I spotted a rhino lying down, only about 25ft away. Chris was looking in the opposite direction. 'Look! Look!' I whispered in a trembling voice while searching in vain for a tree to climb. It took Chris a while to turn round, but then his reaction was dramatic. In seconds he had assumed the Wild West pose with rifle cocked and safety catch off. The armed Zulu at the rear of the group did the same. The disconcerted rhino jumped to its feet and stumbled off into the bush. It was a white rhino, Chris explained, generally quite docile. Black rhinos were a different matter and we would avoid crossing their territory.

The three-day safari was wonderful although, rather annoyingly, you can't get nearly as close to animals on foot as you can in a vehicle. But we saw both rhino species, lots of birds and an impressive snake. No lions, somewhat to my relief.

The final extravagance, when we knew we should be saving every penny, was to hire a car with a couple of friends to visit the Cape of Good Hope Nature Reserve and to stand at the (nearly) southernmost tip of Africa to watch the turbulent sea whipped up by the usual relentless southeasterly wind. It was hard to stand upright and as we discussed the hazards which faced sailing ships in the olden days as they battled their way around the Cape I had an idea. We were concerned that we were about to run out of petrol, having filled the car with the minimum we thought necessary for the trip, so maybe we could return using the car doors as sails? It worked! We'd hired the smallest car possible, with two doors, and with both fully open and the wind behind us, we sailed, with the engine off, the 20 miles back to the park entrance.

On January 4 1976 we assembled with friends on the platform of Cape Town's railway station, popping champagne corks and toasting our next venture. We were expecting to write another backpacking guide, so finding rewarding walks in every country we happened to find ourselves in was part of the plan. Actually the only plan. We would take Africa as we found it and change our route accordingly, as long as we ended up at the top, in Cairo. Our nation's flags were stitched on to our backpacks to facilitate hitchhiking and all of Africa lay ahead.

INTERLUDE
JOSEPH

Joseph was late for work. Proud of his status as a skilled worker – he was a welder – he was conscientious about timekeeping. Hastily kissing his wife and children goodbye he stepped out of his neat house into the Gugulethu street and started walking briskly towards the bus stop. Rounding a corner he saw his bus approaching and broke into a run. 'Stop! Police!' But Joseph didn't hear the shout. Perhaps he heard the gunfire before he dropped to the ground, his cervical vertebra shattered, his spinal cord severed.

Joseph was taken to Conradie Hospital. All he could move were his eyes. A mirror above his head allowed him to see his surroundings and it was through this mirror that he saw two policemen coming towards him, accompanied by the ward sister. They lifted his paralysed hands, dipped the unfeeling fingers into black ink and took his fingerprints. Then they left.

Joseph's rehabilitation began almost immediately: physiotherapy to strengthen the few functioning muscles in his arms and occupational therapy to help him relearn some basic tasks like cleaning his teeth. Most importantly, he exercised the muscles which would later operate the wrist-driven hand splints to enable him to use a pinch grip. Joseph was one of my star patients. His intelligence and motivation were clear from the start and he was ready to use the splints in record time. The day that a patient is first fitted with a flexor-hinge splint is momentous: a hand that has been a useless appendage becomes, once again, serviceable. I fastened the splint on to Joseph's right hand and asked him to bend his wrist back. His fingers closed. I gave him a small ball to pick up. He grasped and held it. I expected the usual smile of joy but his body shook as tears rolled down his cheeks. 'I used to be so strong!' he sobbed.

The police were still on the scene but now on the defensive. Despite their efforts to justify the shooting, they found that Joseph was carrying his passbook, which entitled him to be in the area, when they felled him, and that he had committed no crime. Ever. His social worker assured me that he would receive compensation. A white lawyer came to see him during one of his OT sessions.

'Tell me what happened,' he asked gently.

Joseph kept his eyes down. 'I don't remember.'

'You remember nothing? Where were you?'

'I don't remember.'

Weeks went by. Joseph would soon be fit enough for discharge, but how would he manage? He had five children and a wife who would have to give up her job as a maid to look after him. Compensation for his injuries was essential but there had been no progress. My visits to the social worker brought vague reassurances and then the news, 'The Attorney General has ordered the case to be dropped.'

I went to see my friend Joan, a feisty young nurse who had spent thirty days in solitary confinement undergoing daily interrogation, suspected of aiding a terrorist.

'Believe me,' she said, 'if I'd known he was a gunrunner I would have cracked the third day.'

Now committed to work for political change within the law, she listened to my story about Joseph.

'Leave it to me. I know someone who can help. He's a very, very good lawyer and he specialises in cases like this.'

Some time later Joan phoned me. 'We won!' The case had been reopened, the officer who had fired the shot disciplined and Joseph would be awarded compensation.

After a year of denials the police had admitted their mistake.

12

LESOTHO

We set off for the northern part of southern Africa in midsummer. Nice! But the summer in this part of the continent is the rainy season, a detail which had rather escaped our notice. Every afternoon, after a generally sunny morning, the clouds would build up and the rain would come down with monsoon ferocity. It was something we learned to plan for, except for the time in Bloemfontein, en route to the Lesotho border.

It was only while drinking coffee in the zoo café, after a happy time watching the animals, that we noticed how dark the sky had become. The rain came down in sheets accompanied by ferocious wind. Then we remembered our tent. We had pitched it in haste, without even bothering to put up the fly since we hadn't expected to stay so long at the zoo. Everything would be soaked. Begging a lift from a departing customer we braced ourselves for a scene of devastation. To our astonished relief we found our tarpaulin pegged neatly over a pile of our – admittedly soggy – belongings. Our saviour, Hansie, appeared and explained that as the rain hammered down on his tent he became increasingly worried on our behalf. 'Your tent was flapping around from just one corner. So I had to do something.' Brushing aside our thanks he surveyed our sodden sleeping bags. 'I can lend you two bags for tonight,' he said. 'I don't need them.' All we could do was invite him to share our soup and conversation. And to be good listeners.

Hansie was a farmer. He had a strong Afrikaans accent which, to our prejudiced minds, meant he would not be open to any sort of discussion about apartheid, but it was he who introduced the subject. From our accents he had also made assumptions and expected us to be critical. 'You know, I think our country has been checkmated. I see no way out now except revolution. I hate conflict but I think it's inevitable.' He sighed, and took another spoonful of soup. 'I have to tell you that I could never sit at the same table as a black man. Nor use the same cutlery. I just couldn't do it, no, not even if it's been washed a hundred times.'

Our own re-education was almost as abrupt as Hansie's would have been in the 1990s. Unquestioningly we walked to the head of the long queue of Basotho people waiting to leave South Africa, were stamped out of the country by a courteous white official and then stared in dismay at the scene at the Lesotho border. And I was shocked at being shocked. What had passed through my mind was: 'What, join this queue of Africans to go through the border? And get on the same bus?' Eighteen months in South Africa had left its mark. The privilege of simply being white had become normal. The physical border we were about to cross was nothing compared with the cultural one.

Within a day, however, those borders had been crossed, despite scarce and hopelessly crowded public transport and roads transformed into slithery quagmires after the relentless rain. One look at Maseru was enough to persuade us to head east along the Mountain Road, one of the very few motorable roads in Lesotho. The country – which is an enclave, completely surrounded by South Africa – has the distinction of being the only one on earth entirely above 1,000m (3,281ft). We took a series of kombis (VW minibuses), all of which are designed to hold nine passengers; at one point ours held nineteen.

Our plan was to get as far as we could by vehicle, then continue on foot through the mountains, still in an easterly direction until, with luck, we came to Sani Pass (or Sani Top as it was known locally) and the road back into South Africa.

After a night in Mantsonyane stocking up on food, we found a truck operated by the Save the Children Fund. It was transporting flour and dried milk – and a few passengers – to isolated communities in the interior. This was far more interesting than a crowded kombi. We made ourselves comfortable among the sacks, shared our food, and gawped at the mountain scenery, so green after weeks of rain, and the blanket-swaddled Basotho men riding wiry ponies. Their wives were invariably walking behind, usually carrying a suitcase or other luggage on their heads. Time and again the vehicle became stuck in mud and all the men, including George, hopped out to push. Finally it stopped abruptly and gently subsided. We fell or jumped out and saw that the rear wheel had completely disappeared into yellow, sticky clay. An hour was spent trying to dig it out but it was a hopeless task. No help would be available until the following day, so while the crew unloaded the cargo we cooked soup for them before pitching our tent. They walked off to the nearest village to find help and lodging.

We were woken the next morning by shouts and the lowing of cattle. The crew had returned with six oxen which pulled the truck free with a satisfying slurp. The men also had bread and milk, and we sat down together to share this breakfast before reloading the cargo and continuing to the Orange River.

There was a bridge across the river at Koma-Koma, we'd been told, but no sign of one as the truck drew to a halt where the road disappeared under a brown torrent of flood water. Our driver was unfazed: 'Koma-Koma low-cross bridge,' he explained. The end of the journey for him and the start of our walk for us. Except that even with a firm concrete base this ford was far too dangerous to cross on foot.

We found a flat area to pitch our tent and waited for the rain to stop and the flood to subside. We waited for three days. I'd finished my book, had played enough Scrabble to last a lifetime, and investigated every aspect of the natural world outside our tent. It was time to go. As the taller and heavier of the two of us, I went first to test the waters. Leaving my pack and boots with the tent I gingerly entered the flow. By mid-river it raged against my thighs and I was nearly swept away. But the concern about having nothing to read was stronger than the fear of death so I made it to the other side – and back again. It would be easier with the weight of my pack, I reassured myself. And it was. We both made it safely across and the adventure of finding our way on foot to Sani Pass had begun.

All too soon we came to another river. The Linakeng looked deep, with loose boulders and rocks covering the bottom, and I was not going in. Although I'd made light of the hazardous crossing of the Orange, the experience had unnerved me. We turned right and followed the river upstream, hoping to find a safer place to cross.

The little schoolhouse was perched on a low hill overlooking the river with a scatter of huts nearby. Through the open windows we could hear the children chanting their lessons. We sat down to wait for classes to finish, knowing from experience that anywhere in the world schoolteachers are the best source of help in isolated areas: they usually speak English and their local knowledge is good. A small face appeared at one of the windows. Then another; it seemed that the whole class was peering at us silently. Then pandemonium. Children poured out of the door – and the windows – and raced towards us shrieking. They were followed by a harassed-looking male teacher. We explained that we were heading east to Sani Top but couldn't find a safe place to ford the river. 'No problem,' he said, 'I'll show you the place for crossing.' He shouted at the children in English to return to their classroom. They ignored him. He repeated the request in Sesotho. No response. He shrugged and told them something in a quieter voice. There was a whoop of delight and we and fifty or so children followed him along the riverbank.

'What did you tell them?' I asked.

'I said they could come with us but must write an essay about it afterwards.'

A little girl held my hand and asked me repeatedly, 'Where is my father?' It was a question I felt at a loss to answer. The teacher collected two female relatives to carry our packs on their heads and soon stopped at a stretch of river that looked much the same as anywhere else but was, he said, easy underfoot.

We sat down to take off our boots and socks and the children clustered round like bees, buzzing with excitement. They fought for the privilege of carrying a boot each, and a smelly sock each, and to hold our hands to support us. One child on each side chivalrously hoisted up the bottoms of my shorts to keep them dry. The river bottom was indeed soft and sandy, and with so many helpers we were practically borne aloft through the flood. The final luxury came when we sat down on the far bank to put our boots back on. The towel was whisked out of my hands and a small girl dried my feet, carefully separating each toe in order to dab the last moisture away. Her brother insisted that he eased the boots on, and a further boy did up the laces.

I would have loved to have read those essays!

Our walk continued for four days, guided by compass and passers-by. Every day we were greeted with curiosity and friendliness, offered shelter in huts, and sometimes eggs. A boy sold us two fat trout. Initially our asking the way to Sani Top was greeted with puzzlement and directions to the nearest road (which wasn't near, and headed north not east), but as we progressed our request was met with recognition and specific directions.

One evening, after a particularly tiring day, we struggled into a village and asked to speak to the headman for permission to camp nearby. Chief Frank introduced himself and said, 'Please be condescended to accompany me to my very respectable home.' We were dumbfounded. Frank explained that he had visited the United States as part of a UN delegation when he was an MP some years ago. It was hard for us to imagine this urbane politician living in a traditional hut some three days' walk from the nearest road, but his was a hut with a difference. Modern, Western furniture was arranged on the carefully swept dirt floor, and a carpet and curtains for the glazed windows gave it a homely feeling.

As we sipped our maize beer he chatted to us about Lesotho. 'Our biggest export is men,' he told us.

'Many, many Basotho work in South Africa's mines.'

'How awful for them to go from the freedom of Lesotho to apartheid in South Africa,' I commented.

Frank's eyes flashed with anger. 'Don't tell me how my people should feel! The money is good. It is their choice.'

The uneasy atmosphere was broken by the arrival of a beautiful teenage girl wearing a white petticoat. 'Ah,' he said. 'This is my daughter, The Queen.'

'And what's her name?'

'I told you – The Queen. She will dance for you.'

More teenagers appeared, some carrying drums and whistles. A dozen girls knelt on the ground in front of us and the drums began to beat. The dance began simply, almost imperceptibly, in their head movements. Gradually the rhythm moved down into their bodies, and became stronger; a beautifully sensuous dance. Then The Queen had her solo. All movement was concentrated on her body, shoulders and long, curved neck. The hips and head stayed motionless. While we watched, mesmerised, the setting sun touched the scene with orange and turned the distant mountains purple.

I felt a surge of happiness. This was Africa and the entire continent lay ahead of us. For the next eleven months we would depend on the kindness of Africans and occasionally we could give something back in return. Not physically, perhaps, but in appreciation and understanding.

INTERLUDE
A SWAZILAND DILEMMA

'It is a very small place. Do you think George will fit in there?' We shared the German's concern as we investigated the space, designed for one suitcase, behind the back seat of his VW Beetle. But our options were limited. We had just learned that George, with an American passport, needed a re-entry visa to get back into South Africa. The permit could only be issued in South Africa. We were in Swaziland.

We'd met Hans at Mlilwane Game Sanctuary, where we were relaxing after an exhilarating few days hiking in Malolotja Nature Reserve. No one had told us Swaziland was so beautiful! Casinos and pornography, yes – sin was the big attraction for most South African visitors in the 1970s – but here were green mountains, meadows full of flowers, simple campsites, and miles and miles of hiking trails. It was November, spring, and the long-tailed widow birds were doing their thing, popping up out of the grass then fluttering down trailing their long tail feathers like a child's kite. We saw wild antelope for the first time – blesbok (silly-looking animals, we thought, with long, lugubrious faces) – and I was enchanted to spot dassies, or rock hyraxes, smiling sweetly from the *koppies* (rocky prominences). They reminded us of cheerful guinea pigs.

Mlilwane also had its sweetly smiling resident, though Rosie's nature belied her appealing expression. The little warthog had been bottle reared and was now an overconfident and bumptious adolescent. I'm sure (am I?) that her charge and the sideways thrust of her little tusks was supposed to be friendly, but it left a permanent dent on my cine camera which I'd used as a shield. The hippo, Somersault, had an even bigger smile, and had reversed the usual hippo behaviour of snoozing during the day and eating at night so he could enjoy the snacks fed to him by the wardens.

Then there were the blue cranes. Very elegant, dressed in haute couture blue-grey, but with a mean streak. We watched one chase a visitor round the rest camp and into the thorn bushes.

For one of our first African game parks we were not doing badly, but we wanted a game drive – that's what you do in a game park – and for that we needed a car. Enter Hans. He was taking a short break from his engineering job in Johannesburg, and was glad of the company (so he said). It was while we were watching, in some astonishment, a pair of male nyala performing some sort of stiff-legged dance that Hans broke the news about the re-entry permit.

We were getting ready to leave. Our rucksacks were packed, and I'd insisted that George ate a small breakfast. 'After all, if we're going to fold you up into that space, there's no room for a full stomach.' We stopped a mile from the border, and George climbed over the back seat. There was just room for him to assume a foetal position, kneeling on the floor with his head between his knees. 'Whatever you do, don't sneeze,' I said, covering him with a rug and a road atlas.

'Passports?' Hans and I beamed at the border guard as we handed over our documents. 'Lovely day, isn't it? Thank you so much.' And we drove across the frontier into South Africa.

13

RHODESIA AND MALAWI

The border official at Beit Bridge, between South Africa and Rhodesia, made it quite clear that he disliked hitchhikers. We knew our documents were in perfect order. And we'd taken the precaution of buying air tickets to Malawi since we knew that evidence of onward travel was a requirement. His response was that we should have air tickets to America, but we thwarted this by showing him our traveller's cheques, demonstrating that we had 'sufficient funds'. He countered, lamely, with 'Well, you won't get a lift to Salisbury, so won't be able to use your air tickets', before providing us with a visa for the shortest permissible period and grumpily stamping us in on a separate piece of paper in order to avoid the problem of having a Rhodesian stamp in our passports when entering the countries further north. As he did so he added, 'If I had my way I wouldn't offer you this courtesy.'

A few words about Rhodesia, as it was then. In 1965 Prime Minister Ian Smith hit the headlines by instigating UDI (Unilateral Declaration of Independence), but the country had, in fact, been self-governing since 1923. The white, mainly British, population, though believing themselves more liberal than those in South Africa, would not agree to the British stipulation that they accept Majority Rule before they could achieve full independence. International sanctions were imposed on Smith's rebel regime, but rather than crippling the economy they inspired an entrepreneurial spirit among the remaining white population which hadn't given up and left for South Africa or Britain. When we arrived, early in 1976, the white-dominated government was grimly hanging on, despite ever more successful guerrilla activity. With 270,000 Rhodesians of European descent, and more than six million Africans, the system was clearly unsustainable and four years later Rhodesia became Zimbabwe, under the leadership of Robert Mugabe.

Annoyingly, the border official was right. We waited four hours for a lift to Salisbury but eventually arrived at the very British-looking Triangle Country Club where we wandered around for a while trying to find Mr Brockway. We'd met his daughter in South Africa and she'd told us we should stay with him because the old chap, a recent widower and in charge of the golf club, was lonely. When we finally tracked him down he almost immediately said, 'I hope you've come to stay with me.' So we did. He was a lovely old man from Bournemouth who had been in Rhodesia twenty-seven years but had retained his liberal outlook. A generous host, he was keen that we should meet a cross section of (white) Rhodesians. Although segregation was not official government policy in Rhodesia it was still very evident. The evening before our departure he invited some friends round, including a man he wanted us to meet because he was chairman of an embryo opposition party to Smith's Rhodesian Front. He described enthusiastically what his party hoped to achieve. Then the conversation moved to family matters and we learned that his daughter was at a South African university. 'Why not Salisbury?' I asked. 'Well, it's fifty per cent black!' he responded. And then he realised what he'd said.

Lifts were, indeed, not easy to come by in Rhodesia, but once we did get them we met interesting and hospitable people who were keen for us to see the country's main sights. Our job was to listen and learn. The many conversations we had with white Rhodesians drove George to write in the first edition of *Backpacker's Africa*: 'Frankly, our political impression was that with independence [ie majority rule] a lot of good people will either be killed or forced to flee. Those remaining, black and white alike, will suffer a tremendous slump in their standard of living.'

It was time to use those air tickets to Malawi.

❖ ❖ ❖ ❖

Malawi (formerly Nyasaland) was an oddity. It was one of the most stable African countries that we travelled through, despite (or perhaps because of) it being a one-party state ruled with a rod of iron by Dr Hastings Banda, who managed to retain a sizeable number of British expats working in schools, hospitals and the like. It was also thoroughly and exuberantly African. It both provided us with our most enjoyable and civilised mountain experience – Mount Mulanje – and our most uncomfortable, but interesting, few days of travel, on Lake Malawi.

That was all to come. First we had to get there. Since we were flying it should have been the easiest border crossing of our trip. We just had to look respectable. By law. That meant that George's hair couldn't touch his collar and his beard would have to be neatly trimmed. Stories abounded of 'hippies' being given a short back and sides and a shave at the airport and this, in the decade when men's hair routinely hung halfway down their backs, was an indignity not to be risked. I did a rather splendid barber job with some borrowed scissors, and looked out the long blue dress that was bundled, rather damply, in the bottom of my rucksack for an unexpected formal occasion. Women were not permitted to wear trousers or shorts, and skirts had to come well below the knee. George changed into a crisp(ish) long-sleeved shirt and straight-legged trousers (flares were forbidden). We also checked our reading matter for anything that could be construed as politically subversive or pornographic. So all we needed to do was get to the airport. Our hosts – we were now staying with Mr Brockway's son, Chris, and his wife, in Salisbury – were rather too keen to drive us there and say goodbye. As we were gathering our stuff together Chris received a phone call. A state of war had been declared between Rhodesia and Mozambique, so our Air Rhodesia plane was cancelled; its flight path was over Mozambique and any Rhodesian plane found violating their airspace would be shot down. That evening the smiling (white) Minister of Defence appeared on TV, told us not to panic, it wasn't war, just a border closure which would affect Mozambique more than Rhodesia. Our hosts were panicking but it was less a fear of war than the prospect of our indefinite stay that motivated them to move heaven and earth to get us out of Rhodesia. Chris found an Air Malawi flight the following day, routed over Zambia, and all seemed to be well. At least we reached the Departure Lounge before being told that the plane had been delayed indefinitely while negotiations took place.

Eventually we got there. As a final indignity we were refused entry because we didn't have return tickets. George showed the man their official leaflet saying that proof of adequate funds was acceptable and flashed our impressive number of traveller's cheques. We wore him out, finally, and were crossly granted a 24-hour visa which could be extended at the immigration office in Blantyre.

Blantyre was, and is, the commercial capital of Malawi, and we were destined to wait a few days there in order for me to get a new passport. My existing one showed that I had worked in South Africa which would have prohibited me from entering any country to the north. The British Embassy in Blantyre must have been fed up with the backpackers claiming to have lost their passports, but a new one was provided in a matter of days. We holed up at the Government Rest House, a splendid remnant of colonial times, with other branches providing inexpensive accommodation all over the country. The rest house in Blantyre, however, was not conducive for rest. Malawians, we discovered, were the most irrepressibly happy of any nationality in Africa. At 5am each morning the surrounding rooms would erupt into a cacophony of shouts, whistles, door-slams and snatches of song, and radios would be turned up to full volume. The local preference for a good time over our rather boring need for sleep was much in evidence later when our night bus broke down.

We spread out our sleeping bags in a doorway, while the passengers remained in the bus laughing, chatting and singing all night. They seemed almost disappointed when we finally got going again at dawn.

In Salisbury we'd told a keen walker about our aim to find a good hike in each country we visited for our intended guidebook. 'Oh well, in Malawi you must get in touch with the Mulanje Mountain Club. They usually go somewhere interesting at the weekend.' We obediently wrote down the name and phone number of the club's president, despite hesitating to impose ourselves (yes, I know, but it's different when the offer is freely made rather than requested). And the president of anything is particularly frightening. However, we were stuck in Blantyre for about a week waiting for the new passport so what better than to do some hiking. George phoned the president who, as we had expected, sounded a bit huffy but gave us the number of the chap leading the trip up Mulanje that weekend. Peter was friendly and encouraging. Yes, of course we could come. He would arrange for someone to pick us up at the rest house at 8 o'clock on Saturday morning. We explained that we'd like to stay on the 'plateau' (it turned out to be anything but flat) for a few days rather than descend on Sunday, and learned to our considerable relief that there was no need to bring our tent because there were cabins for Mountain Club members which we were welcome to use.

As I reached the door of the rest house I was told by the warden to change out of my jeans into a long skirt. 'But I'm climbing Mulanje! We've been told we're allowed to wear trousers for sporting activities!' I was still arguing my case when the five other hikers arrived, the women all wearing long skirts and hiking boots. I went back inside and changed. We drove down dirt roads and through tea plantations, while the distant blue mountain got larger and more imposing. I felt a frisson of anxiety when Peter showed us the ascent route on the map, with massed contour lines. Parking in a tea plantation, we met our porters, and the women slipped out of their skirts and into more suitable climbing apparel. Having been sceptical about the need for porters I now thought they were the best idea ever. I was happy to let them carry my pack while I shared George's, but even so the path up was one of the hardest yet: almost vertical and slick with mud (of course it was raining), so had we been on our own I think we would have given up. But there were compensations. The greenness was brightened by huge flowers, streams cascaded into waterfalls, and at one point one of southern Africa's most spectacular birds, Livingstone's Lourie, glided past, its green and red plumage bright against the dark forest.

Sometimes the real pleasure of hiking is to stop, and so it was on Mulanje. The leaders had set a cracking pace and we had no choice but to try to keep up. When we finally reached the cabin where we were to stay overnight we stood wetly in the doorway in a state of disbelief. We had never expected such luxury. The warden had lit a fire and collected water prior to our arrival so the club members were already sitting in comfy chairs drinking tea. Looking back, I find it hard to believe that these cabins fitted with an independent African country. Maintained by the Department of Forestry and the MMC, they were exclusively used by whites, mostly expats on a working visa, and the set-up was not really any different from apartheid South Africa, with black servants doing the labouring. I suppose no one in authority had got round to changing all this after independence.

The next morning, after a sumptuous breakfast of bacon and eggs, our new friends set off down the mountain and we struck out across the plateau towards the furthest cabin and a forestry station three days' walk away. It was a gorgeous walk, with scenery varying from alpine meadows full of flowers to deep valleys of cedar trees hung with lichen, and dramatically eroded towers of granite sheltering deep pools of warm water, perfect for a bath. Each night we slept in a comfortable bunk bed in one of the cabins, after an evening warming by the fire. The wardens even insisted on washing our dishes.

Every so often we'd pass men jogging along the trail carrying enormous planks of wood on their heads, weighing, we learned later, at least 80lb. The valuable cedar which grew on Mulanje was destined for a sawmill, some 20 miles away, but first the logs had to be sawn into rough planks – all done by hand by two men and a double-handled saw – then carried down the precipitous slope of Mulanje with a further day's jog to reach the mill. The men then stocked up on provisions for their mountain camp and came back up Mulanje with sacks of flour and sugar on their heads. They'd been doing this for decades, for a lifetime, father and son. Peter told us a story about one of these men. During the days when Malawi was the British Protectorate of Nyasaland one of the timber carriers stopped off at a village beer hall, got into a brawl and murdered someone. He was tried, found guilty, and sentenced to death by hanging. They attempted to hang him three times, and each time his massive neck muscles saved him. So they were obliged to let him go free.

Look at a map of Malawi and the one thing that stands out is that much of the country is covered by water: Lake Malawi. So our plan was to travel north by lake rather than road. That was before we learned, to our immeasurable delight, that it was possible to buy a cheap 'excursion air ticket' from Blantyre to Madagascar, changing planes in Dar es Salaam. It seemed almost too good to be true; the trek through southern Tanzania to the capital was known to be long and arduous and not very rewarding, and we were determined to get to Madagascar whatever the cost. So we could fly there from Blantyre, with a stopover in Dar, to which we could then return after our trip to Madagascar. And although we wouldn't use the Dar to Blantyre bit we would be complying with the usual requirement to have an onward plane ticket. Perfect! We still wanted to take a boat trip on the lake, however, so planned a round trip: two days from Monkey Bay to Nkhata Bay via Likoma Island, and back to Blantyre by bus.

While waiting for the weekly boat, we stayed a few days in Blantyre with Peter and his partner Eirene, and listened to their stories of what it was like to be an expat in a totalitarian country. We'd noted in that Mulanje cabin that the main topic of conversation was who had most recently been P.I.ed – that is, labelled as a Prohibited Immigrant – and Peter filled us in on what sort of activities risked deportation. For instance a houseboy reported a chap for possessing an obscene photo. He was deported, despite the fact that the photo was in his wallet, which the houseboy just happened to be looking through, and that it was of his wife in a bikini. Another man was given twenty-four hours to leave the country because he had shown disrespect to the president. He had pulled out of a side road on to the highway without realising that the absence of traffic meant that the president's cavalcade was about to pass through. Expats merely got deported for these misdemeanours. Malawians went to prison. Censorship was unsubtle, with foreign newspapers and magazines a chequerboard of black redactions, while anything about Malawi was just snipped out. Nothing bad ever happened in Malawi – only good news was reported – so the local English-language paper was pretty bland. The upside to all this was that, in contrast to the two countries we had come from, whites treated Africans with a refreshing courtesy and respect.

While in Blantyre we were invited to attend the Malawi Schools English-speaking Drama contest. Each school put on a 25-minute play, with the child actors facing substantial obstacles just to be heard. The hall had a tin roof and of course it was raining, hammering down like a drum roll, so they had to shout at the tops of their voices. The hall was packed with excited children who entered into the spirit of the thing with Elizabethan fervour, shouting, booing, throwing things, and stopping the action for several minutes on the rare occasion that they understood a joke. Our favourite, because it was so gloriously shambolic, was the ambitious 25-minute performance of *Hamlet*. I'm not sure if it was using Shakespeare's text or a Malawian version, but it didn't matter because it was inaudible, with the audience providing all the dominant sound. The director knew that the play was full of soliloquys but also that these would be too challenging for the lad playing the prince, so had opted for dumbshow to the confusion of the onlookers. Hamlet reappeared with a cardboard dagger and stabbed a few people, which went down well. Then Ophelia wandered in and went mad. More stabbings followed – rather more, I think, than in Shakespeare's play – and the stage filled with dead bodies, to the delight of the young audience, who may have found that future productions of Shakespeare fell below expectations.

I wouldn't say our lake voyage on the MV *Ilala* was an unqualified success but we couldn't leave Malawi without experiencing the country's main feature. As so often here, the planned four-hour journey to Monkey Bay by Express Bus was a figment of the bus company's imagination, and waiting for the slow service the following morning gave us the opportunity to experience a night-time tropical thunderstorm inside our little tent. I wrote:

> The lightning didn't just light up the landscape, it absolutely blinded us. The thunder shook the earth and the rain crashed down on our tent unremittingly for two hours. Next day we found a tree not far from our campsite split and smouldering. I've never been frightened in a storm until this, but knew that in Rhodesia they had already had 85 deaths from lightning strikes that year – and it was only February!

Built in 1949, and transported in bits to Nyasaland, the *Ilala* is still doing the six-day, 745-mile round trip from Monkey Bay, stopping at twelve ports and providing the main transport north in this landlocked country. We couldn't afford the relatively comfortable first class so settled for second, with the cargo, and which had fixed tables and benches. It was preferable to third class which was packed, excited families with wailing children occupying every possible space; there the only option was to sit on the wooden benches all night – if you could find a space.

After a few hours we made our first stop to load up with more cargo and a lot more passengers. A wonderful old black steam crane was called into action, puffing and wheezing as it accomplished its task and belching out red sparks at intervals. We watched a car being loaded, using the trial and error method, after which we took the opportunity to disembark and visit the market and its pharmacy section and learn how to improve our health and quality of life. Ground-up hedgehog quills and pangolin scales would make us strong; crushing up turtle shell with various roots and mixing with hair oil before going to work would guarantee promotion; and slipping your unfaithful wife a potion would mean she would never look at another man again. The display was a macabre introduction to the wildlife of the region: a hedgehog skin, an owl's head, a hornbill's beak and a baboon's foot along with a variety of snake skins.

We sailed in the evening and when night fell we initially spread our sleeping bags on the cargo and slept reasonably well – until the inevitable rain arrived, when we hunched under a table that was covered in sleeping children.

Next day we called at several islands and at each one the passengers crowded to the rails to buy fish. Soon the deck was slippery with discarded offal and fish heads, fish-smeared children raced around shrieking, and the whole place stank. The voyage had become a bit of an ordeal but was made worthwhile because of Violet, a delightful and erudite woman who had spent nine months in London learning shop management on a course run by Marks and Spencer. She now owned a successful business in Blantyre and was about to expand into Zomba. She told us a lot about traditional practices such as circumcision rituals and how pubescent girls had to stay alone in a special hut during their first period. When we remarked on the incredible good cheer of her fellow countrymen she said: 'It's said that it's because they eat fish. There's something in the fishes' brains that makes them excited.'

By the time we reached Nkhata Bay, after thirty-six hours, the stench was almost unbearable and I was very happy not to be spending another night on board.

At least the series of buses which eventually got us back to Blantyre didn't smell of fish, but our patience was worn thin by the numerous breakdowns, which of course were taken by our fellow passengers as another opportunity to celebrate life. During one prolonged breakdown I was encouraged to see the legs of the driver and conductor sticking out beneath the bus in characteristic 'men fixing vehicle' mode only to find, on closer inspection, that the driver was asleep and the conductor eating fish.

INTERLUDE
LEARNING TO LISTEN

Hitchhiking is perhaps unique in its requirement that you, as a passenger, listen courteously to opinions which you vehemently oppose, hear out mind-numbingly boring or eye-poppingly dreadful life stories, or simply spend hours with someone whom you would never normally meet, all the time being a good listener and keeping your own story and opinions to yourself unless asked. It's one of the most challenging, and perhaps dangerous, aspects of travel, not because you might be picked up by a murderer – very unlikely – but because a lonely driver's need to show off can result in some terrifying journeys. One in Malawi stands out as perhaps the most frightening ever. I described it in a letter home:

> We hitched a lift from Lilongwe, getting to Blantyre in record time, mostly with a terrifying Portuguese man from Angola who drove at 80mph, meanwhile telling us a long, complicated story about how he had threatened to shoot the chief of police in Lusaka so had left Angola in a hurry (some years back) and how much money he'd made in Malawi, meanwhile releasing the steering wheel to shuffle through his papers so I could see the cheques he'd written recently and the ones he'd received. Once a car overtook him and this was an insult to his nationality, his driving and his manhood. He got his revenge at 90mph on a blind bend. We did the 220 miles to Blantyre in three hours. Gulp.

A lift in Rhodesia gave us the opportunity to meet an American whom I described as 'quite fascinatingly ghastly'. He stopped for us about 100 miles from Victoria Falls to tell us he was only going a mile or so, but on recognising George's accent said he might as well take us to Vic Falls although he hadn't been planning to go there – he'd seen Niagara, so what was the point? He talked non-stop, telling us he was a salesman and describing his tax fiddles and, proudly, how he once overcharged someone $800. He took us for a brief look at the Falls – 'Can't see much, can you?' – before disappearing into the hotel casino.

Most of our lifts in South Africa were with Whites, but one of our best hitchhiking experiences was the time we were given a lift by two Coloured people in a pick-up truck, or 'Bakkie'. We rode in the back, well separated from the drivers, obeying the law of apartheid, but the look of shocked disbelief from all who spotted us, White and non-White, has stayed with me as one of my most treasured hitchhiking memories.

14

MADAGASCAR

We arrived in Madagascar in a state of blissful ignorance. And left a lot wiser, and so passionate about that glorious, and sometimes tragic, island that I have returned more than thirty times in the ensuing years. In 1976 everything we saw surprised and enchanted us. There were no guidebooks on the country in any language so our ignorance was almost total apart from the smattering of wildlife knowledge that I had picked up from that Cape Town lecture. That innocence led to serendipitous wildlife encounters at almost every turn, but also to the experience which remains the worst in my travelling life.

That was all to come, and as we approached the Big Red Island we got our first dose of information from the twinkly steward on our Air Madagascar flight. He filled us in on the origins of the people and explained about the extraordinary racial diversity that reminded us of Brazil, with people of all colours and facial features mingling together. Something else reminiscent of Brazil was George trying to communicate in Spanish while I struggled to recall my French from (failed) O-level days.

Madagascar had gained its independence from France in 1960 but the West-leaning honeymoon period was short. In 1975 the country became a self-proclaimed Christian Marxist Democracy, which meant that young men were sent to Moscow to study and returned as devout capitalists, which perhaps explains why the country's particular brand of socialism didn't last. When reflecting on Madagascar's poverty it's worth noting that the population when we visited in 1976 was around eight million. In 2020 it was reckoned to be 27 million.

Our bargain Malawian air ticket allowed for a stop in the port city of Majunga (now known as Mahajanga) and then on to the capital Tananarive (Antananarivo), but we were able to swap the onward section and fly from Majunga to the island of Nosy Be, which seemed a brilliant move and cause for celebration. It was easy to live it up in Madagascar with its wonderful seafood and good beer – and a favourable black-market rate for our dollars.

The main town in Nosy Be is called Hell-Ville, which was suitably descriptive when we arrived during the tail end of Cyclone Gladys, although we learned later it's named after a French admiral. Rusting corrugated iron buildings were jumbled haphazardly along streets swirling with mud and garbage. And there were no hotel rooms available. After eating an enormous lunch we persuaded the restaurant to let us sleep on their floor after closing time and to keep an eye on our packs while we took a look at the island. If it ever stopped raining. By this time we'd found a map and a few brochures and learned that the best beaches were in the northwest, and that if we wanted to see lemurs the smaller island of Nosy Komba was the place to go. I confidently wrote home that Madagascar had 'seven varieties' of lemur. Actually in those days there were thought to be thirty-one species, and that number has now grown to over one hundred.

Nosy Be is a very different place these days. In 1976 we believed, once the rain had stopped, that we had stumbled on Paradise. We woke to a cloudless sky and the air washed clean, and wasted no time in finding a taxi-be (shared taxi) to take us into the countryside. Staring idly out of the window I saw what I thought at first was a sheet of bright green plastic wedged in the hedgerow. When I realised what it was I was struck dumb with excitement: an *enormous* emerald-green chameleon! Remember, the only chameleons we had seen hitherto were the dwarf species in South Africa. Once I'd found my voice and alerted George, we spotted four more. I vowed I wasn't going to return to Hell-Ville until I'd had a proper look at one. First we wanted a swim, and had been told on good authority that Andilana Beach was the prettiest on the island, as indeed it was. A picture-postcard scene with palm-fringed sands and a coral reef within wading distance. I had prudently bought a mask and snorkel in Dar es Salaam, so could marvel at this underwater world – I hadn't snorkelled for years, so everything was amazing: corals, sponges, sea anemones, fish of all sizes and colours... it was almost too much and I had difficulty not gasping in delight and drowning. Later we had our picnic under the palms and somehow managed to knock down a coconut. But what to do with it? We approached a group of men who had been watching us from a distance, and held out the coconut with a question mark on our faces. One handed George a machete which was no help at all. Taking the knife back, the man expertly cut the top off so we could drink the water and then fashioned a spoon from the husk and cut the coconut in half so we could eat the flesh. Yum.

As we were starting to pack up I saw, out of the corner of my eye, a hawk-like bird flying overhead. But it wasn't a bird, it was a bat! 'One of those huge, foxy-faced creatures you see in zoos,' I wrote. Yet another first. I'd never seen a fruit bat in the wild. It flew around examining us before hanging upside down from a palm tree. All that was needed before we looked for a lift back to Hell-Ville was to find a chameleon. It didn't take long. Reading my description written at the time, I think it must have been a very large panther chameleon:

> About a foot long excluding the tail, brilliant green with a turquoise stripe down the side, and lovely scarlet lines radiating out from his eyes.

And it got even better.

> Picture the scene: a horseshoe-shaped beach of golden sand fringed with palm trees. Resting nonchalantly on the beach is

Above: Outside our shared house in Cape Town, 1975
Inset: Cape dwarf chameleon. We sometimes found one in the hydrangeas.

Below: Rondebosch station send off, Cape Town, January 1976

Above: 'Welcome to my village!', Lesotho

Below: Crossing the Linakeng River with the help of an entire school

Below: A Basotho woman lends a hand – or head

Above: Chief Frank's family in Lesotho

Below: Typical African scenes in the 1970s

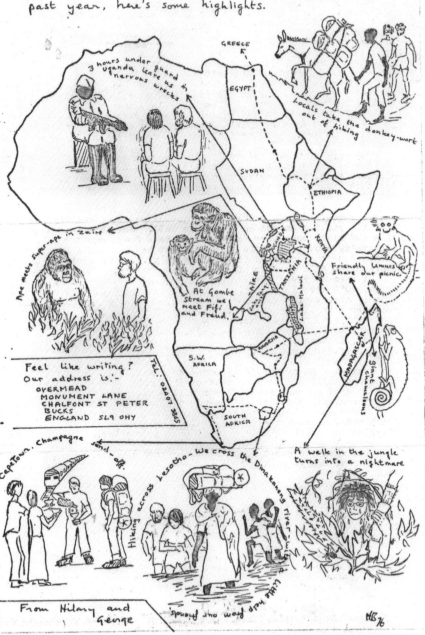

Above: Christmas letter, 1976

Above: Printed by George, 1977!

Below: Sketch for Bradt Enterprises logo

Below: Our first catalogue

Above: Rosita, the baby squirrel monkey, with her surrogate mother in the Darién

Above: Young Cuna girl with baby brother, Paya village

Below: River crossing, Darién

Below: George won the competition for the most insect bites!

You may wonder who runs Bradt Enterprises while we slog up volcanoes and tromp through jungles.

Two 'volunteers' were pressed into service before our trip to Mexico and Central America, and the fact they are our parents probably has something to do with their willingness to take on such a thankless task. Of course at intervals they threaten strike action, and more serious measures such as going on vacation or eating all the asparagus before we return. But you will find your orders filled promptly and letters answered or forwarded to us wherever we are in the back of beyond.

LET'S INTRODUCE YOU TO:

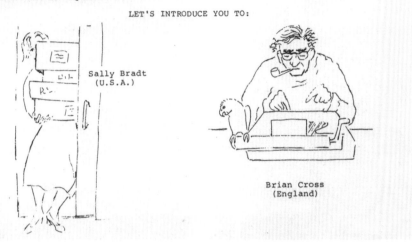

Sally Bradt
(U.S.A.)

Brian Cross
(England)

Above: Tribute to our parents in *Backpacking in Mexico and Central America*

Below: We were so proud of our first 'proper' book, with its wobbly text courtesy of Letraset

Below: We celebrated its publication with a cake that declared: 'We'll eat our words'

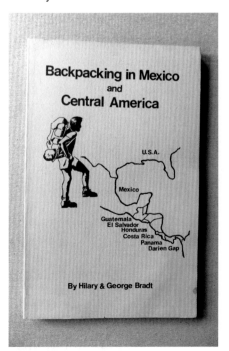

Above: Christmas dinner 1978, under Pico Bolívar, Venezuela

Above: On our first organised trek as joint leaders (1979), this donkey needed some persuasion

Below: Cooking our soup under Mount Salkantay, Peru, 1979

Below: The pre-Columbian Takesi Trail, Bolivia

a huge, pink-lined conch shell, and a few yards into the sea is a multicoloured, multi-fish coral reef. A large tropical tree spreads its shade over the beach where we sit eating our picnic. In the branches are lemurs, peering down anxiously to see if we are going to share our bananas. That's Nosy Komba!

I went on to describe the 'two types' of lemur, one chestnut with splendid white side-whiskers, and one coal black. (See what I mean about ignorance? They were both the same species – the chestnut ones being the females.) The snorkelling was the best I'd ever experienced and I describe the beautiful clawless lobster I watched cruising along the seabed, and the shoals of multicoloured fish.

When I returned to Nosy Komba in 1984 there was no coral. It had been dynamited by the local fishermen, and the lemurs were 'managed' by the island's villagers, who charged a fee to see them.

With only a month in Madagascar we couldn't linger so the next stop was Diego Suarez (Antsiranana). The ferry from Nosy Be was met by a skirmish of taxi drivers all trying to grab anyone who looked as though they might want to go to Diego. Without having any say in the matter, our packs were loaded on to the roof of a Peugeot 404 station wagon which already had eight passengers. 'But it's full!' I said. The driver just laughed and opened the door. Two more passengers got in after us and our driver sulkily started the engine, clearly thinking it was hardly worth making the journey with a half-empty vehicle. After about half a mile he gave a whoop of delight, slammed the vehicle into reverse, and collected two very large ladies who somehow squeezed in. Satisfied, he roared off with fifteen passengers. In case we felt lonely he put on the radio at top volume, and drove at breakneck speed, hand on horn, scattering chickens, goats and children at every village. I was sitting next to the driver in relative comfort, except when he changed gear or turned right. Two people were squashed in next to me. I looked behind for

George but found that he had entirely disappeared underneath an enormous woman.

Hitching from Diego's best beach we were picked up by two animated Indian lads who invited us to eat at their brother's restaurant. Quite apart from the delicious food this was a stroke of luck since he had a friend who spoke English and told us about Amber Mountain National Park and where to get a permit. It all seemed so easy.

We found Amber Mountain NP very much to our liking: overgrown, neglected, with a few rusting signs but also the freedom to camp and explore. The banyan trees, baobabs, tree ferns and other, to us, exotic flora made us long to do a proper hike of several days on this magical island. And when we found a beautiful, detailed topographical map of the north of the island we saw where we should go: the Preserve Naturelle of Marojejy. What we didn't know was that these 'natural preserves' were usually closed to visitors. The forested mountains of Marojejy are near the east coast and accessed, we guessed, from the town of Sambava. The maps showed a footpath running across the reserve. It seemed to be about nine miles long, just right for a couple of days' walking and wildlife viewing. Already we could visualise the leaping lemurs, creeping chameleons and myriad butterflies.

As we flew into Sambava we could see the green peaks of Mount Marojejy sticking through the clouds, but there was something strange about the forest – it looked as though a box of matches had been strewn over the soft, crumpled landscape. Cyclone Gladys, which had given us such a wet few days in Nosy Be, had struck the northeast coast with full force, destroying sixty per cent of Sambava and toppling trees in the reserve. We ignored the likely difficulties of walking in cyclone-damaged forest listening only to people who shared our enthusiasm. We understood that we did need a permit, obtainable from a village near the reserve. Ah, no, said the headman there, but we could get one from the next village, closer to the mountain, and he would write a letter to facilitate things. By now a sizeable crowd had assembled and followed us to the next settlement, chattering excitedly. People read the official letter, nodded seriously, shook our hands and selected a woman with a face like a tortoise to guide us to yet another village, a challenging hike over landslides and across rivers. The folks we met on the way read the letter, nodded seriously, and shook our hands. It was getting dark when we finally reached our destination, where tortoise-face led us to an official-looking man who read the letter, regarded us sorrowfully, and summoned the only man in the village who could speak any French to explain, emphatically, that yes we did need a permit and no, it was not available at this village. We must go to Andapa.

Our gloom was lifted when the chief said we could spend the night in the village, prepared an empty hut for us, and invited us to a very good meal of freshwater shrimps, rice and peppery-tasting greens. Our meagre French was no problem since our interpreter talked non-stop and answered his own questions. He did make it quite clear that to proceed without a permit was both dangerous and illegal.

Before leaving the village we spoke to a man who had guided a group of French naturalists up the mountain. His description of the large, snow-white lemur which lived in the highest part (the silky sifaka) spurred us on and next day we hopped on a bus to Andapa and, after many enquiries, found the private house of the officer who worked for the Département des Eaux et Forêts. He eventually appeared wearing blue-and-white striped pyjamas and an angry expression. George pushed me forward to explain what we wanted to do. The permit was only available in Tananarive, he said. Couldn't he make an exception? '*Non, non et non,*' he shouted, and slammed the door.

We were not going to give up – how could we? We'd come to Sambava for this sole reason. There was only one option – to proceed on our own until someone stopped us. Our map showed the path leading up from a village north of Andapa. We hitched there with the owner of the general store who invited us to sleep in the shop and share their evening meal. The family were fascinated by us and by our plans. Why did we want to go there? We explained about how rare Madagascar's lemurs were and how much we wanted to see them. 'Well, they certainly taste good,' said the oldest boy, spearing some meat with his fork. 'A bit like cat.'

The following day, after a breakfast of rice and chicken, we were preparing to leave when we heard excited chatter in the shop. A little man was ceremoniously led towards us and introduced as a representative of the Département des Eaux et Forêts; he could provide the permit. Fabulous! We were legal! Huge smiles all round and lots of handshaking. He carefully copied out details of George's passport, including 'name and adres of bear', and spread a detailed map of the reserve on the table. Sure enough, there was the trail. Our relief was tempered by doubt when he said he was coming with us. He didn't really seem dressed for a two-day backpacking trip: he had no luggage apart from a briefcase carrying his official papers, a clean shirt and three hats. He was wearing plastic sandals. We bought a packet of biscuits from the shop just in case his declaration that he wouldn't eat anything proved false, and he borrowed a blanket from the shop owner which wouldn't fit in his briefcase so George added it to his already heavy backpack. Communication was going to be a problem – his French was barely better than ours.

Once on the trail we agreed that we would never have found the way by ourselves. The narrow, barely discernible path climbed steeply up the mountain, through vanilla plantations, to a large stone which marked the edge of the protected area. Our Man then told us that he had never actually walked in the reserve. Never mind, the trail was now clear and we made good progress, until the first fallen tree blocked our way. For the rest of the day we scrambled over or crawled under trees. Our heavy packs unbalanced us, the heat debilitated us, and sweat ran into our eyes. That night we cooked a sumptuous supper, and of course, shared it with Our Man. It had been a strenuous day, so we deserved a treat.

The forest was strangely silent. No birds sang, no lemurs grunted, no insects chirruped. Our much anticipated wildlife would come later, we supposed. I was relieved that we would be finished by the following day; this walk had been something of a disappointment. Next morning, after a generous breakfast, we followed the clear path to the river, which we crossed, taking off our boots and cautiously finding soft places for our feet. There was no continuation of the path on the other side. We boulder-hopped after Our Man as he followed the river upstream. With a heavy pack this was very tiring, and we asked plaintively where the trail was. He didn't know. Should we turn back? No, if we followed the river we would soon find another path. We didn't.

The river entered a canyon, impossible to boulder-hop or even to wade. We climbed the steep, slippery clay sides, hanging on to lianas and hauling ourselves up to the overhanging jungle. I learned later that the high-altitude rainforest in Madagascar is the densest in the world. I believe it. Without a machete to slice away the vegetation we could only move very slowly, forcing our way through the jungle. The forest floor – what we could see of it – was composed of moss-covered logs and spongy leaves. Each step was likely to be a false step, the rotting matter giving way and plunging us into hidden holes. When we grabbed at plants or branches they hit back. There were plants that stung, plants that stabbed and plants that sliced. Giant bamboos had tiny hairs on their stems that embedded themselves in our hands, stubby palms had saw-edged leaves, and vines tripped us up or caught round our packs. Blood soon mixed with the sweat that ran down our bodies. Huge trees, toppled by the cyclone, blocked our passage. One time, when crawling under the branches, I brushed against a fire-ants' nest. Furious at this disturbance, they got their revenge. I had ants in my hair, ants in my ears, and ants inside my clothes. I started to cry.

Back at the river, we sat down to consider our situation. We were lost. The map didn't make sense, Our Man was silent. We turned our attention to our blotched and blood-streaked arms and legs. Fat leeches were fastened to our ankles and between our fingers. Since I refused to turn back and repeat the cliff and jungle trek, the only course was to follow the river, and when this was blocked by giant boulders there was no alternative but to struggle up the steep sides back into the jungle. We no longer cared about wet boots nor safety when we crossed the river on moss-slippery tree trunks. Your sense of balance seems much better when you don't much care whether you live or die.

After twelve hours of unmitigated effort we stopped for the night. Wordlessly we set up the tent and cooked the last of our food: soup followed by tea and raisins. We were up at dawn. Knowing the rigours ahead, we drank our tea and ate the last three raisins in even deeper gloom. The first six hours were the same as the previous day: slither, trip, sweat and push our way through water and jungle with no lunch to give us renewed energy. Then, in the early afternoon, Our Man shouted in delight. He was pointing to a human footprint in the damp sand by the river. This surely meant that our ordeal could be coming to an end. A few hours later we saw the sight we had long dreamed of – a solitary hut on the mountainside above the river.

The climb up was one of the hardest yet and we were bitterly disappointed to find the hut had long been abandoned. Still, there were some edible plants growing in the garden, including sugarcane, and Our Man was thrilled to find tobacco. He was also excited to find some strange large insects, with long snouts, which he said were delicious roasted. He saved some in a plastic bag. Supper was an almost cheerful occasion. We ate boiled leaves, Our Man coughed happily over his home-made cigars, and we found one last teabag at the bottom of my pack.

Our buoyant mood was shattered again the following morning when we topped the hill above the hut and saw, not a village, but miles and miles of unbroken jungle. Six hours later we reached a trail but felt none of the anticipated elation. We were just too tired. We just trudged onward until a voice greeted us from behind. We sat down and let Our Man and the woman chatter away. 'She knows my family,' he told us excitedly. 'My wife is wondering where I am!'

The woman led us to her village and we lay down on the palm-leaf mats while the family regarded us with gratifying respect and sympathy as Our Man told our story. Each newcomer was entertained with an ever-lengthier version. Then a huge bowl of rice was brought in, along with several kinds of vegetables, and we stuffed ourselves. Feeling almost human, we set off along the path to the village of Ambatobe. The animal kingdom that had been so mysteriously absent while we were lost, appeared to taunt us. A rustle in the trees made us look up, and there was a troop of lemurs; butterflies danced by, and I spotted a new species of chameleon. With civilisation at hand we realised the appearance we presented: our clothes had been wringing wet with rain and sweat for four days, we were covered in dried blood from scratches and leech bites, and we stank. When we came to a stream we motioned to Our Man to go ahead. With clean bodies and fresh clothes we approached the village. The inhabitants were all lined up on each side of the path, hands outstretched, shouting 'Salama! Salama!'

'Salama!' We grinned, shaking the outstretched hands. It seemed a huge population for such a small village. Then we realised that the people at the back of the line were running to the front for a second go. Reverently we were guided to the biggest hut where we found Our Man already enthroned and talking. The room filled with people and we smiled and nodded as the epic journey was described. It had the audience enthralled. Our Man was evidently a master of the art of storytelling. Then supper arrived. They had killed a chicken in our honour, so we had not only rice and greens, but chicken stew. Then came a plate of what looked like large peanuts. The insects! They had a pleasant nutty flavour (I learned much later that they were leaf-hoppers). The next day two youths were enlisted to carry our packs and we almost floated along the trail to the road. We arrived in under two hours, having covered about the same distance that we'd achieved in the previous three days.

Arriving at last in Tananarive we learned that we wouldn't have been given a permit anyway: only expeditions involved in scientific research could enter this nature reserve. I'm still not sure whether this was good or bad news.

INTERLUDE
THE STORY OF BEDO

I had been warned, but even so I was disappointed. In 1982 there were no trained guides in Périnet because there were so few tourists. But, leading my first trip to Madagascar, I did at least expect an adult, not this spindly child.

Bedo was twelve years old but looked much younger. He wore an old T-shirt, once black but faded to a pale khaki by soapy poundings on the river rocks, and enormous shorts like upturned flowerpots from which brown skinny legs protruded like twigs. His feet were bare and his huge eyes and enormous grin seemed too big for the small, bony face. He spoke French and only a few words of English.

We walked down the track to the forest where the wet foliage steamed in the afternoon sun, joining the smoke seeping through the thatched roof of the warden's cottage. 'My house!' said Bedo. He was one of five children, we learned later, who had grown up in Périnet. While other kids were kicking a ball or bowling a hoop along the village street, Bedo was out with his father or a visiting naturalist learning about the rainforest. Motioning us to wait, the child scampered into his house and emerged with a stick on which clung a huge and very cross chameleon. Bedo beamed with delight at our excitement. 'Parson chameleon,' he said carefully.

The five of us walked through the forest, wrapped in the damp smell of leaf litter, our eyes picking out movement or sudden colour against the browns and greens. There was little that Bedo didn't know but a lot that he couldn't name. Except in Latin. '*Neodrepanis coruscans*' he whispered urgently, pointing to the dark interior of a shrub. What was this? A reptile? A bird? All we could see was leaves. 'Yes, bird!' Then it moved. A shiny black ball of a bird, with a slice of brilliant green above its eye. Bedo wrote the name in my notebook and I found out later that it was a velvet asity, a rare endemic that we were lucky to see. Next he pointed to a plant with huge, spear-like leaves. '*Pandanus*,' he told us. And, look, *Phelsuma*. We could see nothing. Then the sun slid out from behind a cloud and brought the lizard hiding behind the green leaf into sudden silhouette. 'How does he *find* these things?' marvelled one of the group as he wrote down the name. There were no field guides to Madagascar in those days. Just Bedo, our child wonder.

'Where are the indri?' we asked. 'Indri. Yes, I show you.' He knew that name. All the visitors to the reserve wanted to see indri but I knew it wasn't easy. Hadn't David Attenborough spent a week in Périnet looking for these lemurs, and trying to record their song? That was twenty years earlier, but there was no reason to think that we would be lucky in the two days available to us. Bedo motioned to us to stay where we were and trotted away down the path. We felt bereft. What were those birds we were watching through binoculars? Could they be parrots? But black parrots? Surely not. And what was that blue job that looked, so the Americans said, a bit like a blue jay? We needed our walking field guide.

Bedo returned wearing a look of triumph. 'Come.' We went. The sun was disappearing behind the trees; darkness would soon follow. Bedo put his fingers to his lips and cupped his ear with his hand. 'Listen!' All we could hear was the moaning of wind in the trees far, far away. But it was not the wind. A wail like the first, despairing cry of a small baby erupted from the canopy just 100yds away. The indri were calling! Like the song of whales, we agreed afterwards, but louder. The song rose and fell, sometimes in duet, sometimes a group harmony, sometimes a solo. We were transfixed, our grins as broad as Bedo's. 'Tomorrow,' he whispered, 'we see them!'

Years passed and Madagascar started to open up to the outside world. Lemurs were *in* and the world's animal lovers couldn't get enough of them. Television teams and photographers spent months capturing them on film, and when they came to Périnet they asked for Bedo. Ornithologists, too, and zoologists: they all needed Bedo, and rewarded him generously.

The boy learned fast. He not only increased his knowledge of natural history but gained enough English and German to ensure that he was the most sought-after guide in Madagascar. The tips became bigger and he started to present invoices to make sure that they stayed that way. Gone were the ragged clothes and bare feet. The poised teenager now wore Nike trainers and new T-shirts showing the emblem of American universities. His sharp eyes were supplemented by state-of-the-art binoculars. In contrast to the other youths in his village, mostly still in rags, his future looked bright.

By the late 1980s Bedo was, by Malagasy standards, a very wealthy young man. In one day he could earn the same as the average Malagasy makes in a month. And he still lived in a small village where there was nothing to spend his money on – except alcohol. It wasn't just his clothes that set him apart from the other boys; he was becoming more at home with foreigners than with his own people. But naturalists who had employed him for years complained that he was becoming unreliable, sometimes failing to turn up.

One July evening in 1989 Bedo had been drinking heavily. An argument with two other teenagers developed into a fight. Some say that Bedo won and went down to the river to wash, others that he was chased there. As he stood on the riverbank one of the youths hurled a rock at him. It struck him on the head, he fell into the water and was drowned.

I still miss that skinny child with the huge eyes and insatiable appetite for knowledge.

We tourists, despite our best intentions, have a lot to answer for.

15

ZANZIBAR AND TANZANIA

'What's all this?' asked the immigration official at Zanzibar airport, as he checked our arrival cards.

'It's the address of our friends. We've been invited to stay with them.'

'This is a socialist country and you are a guest of the government. You stay at a government hotel.'

Abdul, a waiter at our favourite Indian restaurant in Dar es Salaam, had been thrilled to learn that we were thinking of visiting Zanzibar, and asked if we could take a parcel to his parents who he assured us would love to host us for the night. It now seemed that this might be tricky.

Next stop was the 'Zanzibar Friendship Tourist Bureau' to enquire about buses into the town. 'There are no buses. You must take a taxi.' I asked about buses to take us into the countryside. 'You cannot visit the countryside without a special permit. These can only be obtained from the taxi drivers.' I asked about camping. 'Camping is illegal in Zanzibar.' By this time we were surrounded by such a number of enthusiastic taxi drivers that we had to give in and agree to be driven into town, but not before George asked innocently: 'What holiday was it that you celebrated yesterday?'

'May Day.' (It was April 26.)

'Oh, we were told in Dar that it was Union Day, to celebrate the union of Tanganyika and Zanzibar, but I see there has been no union after all.' I pulled him away and into the waiting taxi.

The first government-approved hotel was full, and the proprietor of the next told us the government didn't 'permit him to take English people'. After a fruitless search for an affordable, permissible hotel we returned and managed to persuade him to let us sleep on the hotel's flat roof – providing we left at six before the possible arrival of inspectors.

Next stop was Abdul's family to deliver the presents. Their greeting left no doubt that we were expected and very welcome. The oldest girl, Katy, spoke good English and invited us to stay. We explained the problem. 'Well, you must come to lunch.' We did, and it was the most memorable and delectable of our whole Africa journey, made doubly enjoyable by observing some of the preparations. Mama, a tiny woman dressed in an orange sari, squatted on the floor over an open wood fire in the 'kitchen' where there was no chimney and the rising smoke made its way out through the blackened palm-thatched roof. Basic stands for cooking pots were incorporated into the concrete floor and on these a selection of pots bubbled deliciously. Katy warned that lunch would be late – our arrival, even though at 7.30am, had delayed the preparations – so we went into another room to play with the children. There were plenty of them – ten altogether, although four, including Abdul, had left home. They ranged in age from Katy and her sister, who were in their twenties, to a thirteen-year-old girl and another of seven, and two delightful, and wicked, boys of six and five.

Finally everything was ready and dinner mats were spread on the floor. We sat cross-legged as dish after dish arrived but no cutlery except serving spoons. The family showed us how to proceed. First a bowl of water was passed round and we washed our right hands, then we heaped our plates with a bit of everything, Western style, though the family just dipped into each pot with their fingers. We followed suit, eating with our fingers, a wonderful sensual, regressive experience, and one that is denied to us Westerners since early childhood. The only problem was that I found it difficult to pick up enough to satisfy my greed, and it was so very, very good! We had rice pilau delicately flavoured with various seeds, fried fish – but exquisite fried fish – mutton curry, and my favourite of all, spinach cooked in coconut milk and spices. We just couldn't stop eating, and the family loved it. We felt uncomfortable at the fact that Mama and Katy didn't seem to eat at all, which is probably the fate of Indian women, but we hoped they'd get their fill later. Then a mattress was laid out so we could have a much-needed nap (we had been up since four for our dawn flight). When the younger grown-up sister arrived from work we agreed with her plan to show us the town and seized the opportunity to take her and the teenage girl for tea at the poshest hotel. The town is, of course, fascinating, as all modern visitors know. We marvelled at the narrow streets, the aroma of cloves, the carved doorways, and the bubbling cauldrons of street food.

The following day we had a free morning – a long one, since we had to vacate our roof at six – so decided to try to take a bus into the countryside. We'd seen vehicles which we assumed to be buses – wooden contraptions with people spilling out of the open windows – so simply boarded one of them. The driver indicated that we should take a taxi but we just said firmly that we wanted a bus and there was no further problem. Smiles all round, and we had a lovely two-hour trip into the countryside and back. The other passengers were delighted to have this diversion from their normal routine. At one point a hand suddenly appeared from the direction of the roof with a coconut offering, and later with a cassava root. We didn't dare get out and had no idea where we'd been, but it didn't matter when we could enjoy the countryside views of neat little palm-thatched huts, clove and banana trees, and always people strolling, walking, working.

The family had insisted that we return for lunch, which Katy told me would be *ndizi-nyama*, a dish based on plantain and meat which I'd had before and found utterly disgusting. She must have read this in my face and assured me that the way her mother cooked it was different. And of course it was totally out of this world in deliciousness. There was also my favourite spinach and coconut dish, and chapatis. Our eating idyll was about to come to an abrupt end, however, when a police siren sounded in the street outside. Papa's eyes widened in fear and he motioned to us to lie down on the floor, close to the windows where we couldn't be seen, and then crawl into the next room. When all was clear he explained about the long-term persecution of Indians. We knew nothing of the island's history at the time so were appalled by his tale. In a nutshell: in 1964 the sultanate of Zanzibar was overthrown in a violent revolution led by a Ugandan, John Okello, who encouraged the local African population to go on a murdering rampage, killing more than seventeen thousand Arabs and Indians in one night. President Karume was installed in the newly proclaimed People's Republic of Zanzibar and was assassinated in April 1972, just four years before our visit. That day the police roamed the island beating up suspects, which was just about anyone since he was a much-hated man. Papa was beaten unconscious because they found a book published before the revolution in his possession. Since then the situation had eased but the fear remained. Indians were still allowed only a limited education and their staple foods were rationed.

After many photos, some tears, and swapping of addresses we left for the airport. What a strange and fascinating visit, and what a contrast Zanzibar was then to the popular holiday island of today.

We were not enamoured by Dar es Salaam, and had spent just long enough there to get our visa for Madagascar – and to make friends with Abdul because we'd run out of oomph and it seemed easiest always to eat at his restaurant. On our return to the mainland from Zanzibar it was a food craving that took us to Moshi, not the usual tourist urge to climb Mount Kilimanjaro. ('I have no desire to vomit on the highest place in Africa,' said George, and I agreed. We were fortunate that a friend was doing the climb and could send us her account to be included in our guidebook.) Our reason for going to Moshi was that other travellers had reported that the YMCA served fresh milk *and* butter for breakfast. And so they did – our first dairy products for two months.

We needed an agreeable place to rest and gather our thoughts for the next leg of our journey, and to work out what we could see by public transport. Quite a lot, as it turned out. During the bus journey to our next stop, the town of Arusha, the driver had to slow down to let a sizeable herd of zebra gallop across the road and we caught sight of a group of giraffes loping through the savanna. However, we'd seen many of Africa's mammals before, so what enthralled us most were our fellow passengers: the Maasai. The beauty and tribal integrity of these people is now well known but came as a complete surprise to us. Yes, we'd seen photos, but had cynically wondered if they were real or just set up for the tourists. We would have admired the people even without the hairdos of the young *moran* warriors, or the elaborate beadwork, the many bracelets, or the extraordinary things they did to their ears. The young men were so beautiful – long limbed, fine-featured, and proud of bearing – but their ears were often the most intriguing thing about them, with the lobes swinging just above their shoulders, hung with beads or copper ornaments. One had a row of little bells, while another had a film canister stuffed into the hole, presumably to widen it.

Talking to other travellers in Arusha convinced us that Ngorongoro Crater was a must, so we assembled a group of fellow backpackers and hired Ali, the driver, and his Land Rover. The crater was sublime – and is still one of the top wildlife experiences in Africa – but not so Ali. He went out of his way to be uncooperative, jerking forward as we were taking photos or refusing to stop, using a special bored, superior voice to identify things, and purposely provoking a black rhino to charge by revving his engine. The only other time we saw him smile was when we were eating our sandwiches and a hawk swooped down and snatched mine from my hand, just like a seaside seagull. 'African kite. Very much danger,' he smirked.

We had one more visit to make while in Arusha – to the national parks office to see if there was any possibility of visiting Gombe Stream to see Dr Jane Goodall's chimpanzees. There was!

En route to Kigoma, the access town to Gombe Stream, we stopped at Tabora to change trains. With a couple of hours in hand we visited the busy market, full of colour and intriguing products including a pile of beautifully woven rush baskets which George photographed. A uniformed man appeared from nowhere. 'Follow me!' he snapped. We were trick-hardened backpackers so I asked to see his identification. Another uniformed man appeared with the same request and it seemed expedient to follow him. We received an explanation at the police station. The problem was, he explained, that it was illegal to take photos in Tanzania without a special permit. Really? Besides, it was offensive for people to be photographed without their permission. 'Is it offensive to the baskets?' asked George sweetly. 'Listen, how can you possibly tell tourists – *tourists*! – that it's illegal to take photographs in Tanzania? Everyone we've seen is carrying a camera!' The official closed his eyes briefly before looking at him in disdain. 'You may take photographs in game reserves only.'

'But how could we know that? Why are there no signs up at the border?'

'Ignorance of the law is no defence.'

The small local police station was apparently inadequate to deal with such exotic criminals. We were driven to a larger one where we underwent more questioning, and where we learned that the real reason we were being detained was that there was a military installation near the market. We were then driven to the regional police headquarters a few miles outside the town. No one quite knew what to do with us. It was George who suggested the solution.

'If you're worried about that photograph why don't you have the film developed and see for yourself that we are telling the truth?' We were taking black-and-white photos, which we hoped to use in our next book, so this could be done relatively quickly, we hoped. We still had an hour before our train was due to leave. He wound the film back, removed it from the camera and gave it to the chief of police.

We waited. It was hot in the police station and we had no way of passing the time except to watch the minutes turn into hours and study the 'Wanted' posters on the wall and the many newspaper cuttings about the activities of the CIA. The police *had* shown great interest in the fact that George was American. Noon came. Still no photos. In the distance we could hear a faint whistle. The train to Kigoma was drawing out of the station. I started to cry. George started to fume. When the chief arrived back with a sheaf of black-and-white prints he ignored us and conducted an animated conversation in Swahili with his assistant. They were holding up each print and pointing out suspicious features: views from the train window and some market scenes including the pile of baskets. What was strange was that each photo seemed to feature a flock of large black birds. George leapt to his feet. 'What the fuck have you done to my photos?' he yelled. It was the policeman's turn to look alarmed. 'You damaged them, didn't you?' shouted George. 'You've ruined them!' The two police had a whispered discussion and then the chief turned to us with a magnanimous smile. Handing George the photos he said, 'You may go free!' We walked out into the sunshine and began the long trek back to Tabora.

George wrote a letter of complaint to the Director of Tourism following this incident and we were surprised and impressed to receive a charming letter of apology.

At this point it is worth reflecting on Tanzania as it was in 1976. In that decade many countries in Africa were going through a love affair with socialism, all doomed to failure. At the time, George and

I came to the conclusion that this was largely due to what we saw as humankind's innate attraction to self-serving activities rather than working for the community. However, Tanzania's experiment with *Ujamaa* (brotherhood) rural village cooperatives was noble and could have worked. Everyone agreed that President Nyerere was incorruptible and genuine in his aims. An English girl, shiny-eyed at the glory of socialism, who was working as a teacher in Tanzania, explained how it was supposed to work, but admitted the shortcomings. Every villager had his own plot and the collective *shamba*, the profits from which went towards village improvements, social security, disaster funds and so on. Each worker spent the morning on the *shamba* and the afternoon on his own plot. 'But of course he doesn't,' the girl admitted. 'They usually skip the *shamba* and spend all day on their own plots.' We asked about her school. 'We also have a *shamba* and are supposed to grow seventy-five per cent of our own food. A good idea, but it does mean that the students are too tired to do much book work.'

George later wrote in *Backpacker's Africa*, 'There's something slightly inconsistent with the puritanical, zealous socialism of the leadership when balanced against the conniving, dog-eat-dog atmosphere of Dar. We hope some day it will all come together... but that's not going to happen for a while.'

Our arrival at Gombe Stream on the shores of Lake Tanganyika via water taxi from Kigoma was expected: we'd arranged the date in Arusha. The Tabora police, however, had caused us a day's delay. We were welcomed to the Research Station with some ceremony, being the first tourists they'd seen in several years. There was a comfortable hut for visitors and the following morning we were led to the observation hut and asked to wait. We waited. And waited. The clearing was devoid of life – not even a bird. A feeling of despondency settled over me. We had to leave that evening to catch the weekly ferry to Burundi, so it was quite possible that no chimpanzees would make an appearance. Then an excited member of staff appeared with a message for our guide. He whispered in Swahili and our guide's face cracked into a huge grin. 'Fifi come!' he said. 'And Freud.' A chimpanzee ambled into the clearing and looked at us appraisingly. To say that we were thrilled would be an understatement. Celebrities usually avoid bold eye contact with their fans, and Fifi was undoubtedly a celebrity. Part of our pre-travel reading had been Jane Goodall's *In the Shadow of Man*, in which Fifi, a playful three-year-old in 1960 when Ms Goodall began her studies, featured in such detail that we felt we knew her intimately. Dancing around her was little Freud. He was six years old and, like any six-year-old, full of mischief. He had that comical pink rubber-mask face of all young chimps, huge ears and an endearing tuft of white hair where his tail would be – if great apes had a tail. Today he was Tarzan, climbing up a young sapling, grabbing a vine whose end was worn smooth from the grasp of many hands, and pushing off with his feet to get a good swing. But he pushed too hard, swung too far, hit a neighbouring tree and tumbled to the ground. Oh the humiliation! He cried. He banged the ground petulantly with the palms of his hands, and then ran to his mother for comfort. Her mind was on other things. Absent-mindedly clasping her youngster to her chest, Fifi continued her search for bananas.

Banana feeding was employed by Jane Goodall and her research team in the 1960s to facilitate the study of the chimpanzees. It ensured that the animals would regularly visit the area near the observation hut and sped up the long, slow process of habituation. The practice had been discontinued several years before but chimpanzees have long memories and Fifi lived in hope that the banana machine would miraculously reappear and dispense fast food.

What did appear was a troop of baboons. Freud was delighted and released his hold on his mother to play catch-me-if-you-can with the youngsters. I was astonished to see the two species playing together so happily. I had read that chimpanzees sometimes hunt and eat baboons, so surely the smaller animals would have an instinctive fear of them? Not so, apparently. The adult baboons kept a wary eye on Fifi, raising their eyebrows and half-closing their eyes in a threat gesture. The light-coloured eyelids give the message to other baboons, 'Don't mess with me'. Did the signal work with chimps, we wondered? Difficult to say, since Fifi simply ignored them.

After a gap during which everyone rested in the midday heat, another family group appeared: Athena, with her toddler Afro, aged three, and seven-year-old Atlas. Atlas immediately headed for the young baboons for a game before collecting Afro, who clung to his belly, making frolicking a tricky business. An adolescent baboon snuck up and grabbed the baby and started dragging him away. A hoot of alarm from Atlas brought his mother to the rescue. She grabbled Afro and left the scene, while Atlas stayed behind looking sulky. I had been sitting on the roof of the hut for a better view, but assuming the action had finished jumped down to join the others inside. At this Atlas looked even more belligerent. He grabbed a large rock and threw it, overarm, at me. It fell short but we were told by the staff that he was showing distinct signs of delinquency, often staying behind after his mother had left, hiding behind a bush to throw stones at the field researchers. Several had been hit.

It was time for us to catch a water taxi back along the shores of Lake Tanganyika to Kigoma. We had achieved one of our ten 'Must do's' that we'd set down before our African trip and could scarcely believe our luck in meeting these characters that we'd read so much about.

16

BURUNDI, RWANDA AND ZAIRE

Bujumbura, the capital of Burundi, is conveniently situated on the northern shores of Lake Tanganyika, so after Gombe Stream it made sense to head there and then travel on to its two neighbouring countries, which like Burundi were also former Belgian colonies. The ferry left four hours late and arrived nearly twenty-four hours late which gave us plenty of time to marvel at the African enthusiasm for noise. Any noise would do, but vocal noise was best. Finding a room with a few tables, I sat down to write my journal and record our circumstances:

> At one table a card game is in progress, each card being slammed down on the table with full force and each victory or loss is greeted by shrieks, yells and clapping. Other groups are conducting cross-table conversations at the top of their voices. Others are just wandering around shouting at nothing in particular. This urge to test the range of sounds they can make is most evident at dawn when the full range of singing, shouting, whistling, and shrieking outdoes any rural dawn chorus.

Bujumbura filled us with dismay. A polio epidemic seemed to have ravaged the population, leaving desperate-looking people dragging themselves around, and beggars in filthy rags sheltered in every doorway. I left George on a park bench while I scouted round (unsuccessfully) for a cheap hotel, and when I returned he was surrounded by a dense mass of people – there must have been at least fifty clustered around him, all gazing in wonderment, while he calmly read his book. Tourists were evidently a rarity in Burundi.

Burundi was, quite honestly, a disgrace. Everyone knows what happened in Rwanda in 1994 but not many know what happened in Burundi in 1972, just four years before our visit. We knew because a friend of ours in Cape Town, who had been a VSO volunteer in the country, told us about it. John explained that Burundi, like Rwanda, was populated mainly by two tribes, physically somewhat different: the tall, aristocratic Tutsis, and the shorter, stocky Hutus. Before colonisation the Tutsis ruled in a kingdom, but there was a degree of intertribal mixing. It was the Belgians who ensured that the Tutsis consolidated their power. At independence in 1962 the ruling Tutsis only made up about fifteen per cent of the population so, like the whites in Rhodesia, always felt vulnerable to an uprising. This came a decade later from a small band of educated Hutus in the south of the country – with perhaps a thousand Tutsis killed – and was the trigger for a sickening reprisal. I remember looking in disbelief at John's photo of a group of people proudly holding up a pair of glasses, the symbol, in their minds, of a scholarly Hutu and therefore scheduled for killing. The Tutsis methodically dispatched all the educated Hutus they could find. They entered schools to kill the teachers and selected the top students. A man wearing a watch was considered to be elite and therefore condemned. All Hutu politicians were killed or fled the country, likewise religious leaders. Eventually it just fizzled out, with very little interest from the international community. In four months an estimated 200,000 died. This paints the picture with broad brushstrokes, of course; like Rwanda twenty-two years later, it was not as simple as this, with Tutsis also being killed in Burundi just as Hutus were victims in the neighbouring country. But in contrast to Rwanda, and its surge towards development following the genocide, Burundi in 1976 just seemed to have slipped back into the past, with Belgian expats screaming abuse at the Hutu workers, and all the shops, restaurants and hotels geared towards the moneyed Tutsis or whites. Our impression of the country was that the Tutsis ruled Burundi, the whites ran it, and the Hutus worked it. We were disgusted at the yawning gap between rich and poor, the absence of a middle class, the number of beggars and cripples, the casual abuse from the ruling classes, and the pervading atmosphere of hopelessness.

All this in such a beautiful country.

Rwanda, in contrast, seemed well run by the ruling Hutus, with government support for agronomy, health and education. The people were better dressed and the polio victims wore leg braces. We headed for Volcanoes National Park where we had two goals: to see the mountain gorillas and to climb one of the volcanoes. We managed to hire a guide and porter and spent a challenging morning scrambling up and through the jungle, being stung by giant nettles and slipping and sliding on the cut-down vegetation. We saw lots of evidence of our quarry – snapped-off stems stripped of leaves, and droppings – but no gorillas. Communication with our guide was difficult since he only spoke Swahili, but at midday we understood that he was giving up – we were not going to see any gorillas. We persuaded him to let us stay so we could climb Mount Visoke, the second highest in the park's chain of volcanoes. We wanted another hike for our book but also secretly thought that we might be able to find the gorillas ourselves. What we hadn't realised was that it was a long weekend, and that every French-speaking expat in Rwanda had chosen that day to climb the volcano with the maximum noise – yodelling, whistling and yelling – so no gorilla in its right mind would stick around near the trail.

The climb was physically unpleasant; we sank with each step into the yellow glutinous mud churned up by the French groups, and the stinging nettles and other hostile plants were still out to get us. Visually, though, it was magnificent, with the luxuriantly bearded trees of the *Hagenia* forest taking on a Gothic quality in the mist, and splendid, almost unreal, giant lobelias. At the top, in true extinct volcano style, was a huge crater lake reflecting a rare moment of blue sky before the rain fell again. Our main goal, though, was still to see gorillas, so halfway down we peeled off the main trail and set up camp in a clearing overlooking a promising bit of forest. Next day we just sat quietly and watched through our binoculars, sipping our morning tea. Suddenly George said, 'Look!' and sure enough the trees were moving. A female gorilla with a baby on her back came into view. We were almost choking with excitement, even though it was about 200yds away. We watched while the youngster climbed a tree, before a male appeared. He stared in our direction and then stood upright and thumped his chest, just like... well, a gorilla. We were enthralled, and smugly pleased with ourselves for having seen these animals when our guide had failed.

Crossing the border into Zaire, we were thrilled to find ourselves in a country which actually seemed to want tourists and had a proper tourist office in Goma. The helpful staff told us about another habituated group of gorillas we could visit in Kahuzi-Biega National Park and an active volcano we could climb. Better and better! The downside turned out to be that the only public transport was the occasional pick-up trucks which charged us whatever they thought they could get away with, and were crammed with other passengers. Not surprisingly we favoured waiting in the hopes that a private car would stop for us, even though we sometimes had to wait much of the day. And the waiting brought the crowds. Being stared at impassively for hours is something I never adjusted to.

> I think God has purgatory all planned for me. I shall spend twenty-four hours a day surrounded by a tight circle of mimicking African children, and there's no escape. We've been practising for the last two days, and I feel that we've atoned for all the tourists in the world who have stared at local inhabitants of Third World countries. The entertainment value of us sitting at the side of the road is a bit limited, but not so when we set up our tent and cooked supper. Reluctantly the large crowd dispersed at nightfall when we zipped ourselves into the tent but were jostling for the best position before dawn. Actually the very first 'bonjour!' came at 4.30 but he didn't stay. Our audience weren't disappointed – the business of our cooking breakfast and packing up the tent was the most thrilling entertainment they'd had for years. I expect they're still talking about it.

Our gorilla expedition from Bukavu was much better organised than in Rwanda. We set off with a guide and four helpers and were soon following a recent gorilla trail of snapped-off plants and copious amounts of excrement (they seem a little careless in that regard). The going was as difficult as Rwanda, however, with the same stinging plants and muddy, slippery slopes, but the trail was obviously recent and we were encouraged by the fact that our fee was good for a guaranteed gorilla viewing. If we failed the first day we could return the next.

Suddenly George grabbed my arm and pointed. Not a yard away was a huge male gorilla regarding us soulfully, chin on fist in the pose of Rodin's *Thinker*. George whistled to attract the guide's attention who rather crossly pointed out the gorilla and motioned to us to be quiet. Not that we'd moved or uttered a word. Ape and super-ape regarded each other for a while before he shuffled off for a snack of leaves. Suddenly there was a screaming noise, a crashing of vegetation, and a smaller gorilla came charging straight at us. It stopped a yard or two away and I'm sure it was smirking. The guide had to prise my arms away from his neck. I think you're supposed to squat down in a submissive posture when a gorilla does a mock charge but you try doing that when it actually happens. George, I must say, was remarkably sanguine but I could barely stand I was shaking so much. In all that excitement we hadn't noticed a female reclining in a comfy-looking tree nest, every now and then reaching for a tasty snack of leaves. Her baby stayed hidden, however. The next mock charge was no less sudden and just as frightening and we agreed with the guide that it was time to go.

At the time we thought we were seeing mountain gorillas, as in Rwanda – *gorilla gorilla beringei* – but we later learned these were the highly endangered Eastern lowland gorillas – *gorilla beringei graueri* – which made our encounter particularly important.

Next was our ascent of Nyiragongo volcano, whose eruptions we could see lighting up the night sky from our campsite in Goma. We had arranged to leave in the early afternoon which was fortunate since our start was delayed.

Last night I dreamt we were inundated by mushrooms. They blew in from all directions and accumulated in corners like snow. Then a gigantic mushroom arrived, about ten foot high, with a fluted stalk which acted like a propeller so it twirled along on the base of its stem. A well-dressed man grabbed it by two 'flutes' and went dancing off, twirling, gliding in a very classy polka. Another giant one arrived and I followed suit. The mushroom was a good partner – we waltzed around at ever increasing speed… and I woke up. And vomited. I found I was so dizzy I couldn't stand.

When I did manage to stay upright, I could only go in circles, vomiting as I went. Not a good start for our volcano climb. I supposed it was some sort of middle ear malfunction and it cleared over the next couple of hours. During this delay George took the opportunity to look for eggs for our picnic. Crowing cocks had kept him awake half the night, he said, so they must have hens, and hens lay eggs. He trotted off and returned triumphant. 'They didn't understand my French,' he said, 'so I flapped my arms and squawked like this.' He squatted on the ground and gave a rather good imitation of a hen laying an egg. 'So they said "cuckoo?", and I shook my head and did more squawking. They just laughed and brought me these eggs.' He pulled four small, dung-covered eggs from his pocket. 'And I've learned that the Swahili for hen is cuckoo [*kukoo*]. Isn't that sweet?'

The climb up Nyiragongo was one of the few tourist attractions in eastern Zaire in 1976, and was surprisingly well organised. For a reasonable fee we were supplied with the services of a guide and a porter, plus shelter in a hut just below the summit. We set out after lunch (I had completely recovered from my mystery illness), following an easy trail through luxuriant vegetation which had, over the centuries, colonised the rivers of lava that had solidified on the side of the volcano like petrified tongues. Some were too new to support plant life although a few ferns were bravely gaining a toehold in crevices. It took five hours to reach the hut, where we spread out our sleeping bags then rummaged in our packs to find a torch and snacks for the visit to the edge of the crater. As we scrambled up the rocks a chill mist descended. Our guide walking ahead was a shadowy figure in the twilight. We reached the edge of the crater and saw nothing but mist. I was bitterly disappointed. Had we laboured up here for an expanse of greyness? Our guide motioned to us to sit. We waited. With darkness came a slight breeze, and the mist started to break up. Soon we could see the sides of the crater, lit by a milky red glow. Then suddenly it was clear. We saw orange rivers of lava streaming down the sides of the cauldron to merge with bubbling red lakes. Scarlet fountains shot into the air. Black boulders hurtled up like footballs. Vapour swirled, hiding then revealing this unearthly scene. We couldn't get enough of it! Most memorable views stay constant, but this was ever-changing, from black to red to orange and black again. The smell of the sulphur caught the back of our throats.

Our guide's mutterings got louder and we realised we were cold and hungry. Time for the descent to the hut. We came back the next morning and peered over the edge of the crater but saw only mist. We didn't mind – the previous night's drama had given us a glimpse of biblical hell.

An observation from my journal:

> I know we should be embracing other cultures but sometimes it is a challenge. Today we rode in the back of a pick-up truck piled high with people and produce and I found my aluminium pack frame broken when I finally retrieved it from under a heap of children and potatoes. The woman next to me rested her hand confidently next to my ribs, and every now and then amused herself by picking at my knees (I was wearing shorts). Sometimes men didn't aim their spit quite straight and a gob landed on my arm.

Later I described how a man in our truck planted himself in front of me as I sat demurely on my oil drum, and using my thighs as support shouted questions at me, not because he wanted to know the answers but for the amusement of the other passengers, who felt no embarrassment about discussing us mockingly and openly.

❖ ❖ ❖ ❖

We were ready for Uganda. Yes, we were going to have to be very careful – Idi Amin was firmly in power and was not particularly keen on the English (we learned later that he loved the Scots) – but we were longing to be back in a country where at least we could communicate in our mother tongue. Then we heard the news: 'Haven't you heard?' an expat asked us. 'The border is closed, at least to white people. An assassination attempt has made Amin a bit touchy.' We were only a few miles from the border. The thought of the discomfort and expense of retracing our steps made this option too awful to contemplate. We agreed to press on and see what happened, walking the last 20 miles or so: this was tiring with our heavy packs and added to our anxiety about retracing our steps. At the Zaire border our first question was whether we would be allowed into Uganda. '*Pas de problème*,' said the bored official. We put it more directly. 'We've heard that white people are not allowed in.' He shrugged and said that had changed and stamped us out of his country. Now we were in no-man's-land with a new anxiety. Suppose Uganda didn't let us in, and Zaire wouldn't let us return? Worry worry, walk walk on the rutted road that led to Uganda. George didn't even have a visa – an absolute requirement for Americans.

We arrived at the border to be met by smiling officials. 'Welcome to Uganda! Would you please be good enough to wait a short while. The immigration officer is on his way.' We could see him pedalling towards us with a stem of bananas on the back of his bicycle. He stamped us in with no mention of George's missing visa. 'Anything to declare? No, no, I don't need to look at your luggage. Now, it may be difficult for you to get to Kasese tonight. Let me think... I'll ask our police van to give you a lift there if you don't mind waiting half an hour. Meanwhile would you like a cup of tea?'

We were going to *love* Uganda!

INTERLUDE
AN ACT OF KINDNESS

This is such a clear memory, but I can't remember where it took place except that it was somewhere in Zaire. I can still feel the chill of the night air, and the rough, inadequate warmth of my orange-and-white-striped kaftan. Was it a game park we crossed in that truck or just bush country? I don't know; the geography has become blurred, but the sensations and emotions are still in sharp focus.

It had been difficult to make the transition from anglophone Africa to the French-speaking countries. The everyday aspects of travel that we had come to take for granted, like bargaining for transport, became a challenge. We struggled to find the right words and to understand the response. It was late afternoon when we finally found a pick-up truck loaded with produce and passengers heading for our destination. The price quoted seemed unreasonably high and it took some time to agree on an acceptable fare. We squeezed in and joined our fellow travellers on the hard side benches. Twilight came, and then darkness. The road got rougher and we had to hang on to the sides to prevent ourselves being thrown out. There were no friendly lights from settlements. Nothing but blackness. Then the truck stopped.

Footsteps crunched through the sand as our driver came to our side of the vehicle to speak to us. He wanted more money. If we didn't pay, he said – or we think he said – he would put us out in the bush. He pointed into the darkness. '*Il y a lions*,' he said. We believed him, but lions or not we were not going to pay more than the agreed price. The other passengers watched impassively, only the whites of their eyes visible in the gloom. The argument continued for a few minutes, then he returned abruptly to the driver's seat and we continued on our way. I was frightened. More of the power this man wielded than of the wild animals that no doubt lurked in the bush.

We continued along the dirt road, swaying from side to side avoiding pot-holes. It became very cold. Our warm gear was in our backpacks which were inaccessible under the seats. We sat close, hugging ourselves to retain body heat. The journey seemed to last hours. Perhaps it did. Finally bright lights in the distance heralded a small settlement. The driver stopped outside a house and disappeared inside. We were sure he was visiting his girlfriend and felt bitter and angry at our helplessness. We didn't dare get out in case he jumped in and drove off with our luggage. He was gone a long time. A light drizzle was falling, and we waited. Then the driver reappeared. I have a perfect memory of him standing for a moment in the doorway, a silhouette lit from behind, holding something in each hand. He walked up to our side of the truck and handed each of us a glass of steaming hot milk. As he gave them to us he smiled for the first time.

17

UGANDA AND KENYA

We did indeed love Uganda – right up until the last day when events took an unexpected turn. We loved the scenery and the game parks, but above all it was the warmth and courtesy of the Ugandans that made it so special. We were not the first to make this observation. Winston Churchill wrote in his book *My African Journey* in 1908: '…Uganda is a fairy tale. You climb up a railway instead of a beanstalk, and at the end there is a wonderful new world. The scenery is different, the vegetation is different, the climate is different, and, most of all, the people are different from anything elsewhere to be seen in the whole range of Africa.'

Our enjoyment was certainly helped by the black-market rate for our dollars – we could afford to do the game parks like regular tourists, even to the extent of flying to Murchison Falls, and eat decent meals. We also, to our embarrassment, experienced racism in reverse, being treated especially well because of our colour. When we joined a queue for tickets for an event we were ushered to the front, despite our protests. A grizzled Ugandan explained: 'We have no bad memories of the British. Since Independence [in 1961] we have not been well governed.' Something of an understatement, with the hated Milton Obote being replaced by the detested and brutal Idi Amin.

The ticketed event which we remember for its excellence was an arts festival in Kampala. Schools and colleges from all over Uganda were competing to represent their country at the All Black Arts Festival in Lagos the following year. The acts were mostly, and surprisingly, geared towards European culture, leading off with the music section: 'Western choral', 'Western solo instrument' and 'Western folk music', then 'Scottish dancing'. These were followed by traditional Ugandan dances and compositions for African instruments. It was a bit strange watching Africans in kilts performing the Highland Fling (apparently Amin *loved* Scottish dancing), and singing English folk songs with lots of fa-la-la-las, but the traditional dance performances were by far the best we'd seen anywhere, best described as controlled exuberance. These were followed by the original composition. The one I remember best had a thunderstorm as the subject, using African instruments – drums, a type of harp, and a python's skin stretched between a line of women who tapped it with drumsticks to conjure up the sound of rain. More conventionally there was a sheet of metal for the thunder, and wind instruments for... well, the wind. It was hugely effective. We were, as usual, the only white people there and a teacher sitting next to us made sure that we knew what was going on and translated as necessary.

Contemporary accounts of Uganda in the '70s report the decimation of the wildlife in the game parks – conservation was not a priority for Idi Amin – but this wasn't our experience. In both Murchison Falls and Queen Elizabeth National Park we took launch trips, and one by jeep, and reported the abundance of animals: lots and lots of hippos (admittedly unlikely to be poached), but also plenty of elephants, and our sleep in the hostel was disturbed by the roaring of lions. However, having had no opportunity to visit similar East African game parks, and it being our first trip to Uganda, we had nothing to compare it with – and I must say I don't remember seeing large herds of antelope. The reason for this was made clear when we visited the office of the head warden in Murchison Falls. We'd heard that a member of staff might be driving to Kasese and wanted to see if we could get a lift with him. The head warden seemed rather distracted (although the answer was ultimately yes) and when he had to leave the room, we were able to study the notices on the wall. Someone had been disciplined for 'misappropriating an elephant', rangers were warned not to go into town drinking when they should be on patrol, and there was also a notice stating that many visitors had asked him whether rangers were permitted to kill animals for food. 'I always assure them that this is not allowed. So please, if you are carrying red meat, keep the jeep cover closed and wash the blood off the sides immediately on arrival. Better still, don't kill animals. Indeed, I shall be forced to discipline future offenders.' I have some sympathy with him. During Amin's era, the army was allowed – encouraged, even – to use the game parks as a handy source of meat and the junior staff probably had no choice but comply with its demands.

Our time in Uganda was drawing to a close, and we wandered around Kampala using up our remaining Ugandan shillings. Because of the collapse of the economy compounded by the expulsion of Asians, there were very few goods in the shops. Most shelves were bare, but anything that was there – such as some rather beautiful sable paintbrushes – were a bargain. We still had enough money left for a beer so we drifted into a bar. I sat at a table writing my journal while George moved to the counter to catch the news on the radio. The shortage of newsprint meant there were no newspapers available in Uganda and we had no idea what was going on in the world. He returned looking both anxious and puzzled.

'You're not going to believe this,' he said, 'but apparently Israel has just invaded Uganda!'

'No, I don't believe it! Do you?'

We agreed that he must have misheard and that we would stick to our plans to spend our last day visiting a renowned botanical garden.

'It's in a place called Entebbe,' said George. 'Not far from here. We should be able to get a bus.'

Early the next morning, en route to the bus station, I decided to make the most of the (to us) very cheap international phone charges and call my parents. It was a strange conversation. My mother answered and sounded shocked, rather than pleased, to hear my voice. 'Are you all right?' she asked, then, despite my reassurance that we were having a wonderful time, launched into a monologue about how if we needed money she could send some. That was so completely out of character that I was lost for words and after a few platitudes our four minutes were up. We continued to the bus station, pausing at a bookshop to buy a copy of Alberto Moravia's novel *The Woman of Rome* which was displayed in the window.

Kampala was running out of petrol. We had no idea why. Cars were abandoned by the side of the road; some were being pushed towards the long queue of cars which stretched from the petrol station. We reached the bus depot and asked about buses to Entebbe. The place was full of soldiers carrying machine guns and everyone was strangely on edge. There were no buses because there was no petrol, we were told. There was no petrol because Kenya had closed the land border with Uganda. 'Entebbe? Why are you going to Entebbe?' asked a young soldier. Our explanation about the botanical garden now sounded unconvincing. 'Passports?' We showed him our passports.

'American...' he said, looking at George. 'You're American?'

'Yes.'

'Please come this way.'

We followed him into a small compound where a bus stood that was going nowhere. It had no wheels. A beggar dressed in filthy rags was lying on the ground looking up at a soldier with an expression which I was slow to interpret as I had only seen it acted out in movies: abject fear. Then I saw why. A sergeant arrived carrying a rawhide whip. It had a thick handle tapering to a flexible end. Behind him came two soldiers, dragging a second beggar, even shabbier than the one on the ground. The sergeant began to whip him with all his strength, while the other soldiers gathered round laughing. Meanwhile we were being interviewed but the man's screams made it hard to hear the questions so our interrogator asked them to pause for a while. When the questions finished the whipping continued. Passers-by observed in amusement or apparent indifference before the victim joined the first man face down on the ground.

The interrogation had apparently been inconclusive but at least we learned what had happened the day before, piecing together the full story much later. Palestinian rebels had hijacked an Air France plane which had been forced to land at Entebbe airport where it had sat for several days before being stormed by Israeli paratroopers. At least twenty Ugandan soldiers had been killed. Israel's ally, the USA, was pointing an accusing finger at the Ugandan government for harbouring the Palestinian terrorists. Britain was equally unpopular. No wonder the soldiers were suspicious of two white people heading for Entebbe with the most implausible motive. The more we protested our innocence, the more we convinced them that we were spies. 'You must wait here until my senior officer can interrogate you,' we were told, and motioned to sit on the disabled bus. A teenage soldier guarded us. He fondled his machine gun, and every so often raised it to see what we looked like through the sights. That's where Alberto Moravia came in handy. When George finished a page he tore it out and handed it to me. It was a distraction from the fear that our hotel room would be searched. The day before we had made several photocopies of a letter describing our time in Uganda – mostly complimentary, but truthfully negative about Idi Amin's effect on the country and ordinary people. This was laid out on our bed waiting for the hard-to-find envelopes so we could send it to various friends. The stress of the situation affected my bowels and I asked to go to the toilet. To my surprise this was allowed, but I returned to find our teenage guard had been replaced by an older, crosser one. George explained that the youngster had been reprimanded for letting me go unsupervised.

After three hours the soldier reappeared and beckoned George to the door of the bus. 'Oh my God,' was my immediate thought. 'They're going to shoot him!' After a brief discussion George returned suppressing a smile. 'This gentleman says that his superior officer has no petrol so can't come and interrogate us. He requests that we go to the police station and turn ourselves in.' The soldier described the route we must take and drew a little map.

At our hotel we hastily packed up our things and walked, not to the police station but the railway station. There was a train to Nairobi that evening. Our hearts were pounding as we approached the Kenyan border. Would the train be searched? Had our disappearance been noticed? As the only white passengers we were easy to find. We passed through without event.

In Nairobi we went to the British Council to catch up on newspapers. The first one we saw was the *Daily Express*. 'Get them out alive!' screamed the headline. 'They' were the British expats remaining in Uganda whose lives were considered in danger following the Entebbe raid. Months later, when I returned home, my mother put our strange phone conversation into context. 'I was listening to the 9 o'clock news on the wireless: "Hopes are fading for the safety of the Britons remaining in Uganda..." Then the phone rang and the operator said, "I have a call for you from Kampala". So of course I assumed you were being held hostage and were about to ask for money.'

It should have been a relief to be in Nairobi. You would expect the Entebbe experience to have dampened our enthusiasm for Uganda but it didn't. Army personnel, we knew, were mainly recruited from Amin's tribe, the Kakwa, whereas most of our dealings had been with the debonair Buganda. Somehow what had happened at that bus depot didn't count.

In Nairobi there were no shortages in the shops, we could eat anything we wanted and buy anything we wanted, but we felt tired and dispirited. And unambitious. The country treated us like tourists and we behaved like tourists, or at least backpackers, making regular visits to that precursor of social media, the bulletin board at Nairobi's Thorn Tree Café, to see what other overlanders were up to. We found to our surprise that an English friend we didn't even know was in Africa was heading for Ethiopia. It reminded us that we should do the same, after enjoying some of the coast's attractions – the island of Lamu and Twiga Lodge campsite south of Mombasa where we spent over a week lazing around, swimming and snorkelling. It was here that we met our old Malawi friends, Peter and Eirene, who were heading to Lake Turkana in their Land Rover to do some fishing. They offered to take us along with them and we accepted with alacrity, abandoning, with some regret, our plan to climb Mount Kenya. Never mind collecting hikes for our book, though – we were looking forward to a change of scene, and a change of transport.

It worked. By the time we got to Lake Turkana we felt revitalised and full of enthusiasm and curiosity. Sitting in a comfortable vehicle watching the changing scenery was balm to the soul, but it also highlighted the benefit of bus travel, where you can study your fellow passengers without drawing attention to yourself.

Heading south by bus from Lamu our companions were a strange mixture: a bunch of white travellers, some bare-breasted women covered in babies and beadwork, and Moslem women completely encased in black apart from a slit for the eyes.

As we drove north the landscape changed from cool, green and wet to yellow desert strewn with black volcanic rocks, and ended at the lake, an expanse of turquoise within a setting of ochre. As if to highlight how different it all was, a caravan of camels passed, driven by a woman dressed in animal skins, her silver bracelets glinting in the sun.

Eirene and I – and George when he admitted it – didn't particularly enjoy our time at the lake. Without the men's enthusiasm for fishing – 'Peter, what would we *do* with a 150lb Nile perch?' – the time passed slowly. It was incredibly windy, bending our poor tent into a C shape and whisking my beloved foam-rubber mattress into the lake where it floated merrily away and nearly caused me to drown retrieving it. Later we learned that the lake is full of crocodiles and we were warned not to wade in it.

Peter and Eirene left us at Marsabit National Park to return to Nairobi while we continued towards Ethiopia. Once we were alone two shrivelled, wrinkly-breasted old women approached us to gaze into our eyes, say '*Jambo!*' and admire our backpacks. Beads and aluminium ornaments covered their faces and caused me to reflect on how much more beautiful is the adornment of African women compared with the make-up of their European counterparts.

We were ready for Ethiopia.

18

ETHIOPIA

We needed all the mental fortification we could muster for this extraordinary country which served us some of our highest highs and lowest lows, but was unfailingly and genuinely amazing. Everything – the landscape, the people, the religion, the hassles – was utterly different from the rest of East Africa, and the political situation was the most volatile – and dangerous – of our journey. Only two years before our visit, in 1974, Emperor Haile Selassie had been deposed, and the military government of the Derg took power with lofty socialist ideals before succumbing to corruption and revenge. When we arrived, the country was in the grip of a Marxist regime that was in love with itself and strenuous efforts were being made to educate what the government described as the 'Broad Oppressed Masses' against capitalist invaders, so we knew we must proceed with care. In addition groups of *shifta*, bandits, made life on the road dangerous for everyone and imposed a rather welcome curfew on night travel (we were not fond of night-time buses).

We arrived at our first major town wide-eyed.

> Amazing! The streets are teeming with people like something out of Arabian Nights. Wild-looking men carrying spears, women glittering with silver ornaments with sagging breasts, fuming camels, donkeys, children riding around on billy goats. 'Faranji, faranji!' shriek the children (this word for foreigner supposedly derives from the French who built the first railway). A *faranji* from Lancashire plays a soulful tune on a tin whistle to a camel which dribbles on his shoulder. The children love it. He plays Irish jigs to them and knocks back the beer. I ask him how the local beer tastes. 'Like this,' he says and plays a sweet, lilting tune.

This local beer was *tella*, maize beer, and we became somewhat addicted. It was a cheap, refreshing drink and surprisingly alcoholic. Even better was the *tej*, mead, only available from a *tejebet*, which caused many a diversion. It was the national dish, however, that came as both a surprise and, when we got used to it, a constant pleasure after the blandness of small-town East African food.

> Last night we had our first proper Ethiopian meal. The *injera* is identical in appearance and texture to George's old grey foam rubber mattress. It has a sharp, sour taste. The *wat* is a spicy curry-type sludge, which comes in different colours and heat, and can be nice or only tolerable but is necessary to make the *injera* bearable. Together they're rather good. One sits round a big plate of it, the foam rubber comes folded tastefully over the mound of *wat* in the centre. A short hand-washing ritual is followed by rip, scoop, slurp. Fingers only, right hand only. Apart from bread this is the only food you can buy so it's a relief that we like it.

Even the task of getting a seat on a bus had an Ethiopian twist. Our destination was only about 15 miles away so we thought it would be an easy bus ride, but when we got to the depot we watched a series of buses draw in then leave while we remained behind. The problem was that a horde of the roughest, strongest-looking men imaginable fought their way on board in a surging, punching mass and we didn't want to be killed. After the second bus to our destination had arrived and left there seemed to be rather a sameness about the ruffians fighting for a seat. Hadn't we seen some of them before? A Belgian woman showed us the way. We hadn't thought she had a hope of boarding, but we watched her select a ruffian who then fought his way to a seat; she then took his place calmly a little later. Money was exchanged. Once we'd got the idea we hired a nice tough teenager who succeeded in getting us seats. We paid him off, feeling smug that we'd mastered a new skill.

Later we got talking to the Belgian woman who had a depressing, but all too common, story in this age of 'agrarian reform'. She and her eighty-year-old husband had lived in Ethiopia for more than forty years, running a coffee plantation. It was confiscated two years ago, but the new peasant owners neglected to spray the trees against blight and lost the entire crop. So they dug them all up and planted millet instead. A tragedy considering the price of coffee. She and her husband couldn't afford to return to Belgium so hung on, impoverished and bitter, to an uncertain future.

With no night transport because of the curfew, bus journeys were usually quite a pleasant experience because of the dramatic scenery and fascinating fellow passengers. Turbaned, robed men boarded the bus carrying spears, and a guard with an impressive-looking rifle rode with us to guard against *shifta*. Once a woman got on who'd obviously never ridden in a motor vehicle before. She sat with her head and eyes completely covered, whimpering, while her worldly son grinned with embarrassment.

The biggest trial were those times when we had secured seats but the bus wasn't ready to leave for an hour or two.

> We then felt an empathy with zoo animals since our experiences are pretty similar. Large crowds stare at us, pulling funny faces, knocking on the glass to attract our attention, and trying to feed us unsuitable food.

The proliferation of children with nothing to do but bait foreigners was explained by a teacher we met. Schools had been closed for two years, he told us, because of the pupils' 'high level of political consciousness'. Secondary schools were closed so the students could disperse into the countryside to educate the Broad Masses about socialism and junior schools were boycotting the classroom. It did explain why the children were so obnoxious – they were doing their duty with enthusiasm. Once a crowd of teenagers surrounded the bus, chanting in unison 'CIA! CIA! CIA!' and on another occasion, a kid pressed a piece of paper to the window which read: 'Exploter Yankey Emperiolist go home'.

Once we got moving, however, the landscape was a constant delight. In the dry south we marvelled at the termite mounds, towering like red church spires around 20ft high from a domed base. Later we felt as though we were passing through a huge sculpture garden. The earth here was grey so the mounds resembled Michelangelo torsos in marble or granite, all twisted and muscly or intriguingly abstract, but definitely art.

Watching passing scenery was certainly better than hanging around in the towns which were, in the south at least, utterly squalid.

> The streets run with sewage, people and animals urinate at will, and rubbish (fortunately organic) decomposes in front of the 'houses'. There seem to be a huge number of people dressed in monochrome rags and the angry demands for money follow us everywhere. If we're pestered during the day, the nights are no better, though here it's the fleas that drive us mad. Actually I'm lucky – I apparently don't taste good – but fair-skinned George is persecuted and wakes up each morning covered in red welts. He's taken to sleeping on the floor surrounded by a circle of insecticide (I'm afraid it's DDT) which does help a little although of course fleas are known for their jumping ability.

We were slowly – very slowly – making our way north towards the capital. It was time to escape to the Bale Mountains, sleep in a flea-free tent and do some proper hiking. We were looking forward to it enormously, but had yet to get used to Ethiopian time: each new day starts at dawn, 6am, rather than at midnight, so our 2 o'clock daytime bus had left in the morning. Never mind, there was a later one that stopped at nightfall, thanks to the curfew. This bus was sickly before it started, coughing and wheezing as it toiled its way up the winding road towards the mountains, before stopping in a near state of collapse at a small village. We were told we would stay there for the night and wait for a spare part to be delivered the following day. The little hotel had the best *injera* and *wat* so far and adequate rooms grouped round a courtyard, so we were perfectly happy. Maybe a bit too happy, since they also had *tella*.

It was very cold and we were all huddled around a tea-making brazier by the bar. As always, we were a magnet for the young people and a student started the conversation: 'My teacher says that in America a black man isn't allowed to go into a restaurant.' Another joined in, 'And my teacher says a black person can't go to university...', '... or get a job in an office,' added a third. 'Well, that's simply not true!' George countered, provoked at this swipe at his homeland. 'In fact,' he said, warming to the theme, helped by the *tella*, 'we have this policy called affirmative action. Did you know that it's now easier for black people – men and women – to go to college in America than it is for white people?' They stared. 'But what about the Broad Oppressed Masses?' 'Oh well, in America even poor people have a television. And a car!' George sat back to finish his drink and enjoy the effect. 'Capitalism isn't all bad, you know!'

The students started to drift away, chatting quietly among themselves. It was only then that we noticed the man drinking alone at a nearby table. Wiping his mouth on the back of his hand he rose to his feet and came over to us. 'I'm an army lieutenant,' he said, 'and you're under arrest for promoting capitalism in Ethiopia.' We stared at him. 'What's your room number? I will come tomorrow morning and take you to our army headquarters for interrogation.'

I know the truth of the expression 'my legs turned to jelly'. When I stood up I was trembling so much I had to hold on to the table for support. George was white-faced. We both knew the implications of what we'd done. Even in Uganda there had been a framework of law and order. In Ethiopia in 1976 we felt we could be shot and no one would notice.

We were ready for the knock on the door soon after dawn. Our lieutenant ushered us into the back seat of a smart army jeep and then into a beautifully furnished office where a very good-looking and immaculately dressed district commissioner greeted us with a cordial handshake. 'Do sit down,' the official said. His accent was Eton and Sandhurst. 'Now, what's all this about?' he asked the lieutenant who sat with downcast eyes. 'They were talking about capitalism,' he said. 'They must learn not to do that. We need to teach them a lesson, like those Australians last week.'

'Oh my dear fellow, I don't think we need go to those extremes, do you?'

We quaked.

'I agree with you that they ought to be punished...' The lieutenant nodded. 'So I am going to ask them to leave this district today.' He looked at us intently. 'Did you hear that? And I would advise you to get out of Ethiopia as soon as possible. Now you can go free.'

We didn't continue to Bale, we didn't leave Ethiopia, and we never again expressed our own political opinions.

We heard later on TV that twenty-eight 'enemies of the masses' were 'liquidated' in Bale. I suspect that those students, and the officer, did us a favour.

In Addis Ababa we hit the jackpot, being invited to house-sit an expat's place while he was away, a house complete with chauffeur and maid. The former, sensibly, took one look at us and disappeared, while the latter, less sensibly, snaffled a few of our traveller's cheques which she was unlikely to be able to use. Each day we walked into

Addis, and were struck by the capitalist feel of the place, with swanky government buildings juxtaposed with the rather delightful scene of cattle and sheep being driven down the main highway oblivious to traffic. With many of the citizens speaking English, it cemented our view, expressed in *Backpacker's Africa*, that 'Ethiopians are either unbelievably nice or remarkably unpleasant'. In the latter category came the shopkeeper who called us 'Yankee bastards' because we didn't want to buy his suspect amber, and in the former was the delightful insurance broker who failed to sell us travel insurance but ordered tea and told us about his home in Eritrea and the banalities of the current government.

Addis had a good and helpful tourist office so we were able to get a better idea of where else to go. Lalibela, of course, with its famous rock-cut churches, but it was still the rainy season so the airport was closed. We would need to walk, hopefully with the help of pack animals. The Simien Mountains would provide us with the hiking we were deprived of in Bale, and the town of Gondar was famous for its church paintings.

On our last day in Addis we decided to see some traditional Ethiopian dancing we'd been told about. Not only dancing, we found, but very good *injera* and *wat* and several strengths of *tej*. Music was played throughout the meal, and then the dancing began. Like everything in Ethiopia, it was jaw-droppingly extraordinary. Ethiopians dance as you'd imagine insects would dance: their heads, torsos and hips seem to be three different components, all moving independently. Most incredible of all was the woman with dreadlocks who tossed her head so rapidly and so violently that you expected it to detach itself, sail across the room and land in someone's *injera*. After what seemed like several minutes she stopped, smiled serenely and changed rhythm without apparently having suffered any brain damage.

There was no putting it off – we had to brace ourselves to leave our private house and begin our great Lalibela adventure. I have to admit to being more nervous about this trek than any other, mostly because so many people in Addis had warned us of the dangers. The tourist office said it was 'not advised' to go there. It was *shifta* country and also Revolution Weekend or, to be more precise, 'the people's joyous celebration of the second anniversary of the revolution', with, our friends told us gleefully, plenty of shooting. And it was the rainy season. I found it particularly difficult to contemplate being shot in the pouring rain on a mountain while sitting by a nice log fire in a nice comfy house.

It turned out to be a truly remarkable adventure, literally packed full of wonders. Every day we experienced something special or extraordinary, from the scenery to the encounters with the locals, and the weather was consistently fine. Even Dessie, our first stop and one of the dreariest of all dreary towns, came up trumps when we heard some rather good music coming from a *tejebet* and peeped through the window. We were beckoned inside to drink *tej* and listen to some very good playing on the one-stringed African violin. I never knew that such tonal music could come from such a simple instrument. A song was created for the *faranjis* and then our names were requested and a special song for George was composed. And then for Hilary. Everyone loved it, although we could only understand the names. Then a woman swaggered in, very elegant, and sang a song about George's watch and how nice it would be to have it. We decided we'd better leave, after making an appropriate money donation.

The landscape never ceased to impress us. After taking a bus to Kobbo we took the last vehicular part of our journey by truck.

> The road between Kobbo and Moja was the most spectacular mountain road we've been along in Africa. Beautifully constructed two years ago by the Dutch, it winds up from Kobbo where it's sweaty hot to a pass where giant lobelia grow

in profusion and an icy wind sweeps through the thin clothing of the shivering passengers. A great dome of rock juts up sheer from the road and the surrounding mountains are volcanic in origin and crazy in outline. The people herding their animals are part of the scenery: wild, dark, and dressed in sheepskins. The 50-mile drive took four hours.

Our plans to hire mules to carry us or our luggage came to nothing – too expensive – so in Moja we needed to leave some of our unwanted gear in a safe place in order to lighten our load. The local police station seemed the best bet. A huge, scowling man shouldered his way through the crowd and demanded our passports. Our hearts sank – surely he was going to forbid us to continue. Finally his face cleared. 'Come with me. Yes, you can leave your things, and is there any other way I can help you?' He suggested a 'To whom it may concern' letter asking for every assistance in case we got into difficulties, reassured us that there were no *shifta* in the area, and off we trotted.

The scenery is still gorgeous and the people happily uneducated in political consciousness. Most bow low when we greet them and one yesterday insisted on kissing our feet, which I thought was going a bit far. They were also refreshingly uninhibited. A man accompanying his wife who was riding a mule walked with us and when we came to the river stripped off and had a swim. Then he noticed the poor *faranjis* struggling on the sharp stones and so rushed back to give assistance, one hand modestly covering his privates. Even that was forgotten later when it seemed that he wanted medicine. He pulled his penis out and showed it to me and when I said 'No thank you' showed it to George who examined it politely and said it looked OK to him. We never learned what he actually wanted.

As we gained height the countryside was green with new grass and yellow with *Meskel* flowers, the yellow daisies that symbolise rebirth in Ethiopia. We walked for another two days, leaving the jeep track to take a short cut past increasingly isolated settlements. At one of the larger ones we sought out a *tukul* – a place that sells alcohol – to have some *tella*. It was a lovely hut, the walls beautifully smoothed from cow dung and straw, with moulded cubbyholes and shelves. One woman wanted to know if we had babies and pulled a scraggy breast through the armhole of her dress to make the meaning clear.

That evening we turned a corner and there was Lalibela atop a long, steep hill. A delighted shout rang out across the valley: '*Houlet faranjis!*' We had arrived.

Lalibela is now considered one of the wonders of the modern world and certainly one of the top sights in Africa. I can't pretend it was completely unknown in 1976, but we were, not surprisingly, the only tourists so even more popular than usual. We hired the services of the first boy to greet us – the one who'd shouted excitedly when spotting two *faranjis* coming his way – and promised he would be our guide for the whole of our stay. He found us a basic hotel with hay on the floor and a lovely shower in the middle of the 'landing': a bucket with a shower attachment which the landlady filled with hot water and gave us a bowl to stand in. A large, bearded man appeared and insisted that we ate in his restaurant because it was Christmas (I don't think so, even with the Ethiopian calendar) and gave us such a good meal we promised to return. Lalibela was like that – barely had we surfaced from one meal or drink of *tej* or *tella*, than we were beckoned in for another treat, including a very convivial church feast full of wrinkly, crinkly old priests who pressed yet more food on us.

We still had that 'To whom it may concern' letter so went in search of the Governor of Lalibela. Might as well show it to someone. We found the colonel on his way back from a meeting, surrounded by an impressive entourage. It took some courage to approach him, but after he'd read the note he nodded and invited us to meet him in his house. He was one of those cultured, educated and impressive Ethiopians who sometimes made this country such a joy for inquisitive travellers. George pen-bombed my diary to record some of his background – apparently I was too immersed in discussing and quoting Shakespeare with him to take proper notes. He graduated from military academy in Addis before being sent to Korea to represent Ethiopia in a peacekeeping mission (presumably during the Korean War). He then undertook four more years of study after which he was appointed an Imperial Guard to the Emperor. He saw enough there to convert him to the socialist cause and take part in the abortive coup in 1960 which landed him in jail for four years and then exile in Ethiopia's hostile interior for two years. While in jail he narrowly escaped being murdered, studied accountancy through a correspondence course, and on his release secured a good job until being contracted by the revolutionary government to take care of the Lalibela region as the administrator, governor, peacekeeper... He was a convincing and eloquent speaker and for the first time we were able to understand the context of the Socialist Revolution. Certainly Haile Selassie's rule was unbelievably medieval, which of course seems rather romantic to outsiders but very hard on the rural people confronted by the expense of the emperor's entourage if he chose to come visiting, or the subsequent tax.

Our day touring the extraordinary Lalibela rock-carved churches whetted our appetite for others that were further away, particularly one described in Dervla Murphy's book *In Ethiopia with a Mule,* so we arranged to splash out and hire mules for the six-hour trip to the Monastery of Yemrehanna Kristos. The mules turned out to be most obliging, but couldn't cope with us plus the rocky, almost vertical hillsides, so we walked those sections. While doing so a man passed us on a parallel path, equally steep but heading downhill. He was sitting back to front in the saddle, holding the high cantle, and looking very relaxed while his mule picked its sure-footed way over the rocks. The scenery was unceasingly gorgeous. Lalibela is situated at an impressive 8,628ft so is green and well watered, and surrounded by jagged mountains and deep, dark valleys. Little patches of cultivation were worked at every level, with the proletariat busy ploughing, using oxen and a foot plough, or squatting in rows planting the spring crop. When we greeted them they raised their bottoms in unison in a symbolic gesture. It seemed a long way – it *was* a long way, at least 20 miles – but finally the cave church suddenly revealed itself in a deep valley wooded with juniper trees. It's not a rock church but one built in a cave, extended by granite and wood walls, in horizontal stripes, the latter supposedly imported from Jerusalem some 1,600 years ago, although a more reliable source says the origin of the wood was Egypt. The real beauty of this church is the interior, however, so it was disappointing that the priest's large and impressive torch had a broken bulb. With surprising foresight we had brought our own camping torch but it didn't really do justice to the splendid paintings. Every possible area was covered in geometric designs or little figurative animals – elephants and lions – and lots of angels.

Next day, our last in Lalibela, stiff and sore after our long ride, we got up at dawn to witness an Orthodox Ethiopian church service. It didn't bear much resemblance to our C of E services – but then you wouldn't expect it to. First came a priest carrying a small, ornate brass cross and swinging an elaborate incense burner while the deacon chanted from the beautiful hand-lettered, illuminated parchment Bible which is so characteristic of Ethiopian churches. The congregations came and went, kissing the doorposts on arrival. What else went on inside was a bit of a mystery since our view was obstructed by the mass of devout bodies.

We agreed to hire a donkey to carry our luggage for the first part of the return trip to Moja. At dawn the following day a minute brown donkey appeared outside our hotel. It seemed impossible that it could even stand up under the weight of our packs but with legs well splayed to keep its balance it submitted patiently to all the heaving and pulling, and once loaded set off at a twinkling trot. It was great to be walking without our packs and we made good progress.

After saying goodbye to the boys and donkey it was not long before a *tella* urge came over us so we started walking up to a small village on the hillside. Before we reached it a man emerged and ran down towards us shouting a greeting. It was our friend with the Problem Penis. This time he made it clear that he wanted medicine for an unhealed sore on his arm so we agreed to anoint it with the Mercurochrome we always carried with us. Immediately we were running an impromptu clinic. It was simply appalling. Scores of skinny arms were stretched towards us, covered in scabs and spots, some open sores, some infected. I doubt if our disinfectant would have any effect except psychological. A woman pulled back a filthy shawl so that I could anoint her baby's hands. They were covered in septic spots, and where there should have been eyes were two clusters of flies.

Then the crowd parted and a boy of about twelve was led by the hand towards us. His closed eyes were hugely swollen and pus trickled down one cheek, partly obscured by the mass of flies. The crowd watched us expectantly. We shook our heads and spread our hands to show we had no cure. The crowd continued to stare at us, back at the child, then at us again. We closed our packs and walked away down the track. Neither of us spoke for a long time.

We were ready to leave Ethiopia. Our eight-week visas would soon expire and our spirits felt battered by our encounters with poverty and politics. But first there were the Simien Mountains. Word that two *faranjis* were on their way to Debark had travelled ahead of us, and as we descended from the bus we were met by a jostling crowd of guides and muleteers and a patient queue of animals. We hired two horses, one for riding (taking it in turns) and one for the luggage, and a guide/drover called Andaracho who didn't speak our language. Nor did the horses. It didn't take long the following morning to discover that the riding horse was oblivious to the usual aids. Hauling on a rein made not the slightest difference, the animal continued stubbornly in the same direction, and neck reining was ignored as well. Then I saw Andaracho employ the Ethiopian method, which was to whack it on the side of the face with a stick. Horses soon learn to turn sharply at the mere sight of the stick.

Once in the mountains we were to learn other local methods of horse management. Most evenings as we pitched our tent and cooked our dinner, Andaracho would hobble the horses by tying their necks, behind their ears, to a foreleg – an effective and not unkind method which allowed them to graze with unrestricted movement but prevented them from throwing up their heads and galloping off. One evening I'd set up the tent and came to tell George that supper was ready, and I found him hopping on one leg in front of Andaracho, the other leg hooked over an arm, while he pulled his head towards his knee. The Ethiopian understood this extraordinary display much faster than I did. George was reminding him to hobble the horses. Andaracho did his 'It's all right, don't worry' gesture (which he used frequently) so we left him chewing his way through that day's ration of *injera* and went to our tent. Next morning George, up early as usual, came to tell me something was dreadfully wrong with the horses. I crawled out of my sleeping bag and followed him a short way from the campsite where they were both lying stretched out on the grass looking faint. Anxiously, I urged them to their feet; they were not sick but were dead lame. I insisted Andaracho interrupted his breakfast to come with me but when I pointed out the horses staggering around on three legs he gestured 'It's all right, don't worry'. I gasped when he produced a knife, wondering what gruesome demonstration of Ethiopian surgery we were about to witness. Within seconds of taking hold of a limp foreleg, he held up the source of the problem; a thin piece of cord tied tightly round the animal's leg just below the knee. The other horse was released from its 'hobble' the same way. He smiled at our consternation and shrugged off our anger. 'After all,' he was probably saying, 'it works!' I massaged the life back into their legs and by the time we were ready to leave the horses were sound again.

Animal husbandry aside, this national park was stunning. It sometimes felt like a reflection of high mountains, with all the views looking down, not up. Deep canyons bordered by eroded towers and pillars of rock dropped abruptly from level grasslands.

We started off this morning at the crack of dawn, walking to the escarpment, and stood on a rock overlooking a sheer drop of about 4,000ft. And I mean sheer, and I mean four thousand. You felt as though you had somehow ascended the highest mountain in the world without doing any climbing. Below us were masses of giant lobelia and heather trees – yes, trees! We caught sight of a small group of Walia Ibex which are probably the rarest animals in Africa since they are only found on the escarpment of the Simiens. They have the most extraordinary curved horns of a size that seems totally impractical. We also saw gelada baboons, another endangered species, and not at all like other baboons. They have a nose shaped like a grey peanut, a snooty expression, and a magnificent amber-coloured mane. On their chest is a bare red patch so they're sometimes called 'bleeding heart baboons'.

Before leaving for Debark we found ourselves running another impromptu health clinic despite our protestations. We did provide disinfectant and sticking plaster for a screaming child with an enormous boil and some of our precious antibiotics for a man with VD who was so grateful he insisted on giving George a lift back to Debark – behind him on the saddle of his very lively mule. They were soon out of sight and I didn't see George again until Debark. That evening he showed me two little raw patches on his bum.

Andaracho was in high spirits at the prospect of heading home, and as we approached Debark urged our horses ever faster. It was market day and the place was teeming with animals and people, with donkeys tethered together by their back legs. Our packhorse charged straight across the leg tethers. Pandemonium! Andaracho urged my horse to a brisk trot, yelling and whooping behind, and a naked man ran up, chattering, and snatched my stick (effectively my steering wheel). The horses plunged into the crowd, scattering women, dodging their bundles and tripping over ropes. Andaracho was happy. I was not, and dismounted in a hurry.

Gondar was our last bit of sightseeing in Ethiopia, with the fabulously decorated Church of Debre Birhan Selassie, the ceiling covered with scores of round-faced, rather surprised-looking painted cherubs, but our sights were now firmly set on Sudan before our visas ran out. Gondar was quite a large city, so would surely be served by buses or private vehicles heading for the border. But no, the only possibility seemed to be a tractor, which would take two days. Then we passed an airline office which was open despite it being Sunday, so popped in and poured out our troubles. 'Why don't you fly to Metema?' the clerk asked. It had never even occurred to us that the border town might have an airport, let alone a flight that Friday – the day our visa expired.

Phew!

19

SUDAN AND EGYPT

Metema was bristling with armed men and shimmering with heat. Even the children lacked the energy for more than a half-hearted '*faranji!*' and the customs officials were sprawled around on their beds. They examined our luggage from that position, making a particular point of tasting all the consumables. Thump went the stamp and we were motioned to a footbridge across a small stream, into Sudan and a changed world.

Gallabat, a collection of huts with a police and customs office, was immediately and totally different from Ethiopia. Each house had a neat fence around it so only the well-maintained thatch was in view, and the sandy streets were swept clean. There was an air of ordered calm. Where Ethiopia was beige, our first impression of Sudan was of black and white. The midday sun put the huts in their own puddles of black shade, and the men who strolled the streets wore robes of dazzling white. '*Salaam alaykum!*' smiled an official as he checked our documents, explaining that full immigration formalities would need to be undertaken in Gedaref. We stepped back into the sunlight and stood wondering what to do next. 'Can I be of assistance?' The tall man unfolded himself from the stool where he was chatting to his friends in the shade of a house and walked over. 'No, we're all right, thank you.' Our response was automatic. We had no local currency so couldn't give the expected tip. 'Then may I invite you to partake of a drink?' He led us to a hut with a couple of tables – a café of sorts. Two tall glasses of fresh lemonade appeared in front of us. Our new friend introduced himself and asked about our plans. 'You know there has been much rain and the road to Gedaref is very bad. There are no buses. Please wait here.' We sipped our lemonade and anxiously discussed what payment he would be expecting for his help; we badly needed to change our dollars.

Two tall figures approached: our helper and another man. 'My friend will change money for you' – the man bowed slightly – 'and he will take you to your transport. Goodbye, and welcome to Sudan!' Now we had Sudanese pounds we could pay for our lemonade. 'How much?' we asked. 'Nothing,' the money changer gestured, and pointed to the retreating back of his friend. He led us to a clearing at the edge of the village where a 1950s Massey Ferguson tractor was parked, hitched to a flat wooden platform on wheels. Smiling women moved over to make room for us and we settled down to a long, uncomfortable but convivial journey.

I've never met anyone in the near-fifty years since our introduction to Sudan who hasn't been bowled over by the sheer niceness of the Sudanese people. We felt completely revived, our enthusiasm for travel restored, and were ready to cope with the long journey north by whatever means we could manage.

The heat was debilitating. Only two weeks ago we had been crisping over frost in the Simiens so it took some adjustment. In the towns we lurked in air-conditioned banks or lay motionless on our beds in a starfish pose, leaking sweat. Khartoum Museum provided welcome relief, not just for the air conditioning but the thrill of seeing antiquities dating from 14,000BC after the relative newness of so much of Africa. It prepared us for Egypt.

The journey continued with a 24-hour train ride, then a boat across Lake Nasser to Aswan and Egypt that took forty hours, but it was pleasant enough watching the yellow and brown rocky shore slip quietly by as we sat around playing cards and drinking chai with our fellow passengers. And so by train to Cairo, stopping to gawp at the temples of Edfu, Karnak, Luxor and others, and visit the pyramids and the Egyptian Museum with undimmed enthusiasm. My journal devotes many pages to describing the tomb decorations, the varied and appealing gods, and the whole wonderful experience that is ancient Egypt. But the harassment was even worse than in Ethiopia. We were at that point travelling with two other British women and young men invaded our carriage by whatever means they could manage. If they couldn't get in through the door they poured in through the windows at each station to grab whatever piece of female flesh was handy. George carried a stick to beat them off – yes, really – but it was like dealing with mosquitoes: as soon as one was deterred another would find a way in.

October 31. Cairo. And that appears to be that. George left this morning for Athens (cheap air ticket suddenly available). I'm staying to tidy up odds and ends and will follow tomorrow or the day after. So here endeth the Africa experience and the Africa journal.

INTERLUDE
A NICELY SCARRED WOMAN

'I love to see a nicely scarred woman!' Our companion smiled a little bashfully, knowing that these *khawaja* were unlikely to share his enthusiasm, though by that time, after about eight hours of shared company, we knew each other pretty well. 'You can call me John,' he had said when we first introduced ourselves and complimented him on his English. 'I worked in London, you know. I was a hospital porter. But I couldn't stay. And now I have a wife and children. Gedaref is my home.' George and I had reckoned it would take us about four hours to get to Gedaref from the Ethiopian border – but that was before we saw the road, which was axle-deep in black, treacly mud, and our transport: an antique tractor pulling a wooden platform on wheels.

The first hour was spent in man talk about Massey Ferguson. George, not normally one to enthuse about motor vehicles, managed to dredge up enough knowledge and questions to keep the conversation going. John acted as interpreter for the farmer sitting on his left. 'He uses a camel for ploughing but a tractor like this... he could never own one but he loves to ride on it.' The two men lapsed into a private conversation, every now and then gesturing at the vehicle as its huge wheels dug deep into the mud. We were happy to be silent, striving to keep our balance as the trailer lurched from side to side, and observing the details of the landscape as we passed at walking pace. There was not much detail to be seen, to be honest: acres and acres of arable land growing we knew not what. The sun was now low in the sky, bathing the fields in a golden light. I was jerked out of my dreamy state by what looked like a long green leaf, blowing gently in the wind but attached to a wire fence. 'George! A chameleon!' It was always a treat to see our favourite reptile, especially this far north. I associated them with the forested equatorial regions of Africa.

John was amused at our enthusiasm for the chameleon and we resumed our conversation. The encroaching darkness encouraged the men to reveal more personal details. Like men all over the world, they started to discuss women. That was when he told us about the scarring. Actually it was George who asked him, since there was a young woman bearing lines of facial scars down her cheeks on the trailer. It bothered us seeing her flawless complexion damaged in this way. But we were also fascinated. 'How do they do it?' 'A razor. No, just an ordinary razor. You make the cut, then you rub in ash. From the fire? No, from a cigarette.' He laughed at our dismay. 'It's sterile, you see. It makes a very nice mark. Yes, I love to see a nicely scarred woman. It is very beautiful, very attractive. Very...' – he smiled at George – '... sexy.'

Twelve hours after claiming our space on the tractor we reached Gedaref. It was after midnight and we unfolded our cramped legs and climbed stiffly down to the road. John insisted on accompanying us to a hotel, waking up the owner, fixing an appropriate price, and disappearing into the night, brushing off our thanks in typically Sudanese fashion. Next day, however, he appeared while we were having breakfast. With him was a beautiful young woman with two neat rows of scars running down both cheeks like a row of peas in a pod. 'You know,' said George after they'd left, 'I do like a nicely scarred woman!'

PART 4

BECOMING A PUBLISHER

20

BRADT ENTERPRISES

We were home – my home – in Chalfont St Peter, and if my parents were dismayed at having two demanding lodgers they hid it well. They had entered into the spirit of the two journeys with maps on the wall marking our routes and all my letters saved, filed and returned to me (without which this book could not have been written).

There was one character I was most anxious to see after such a long absence (six years) and that was our African grey parrot, Captain Flint. Flint retreated to the back of his cage, suspicious of the attentions of this stranger. But after a few minutes of puzzlement he did a theatrical double take, gave me the special whistled greeting that he saved for members of the family, and came forward to have his head scratched.

I quickly secured a job in a nearby rehabilitation centre while George, who couldn't legally work in Britain, started writing *Backpacker's Africa*. I contributed drawings, maps (which I took great care over but they still look a mess) and of course plenty of criticisms. Kate, my sister, was inveigled into typing it in exchange for babysitting.

As with our South America guide our focus was relatively narrow – hiking – but with virtually no English-language guidebooks of any sort on Africa we wanted to broaden the coverage to include overland travel. The result was a blend between a guidebook and travelogue, and at nearly one hundred pages it was substantially longer than our first book. As we explain in the back-cover blurb: 'Backpacker's Africa is the first book taking you on a walking tour of Africa. Trekking gets you thinking for yourself, off on your own, and presents you with Africa's astonishing diversity.'

We didn't intend to self-publish this one; we wanted a Proper Publisher, and the only one we knew of who might be interested was

Roger Lascelles who produced paperback books on various aspects of travel. George typed up a Table of Contents and a sample chapter, and made an appointment to see Roger in London, taking along the Little Yellow Book since we also wanted to do an updated second edition of that. He returned crestfallen. 'He hardly looked at our book before saying no. And he wasn't interested in the Africa one either. What he did say was that he'd publish a mainstream guide to Peru. He was confident that he could sell that.'

'Did you tell him we couldn't afford to go back to Peru to research it?'

'Yes, he said it wouldn't be a problem. Just get some brochures from the tourist office and do it from those.' We stared at each other. If this was proper publishing, we'd better find a way of doing it ourselves.

We'd used up all our money in Africa. I had £680 in my bank account in England, the reimbursement of my NHS National Insurance payments, but a few enquiries about the cost of printing a book showed us that the situation was hopeless. We couldn't afford to print one of our guides, let alone two.

George now takes up the story:

> Exactly how I found Ted, the owner of a small letterpress shop in Slough, is lost in the sands of time. He needed cheap help, I needed to get some printing done. I indentured myself for the summer in exchange for printed pages. Ted didn't do trimming, binding, or even print covers, thus the 'finishing' would be sub-contracted.
>
> Throughout that summer I slaved away in the hot attic developing the copper plates that Ted secured to the drum of the press. Any spare moments I spent downstairs with Ted at the press learning the basics of printing.
>
> As my deadline for printing approached he agreed, rather petulantly, that it was time to order the paper for *Africa*. When

the agreed print date arrived Ted said, 'You know what … I'm taking the next two or three weeks off – I'll see you in October'. I wasn't in a position to say anything so clammed up.

I returned the next day with Kate's beautifully typed copy and an imposition plan, and began shooting and developing the plates. It was a thrill to push the button on the large, rumbling machine and have lovely, printed pages land in the out tray to be gathered and sent through the press again (upside down and backwards) with new plates.

After a few days of printing, someone from the finishing house came and picked up my loose sheets. Yes, a few pages were crooked, but by golly the pages were in order: A proud moment for a card-carrying dyslexic.

The process was repeated for the new edition of our Peru and Bolivia book.

The deadline that George talks about was the Frankfurt Book Fair in October. Someone had told us about this enormous trade fair, where a whole hall was dedicated to travel, and where deals were done. If we wanted to make our mark in the travel publishing world we would need to go to Frankfurt. But first, we had a lot to learn. Neither of us knew anything about the business world; indeed, neither of us had even worked in an office. The first shock came when George took a copy of the Little Yellow Book to Stanfords, *the* travel bookstore in London. Yes, they would take it (bless them). What discount did we give? George was flummoxed. Who knew you had to give a discount? He had no idea what to say.

'So what *did* you say?'

'I just said "the usual", and she said "So thirty-five per cent?", and I said "Yes!"'

She had then turned the book over and asked about the ISBN. Even George couldn't bluff this one. The kindly buyer showed him how every book is allocated a defining number which tells a bookshop who the publisher is and identifies the individual book. He needed to contact Whitaker's, the company that catalogues every single book in print.

George established an intense and somewhat prolonged relationship with a Miss Budworth at Whitaker's. She was very patient, and eventually after many letters and phone calls our fledgling company had its own prefix and our two soon-to-be printed books had their unique numbers. George went to the florist and ordered a single rosebud to be sent to a certain recipient at Whitaker's, with the message 'Love from ISBN 0 9505797'.

Our company already had a name but it was not the one we had chosen. When George's mother, Sally, wrote to us in South America to ask what name we wanted, we'd decided on Esperanza Books. The beautiful blue morpho butterfly was known by locals as the *esperanza*, and the word also had several meanings in Spanish: hope, expect… and wait. Very appropriate for a publishing company. However, by the time Sally received this letter she had decided on Bradt Enterprises.

We proudly wrote on the inside back cover: 'Bradt Enterprises is a new publishing house for backpackers. Crazy? No. There's a growing interest in combining the best in travel with the tops in trekking. Exploring the world's wild places, carrying everything you'll need on your back, is the only way you'll ever get to some of these unspoilt areas.'

Finally we needed a logo, something that would define our series, because we were now sure it *would* be a series. I remember my mother coming into the kitchen late one evening to turn off the lights, only to find George, in full hiking gear and wearing his backpack, with his foot on an upturned wastepaper basket while I sketched him. 'Oh God!' she said, and shut the door.

By the end of September 1977 we owned a couple of thousand copies of a mustard-yellow book – or booklet, to be honest, since it was stapled – *Backpacker's Africa: 17 walks off the Cape to Cairo route*, and a green book(let), *Backpacking in Peru and Bolivia: A guide to the ancient ways and Inca roads*. The latter was basically the same as the first edition but without the spelling mistakes and with a new circuit in the Cordillera Blanca, as well as detailed maps of two of the hikes. And quite a few rather pointless illustrations because I liked drawing, though with some useful ones of the wildlife. What strikes me, looking at this book now, is the quotes from reviews of the first edition. The leading magazines for hikers in the UK and US had welcomed this new book. Neither mentioned spelling mistakes or general shoddiness. *Climber & Rambler* (UK) wrote that we had given 'very practical information which newcomers to the Andes, however pedestrian or tigerish, will find invaluable…' while their counterpart in the US, *Trail Walker*, commended in particular the account of the trail to Machu Picchu, summing up, 'all in all a very interesting and informative little book'.

In October George hitchhiked to Frankfurt and returned from the book fair buzzing with ideas and enthusiasm. He had had a wonderful time, meeting other writers in the thriving world of self-published travel guides. The Germans were particularly prolific and George told me excitedly that one fellow, Martin Velbinger, was making enough money from his guides to the Greek Islands that he could afford a fast car to reach all corners of Germany on sales trips. What was more, Martin was interested in translating our books into German, and would visit us in a couple of weeks' time to discuss it.

Martin loved to talk. George loved the buzz of doing business. I got tired and went to bed. The next morning I came down to find them in the same spot at the kitchen table, still talking, but looking a bit the worse for wear. They hadn't been able to reach a financial agreement and after some strong coffee Martin went home, but his example gave us the push we needed. Yes, we would take the risk: I would give up my job and we would become full-time publishers.

My father couldn't bear the thought of his innumerate daughter being in charge of finances, and set up a bookkeeping system to deal with the sales that were trickling in. He sat at his manual typewriter in the kitchen with the parrot on the typewriter carriage, tapping out invoices with one finger. Whenever he did a carriage return Flint would fall off, but nothing daunted would climb back on just in time for the next new line. Sally did the same in Boston (though without the parrot). Yes, we do know how dreadfully we exploited our parents; I have felt appropriately guilty for fifty years.

We had so many ideas for the next book. Should it cover Chile and Argentina, about which we had quite a bit of information already? But it was over two years since we'd been there. Too long. We were anyway thirsting for new adventures. We recalled the start of our top-to-toe South America trip, where we had hunted around in the north of Colombia for boats down the Río Atrato. We'd known then that this could be the gateway to the Darién region, and discussed how much we wanted to cross the infamous Darién Gap, not with a death-defying expedition but by using rivers to get to the head of the trail that we were pretty sure ran between Colombia and Panama. So here was an excuse. What the travelling public wanted more than anything was a guide to crossing the Darién Gap. Furthermore, George had never visited Mexico and Central America, and I had rather whizzed through in 1969. And there were no detailed guidebooks to that ribbon of land connecting North to South America, so here was a gap in the market. Finally, George's father and stepmother had a holiday cottage by Lake Atitlán in Guatemala where we could stay. Whether the book would actually sell was never discussed. The die was cast.

We needed to save money. George, who had entered the country on a tourist visa so wasn't officially allowed to work, managed to get a job as a typist at the Bee Research Institute down the road, and by January we had stashed away enough to travel on our usual frugal budget. We had limited funds but this time we travelled with knowledge. We had a field guide to the birds, we knew about the mammals, and we could expect help from tourist boards and national park authorities. To be genuine book authors made a nice change from pretending to be zoologists or anthropologists.

When it came to taking a transatlantic flight, our timing was perfect. In September of that year (1977) Freddie Laker had introduced his first Skytrain with ultra-low fares between London and New York. A drive-away car to Miami and a short flight to Colombia and we were ready to tackle the Darién Gap.

We flew from Medellín to Turbo in a little ten-seater plane which was heavily overloaded. From my perch in the aisle I had a clear view of the cockpit, and a notice, in English, above one of those complex dials: 'Warning, equipment inoperative'. I decided to look out of the window instead, at the lazy brown rivers snaking their way towards the Caribbean across the expanse of flat green jungle. In Turbo we located a banana boat doing its regular run up the Atrato to Los Katios National Park, where we spent a total of eight days at the three ranger stations waiting for onward transport. The time passed pleasantly, especially at Sautatá, the headquarters, where the staff were in constant conflict with a cunning thief. On our first day we were woken from our snooze with a yell of 'Judas!' A young spider monkey ran past on his hind legs holding a chicken leg above his head, pursued by the cook. She knew it was useless. Judas had a cache of stolen goods beneath the hut that he shared with his sister, Rosita. The two orphans had been reared by the park staff and were completely tame. Judas spent his free time plotting his next entry into the kitchen, but Rosita had other concerns. She had adopted a piglet as a surrogate mother and rode around on its back. Whenever the piglet lay down Rosita would jump aboard, curl up contentedly, and suck an ear.

We thought we were experienced river travellers, but the trip to the next ranger station, La Loma, was extraordinary. Nothing prepared us for our *motorista* steering the boat into a seemingly solid wall of logs and water hyacinth which blocked the mouth of a tributary of the Atrato, the Río Cacarica. This river was seldom more than ten feet wide and only three feet deep. Frequently we had to jump out and help the crew manoeuvre the canoe over fallen branches and other hazards. We were right *in* the jungle. The foliage made a green tunnel through which we passed silently since the motor was useless in the shallow stretches. Birds flew ahead of us: kingfishers, trogons, herons and a host of others. 'Jesus Christ' lizards scurried miraculously across the surface of the water, and double-crested basilisk lizards sunbathed on the banks. Every now and then the excited call '*culebra!*' went up from the other passengers, but their eyes were sharper than ours, and we seldom saw these snakes.

The staff in the final camp, Cristales, knew about the trail and arranged a canoe there. After the gorgeous river journeys we were afraid the walk could only be an anticlimax, but it wasn't. About a kilometre from the start, George said, 'I like this!' My feelings exactly. We were walking along the spine of a sharp ridge with dark green bushes covered in crimson flowers lining the trail. Suddenly the dense jungle fell away revealing the evening sky and flocks of macaws and parrots flying high above us, yelling and squawking to each other. Huge blue morpho butterflies flopped across the path while at our feet armies of well-disciplined leaf-cutter ants carried their green loads to their nest. Admittedly the sweat was pouring off us and ticks were making their presence known, but we had expected as much. The experience was enlivened by our competition for the most red, itchy tick bites. George won with 132.

Our contact with the Indians, too, was everything we had hoped for. The Chocós with their large open houses on stilts, their serene faces and well-ordered lives; the Cuna women with their unique *molas* (clothing with complex reverse-appliqué designs) and gold nose rings. All accepted our presence with friendly curiosity. For three weeks, we saw no car, trod no asphalt, and met no tourists.

Within an hour of our arrival in Panama City my handbag was stolen and buses north turned out to be fully booked for a week.

❖ ❖ ❖ ❖

That we were thrilled by Costa Rica's national parks is no surprise, but for most visitors in the 1970s the wildlife was not the country's main attraction. Americans were drawn by the climate and political stability and many had second homes there which made the capital and coastal towns feel a bit too civilised. But the national parks were terrific, the facilities being basic but with enough explanation and description of the birds and animals to keep us informed. We wrote in *Backpacking in Mexico and Central America*:

> When we met Señor Ugalde, Director of the Parques Nacionales, we introduced the subject by saying we'd heard that the Costa Rican parks were the best developed in Central America. "No," he said, "they're the best protected." This is an important distinction. In Costa Rica, protection of flora and fauna has come before development of tourist facilities. Now that the parks are running smoothly and more land is being purchased and patrolled, the administrators are turning their attention to tourism. But this aspect is still in its infancy so don't expect a situation like the national parks in North America or Europe with their huge information centres, campgrounds, restaurants. On the other hand, this is exactly why Costa Rican parks are so interesting. Here you make your own discoveries. They'll be more instructive and important for being your own. There will be no shouting tourists, no lining up to photograph a special

tree, no litter, nor erosion from millions of feet. We liked the parks just as they were, but we look forward to watching the development of information facilities. Already in Santa Rosa and Volcan Poas National Parks, information for visitors is being developed according to a comprehensive master plan. In the meanwhile, congratulations Costa Rica on winning the Albert Schweitzer Prize for conservation and ecology efforts. We know you're on the right track and will succeed in preserving your unique natural heritage as few other Latin nations have.

How splendid that this prediction has come true. And how sad that the imaginative and dedicated programme of conservation in neighbouring El Salvador has not had similar success. We spent a day with the wonderfully enthusiastic director of national parks there, who laid on transport and a guide to seek out (unsuccessfully) the elusive quetzal. Eighteen national parks and reserves were planned or established in this densely populated country and we visited several of them. Potentially they could have competed with Costa Rica for wildlife holidays but political instability put paid to that.

Guatemala provided a breather, a holiday, and the opportunity to write up most of this trip in the luxury of George's father's house by Lake Atitlán. The country was beautiful, we discovered some good walks, and the local people – as I remembered from 1969 – colourful and still steeped in their traditions (we witnessed the sacrifice of a turkey on behalf of an Indian whose fortunes had taken a downturn). We hired a typewriter and George wrote up our notes. I added some descriptions, and started on the maps and illustrations. By the time we reached Boston we had much of it completed. First, though, we had planned a major adventure in Mexico.

The thing is, if you've walked more than 60 miles in 36°C heat through relatively uninspiring landscapes to some ruins that turn out to be disappointing, you're not going to leave the description out of your book just because it was unpleasant. No, you've taken meticulous notes, and you're jolly well going to include it.

We really did think the walk, across a large area of our Mexico map that was devoid of roads, would be rewarding. I introduce it in my daily letter/diary with great enthusiasm:

> We've set off on a trip that promises to be even more adventurous than the Darién Gap. We hope to walk from this area near the Guatemala border to Bonampak, one of the finest Mayan ruins in Mexico. It's about 100km through mainly unpopulated jungle. And we have no map.

There were several reasons why it was not a success. It was now May, the hottest month of the year, and many of the hillsides had been burned, removing any shade and adding to the heat; I suffered an attack of heat exhaustion – felt very faint and sick – and we had to stop for a while. The jungle paths were so steep we sometimes had to proceed on all fours, but there was very little untouched forest; the area was undergoing a transition from wild nature to pioneering settlement.

There were highlights – of course there were highlights.

> An incredible night! During the afternoon we'd noticed some welcome clouds building up and I asked a local if it was going to rain. Not until full moon, he said.
>
> Soon after we'd got into our sleeping bags the lightning started, and soon it was continuous with no same part of the sky lit up. The flashes were all different colours – blueish, pinkish,

greenish. There were no periods of darkness at all. And the thunder! Like the lightning it came from all directions. And then the rain.

We provided plenty of entertainment for the locals.

A group of Indians have just been witnesses to a scene which will keep their scholars busy for years. An altar has been set up in the middle of the road, and a blonde bearded priest could be seen dancing around it, rhythmically beating an upside-down green vessel on the ground. The ritual was accompanied by a repeated, one-syllable word.

George was trying to rid his backpack of cockroaches, having been distracted from his task of photographing one of our books propped up against a saucepan in the road.

George maintains an upbeat tone in the book:

We arrived at the roadhead with an exhilarating sense of achievement. It was 'our' trail all right. Possibly other gringos have walked it before us, but not many judging by the incredulity shown by Indians when they saw us approaching. One woman was so unnerved by the experience that she grabbed her child and fled as fast as her legs would carry her. The men were braver and more inquisitive. It was they who gasped in amazement at the miracle of instant heat under our cooking pot. Our supper preparations were usually witnessed by several lads lying on their stomachs around the stove trying to figure out what made the water boil. Another contingent watched our every move as we set up camp. Each new item they saw provoked the same questions: what is it, what do you use it for, and how much did it cost?

Rather than being close to nature, as we were in the Darién, here we were observers of the endless struggle of rural peoples to survive and prosper. That, indeed, was the chief reward of this trek – once we had recovered. George wrote:

> We look back on this as one of the most interesting and challenging walks we've ever done. The terrain, vegetation and people we encountered along the way gave never-ending varieties of interest. The whole area seemed in a state of transition; as new settlements were established, old ones decayed; as virgin jungle fell to the machete, *milpas* [areas of cultivation] reverted to jungle; in some villages education and civil peace were well established, while in others there was no school and unrest. In the old days, a century ago, mahogany was taken out of the jungles to the rivers where it was floated down to the railhead. Now mahogany is treated like all other wood – slashed and burned. Corn is the cash crop of the area, being either sold or eaten. It's as valuable and versatile as water; with it everything is possible, without it, only famine. With it, chickens produce eggs, cows and pigs are fattened for market, and tortillas are made. If a family grows enough corn they turn part of their farm over to coffee. *Chicle* (the basic ingredient for chewing gum) is still collected, and we passed many *sapodilla* trees, their trunks cross-hatched by *chicle* gatherers to collect the precious sap. The people who work the land range from the proud Lacandons and the colourful Tzeltals through to the ladinos (mixed race).

My diary ends starkly:

> This morning we went to look at the ruins we'd walked eight days to see. We were dreadfully disappointed. The fame of Bonampak rests on its murals and our two books on the Maya describe the

scenes in great detail. They're now so badly deteriorated that we could hardly make out anything.

My best friend in Boston, Anne, surely didn't know what she was in for when we asked if we could stay for a short time while we finished writing *Backpacking in Mexico and Central America*. We had learned that a local school for children with disabilities, the Cotting School, had a sophisticated printing department, and the instructor was thrilled at the prospect of printing a book rather than the usual brochures. Also they could even do perfect binding which meant we would finally have a book with a spine which could be properly displayed in bookshops. This was real, grown-up stuff. Of course we still didn't have any money, or not enough to print the book, but George's aunt came to the rescue. This was the last time our company had any outside funding. Thereafter if we wanted to continue publishing we had to make a profit.

That was all for the future. Holed up in Anne and Ken's attic we set about designing our version of the perfect guide and established the formula for the next few books, a combination of travelogue ('Our experiences'), tips, teasers (the 'Do you know…?' list inside the front cover) and careful maps (though however hard I tried my lettering still looked sloppy). And I bought fancy pens and Indian ink to improve my illustrations. The book was nicely typed but we needed big black lettering for the cover title and chapter headings. Letraset was the answer. These press-on letters came in a variety of sizes and fonts and, we thought, looked pretty good. Most of the headings are straight.

The book went to press two weeks after our arrival back in the USA. It probably holds the record for the most up-to-date guidebook ever published, but also the one with the most misprints.

This time we didn't see the book until it arrived at my parents' house in England. Sally had been tasked with sending us advance copies and getting half the print run on to a cargo ship.

We were thrilled with our latest effort, and I still think it looks damned good. I do remember someone in the book trade looking at it in dismay and querying why we had chosen a faded green for the cover, and why wasn't it laminated? Because we didn't know about lamination, that's why. I baked a cake, and created a replica of the book in icing, surrounded by the message 'We'll eat our words'. It was our first book launch, though with just my family in attendance.

In 1978 we both went to the Frankfurt Book Fair, travelling respectably by public transport but less respectably parading up and down the aisles of Hall 5 with a home-made mobile display board, created out of George's backpack frame, exhibiting our three books. Illegal, I'm sure, but it drew attention.

Now we were proper publishers we needed a catalogue. An A3 sheet of orange paper, folded into a convenient A5 size, listed our three books, with *Mexico and Central America* retailing at £2.60 (post and packaging free) and a photo of my three-year-old nephew weighed down with a backpack and wearing George's boots. 'You're never too young for backpacking!' we claimed.

Our plans for 1979 turned out to be pretty accurate: we were to publish backpacking guides to the USA, to Venezuela, Colombia and Ecuador, and to Chile and Argentina. It was going to be a busy year.

INTERLUDE
ONCE MORE IN MEXICO

The trail was perfect; an old overgrown logging road, winding slowly into the valley and passing through ever lusher greenery. The smooth path enabled us to look around; no danger of tripping here. We had started at a very high altitude, perhaps 9,000ft, where the pine trees were dripping with bright green feathery moss and the ground was dotted with flowers. As we lost elevation the pines mixed with oaks and other hardwoods, and the epiphytes became more abundant. Streams frequently crossed our path, providing a cool drink. Our attention was caught by a sudden splash of brilliant scarlet high on a cliff. Water dripped down the cliff, which was covered in flowering cacti, the giant blossoms seeming an almost iridescent red. As the day wore on, we started thinking about a campsite. No problem finding the ideal place in this well-watered area, so we would continue just a little longer. Then the road ended. Just like that; one minute we were walking along what seemed like a well-used track, and the next moment saw us floundering about in the bushes.

It had looked like a simple bit of bushwhacking. On the other side of the valley we could see patches of cultivation (*milpas*), indicating that there was a village nearby, and decided to scramble down through the trees to the road or trail that we expected to find at the bottom. What we hadn't taken into consideration was the effect of altitude on vegetation. After we'd descended about 1,000ft our friendly pines became a tropical rainforest and our nightmare began. Everything was damp, furry-green and rotten. The ground gave way beneath our feet, branches we grabbed for support broke off in our hands, and many friendly-looking shrubs turned out to prick or sting. All depressingly reminiscent of that trek in Madagascar. It was also incredibly steep. Our descent was faster than we intended, with plants or branches that we grabbed to break our slide simply accompanying us down. 'Be careful, that's a long drop!' called George helpfully as I glissaded past him hugging a loose tree. 'I'm not doing this on purpose!' I hissed through my teeth, landing with a thump on my backpack. The lower we dropped the denser the vegetation became, until we finally reached the bottom. A road? No, it was a river. Why on earth had we assumed otherwise?

The patches of cultivation that had tempted us down from the top were no longer in sight. All we could see was trees, trees and more trees. And the river. We started to follow it downstream. I was in the depths of depression and anxiety; not because we wouldn't survive – I knew we had at least four days' supply of food in our backpacks – but wondering if I had the guts and determination to put up with several days of making our way through virgin territory. Yet again. At least in Madagascar there had been some novelty value.

We waded or scrambled down the river for several hours before camping for the night. The next morning George persuaded me that we must climb up the almost vertical canyon side since he was pretty sure had located those *milpas*. We climbed. It was a repeat of the previous day, except this time we were sliding backwards. We had to grab any handhold available, relying on luck and balance when there wasn't one. As we got higher the vegetation turned into dense, scrubby thorn bushes which we had to force our way through. Just as I'd reached the stage when I thought that death was preferable, we entered a clearing. A *milpa*! An old one, but a definite sign of civilisation. We soon found a faint path, an abandoned house, and finally an inhabited house with a clear trail leading up over the mountain.

Our ordeal had come to an end; it had lasted for only about eight hours, but this was quite long enough. Looking back on the experience I realised how stupid we'd been to make the initial decision to bushwhack. When you think of the basic rules of jungle hiking, which include never putting your hands or feet in a place you can't see, and not taking undue risks in remote areas, we were extremely lucky. Had we been bitten by a snake, or fallen and injured ourselves, the outlook would have been grim.

This story made it into *Mexico and Central America* with this excuse: 'We hope our readers will profit from our experience. It takes more courage to turn back than to continue on, blindly.'

21

THE END OF THE SEVENTIES

Somehow, between returning to England after our Central America trip in 1978, and travelling once again to South America at the end of that year, we fitted in writing and printing our next book, *Backpacking in North America*. There was a good reason for this: Freddie Laker and low-cost transatlantic flights, and the adjustment of the exchange rate between the dollar and pound which suddenly made the USA affordable. Before 1979 no one would have dreamed of going to New York for their summer holiday. We launched the book in January, with the slogan 'America in '79, there's never been a better time'. Indeed, had we published a series of mainstream guides to the USA we would have been ahead of the game and sold tens of thousands. As it was, our commitment to sticking with the backpacking series kept sales at a modest level, but it was another damned good book, with fewer spelling mistakes, unique descriptions of the main areas for hikers, and advice for British readers on how to cope with America. We were certainly perfectly qualified to write it. George had backpacked in most of the national parks of the USA and I knew all about culture shock and how to explain the American way of life to the Brits. I had a lot of fun writing chapters such as Surviving New York City, Crime, and Language; the Natural History section was, of course, lavishly illustrated.

Sales might have been modest, but this book was noticed when we previewed it at the 1978 Frankfurt Book Fair and we were thrilled to receive a letter from a publisher, Delphin, interested in doing a German edition. *Mit dem Rucksack durch Nord-Amerika* was published in 1979. During the process of translation and editing we developed a warm relationship with the editor Susanne Härtel. I remember a letter of George's, following a photocopy of Susanne's hand holding one of the illustrated pages for approval. 'Dear Susanne, now I have seen a photocopy of your hand I can't possibly go on calling you Frau Härtel...' Susanne invited us to stay with her in Munich to approve the final proofs, and we have been friends ever since. She and I still go on walking holidays together.

During the summer of 1978 it had occurred to me that I couldn't really expect my father to continue filling orders and doing the bookkeeping himself. Besides, we needed a good typist to key in the text for *North America*. We put an advert on the local post office board and Janet Mears responded. She recalled her interview: 'I dressed in my best clothes and took care over make up, so was a bit disconcerted to be met by George wearing shorts (it was winter) and to be eyed balefully by the parrot from his perch on top of his cage.' Janet agreed to help out, submitted to being taught bookkeeping by my father, typed *North America* on a posh Selectric typewriter with a range of fonts, and stayed working for the company until her death in 2018. We quite literally couldn't have survived without her.

No sooner were we home from that 1978 Frankfurt Book Fair than we were planning our next adventure: to discover new hiking trails in the northern Andes. Although we'd explored Colombia and Ecuador on our previous trip we'd not done any hiking, and we hadn't been to Venezuela.

We were now skilled in the niceties of travelling as authors rather than ignoramuses (although the latter had its charms). We had a good field guide to the birds, we prioritised visits to tourist offices – with mixed results – and, most importantly, we knew that we needed to visit each country's Military Geographic Institute in order to get the detailed topographical maps which were essential for working out where we could hike. Most valuable of all, however, were the new friends and informants who had written to update our Peru and Bolivia guide and often had information on the countries we were about to visit.

As usual we got a drive-away car to Florida, from where we flew to Bogotá, planning to do some Colombia treks before crossing the border into Venezuela. On the flight from Miami we noticed an excessively nervous American in the seat across the aisle. He was literally shaking. We could understand how nerve-wracking Colombia's reputation might be to someone unused to South America, so George asked him if he needed any help. His face flooded with relief. 'Oh boy, yes! I'm here to pick up our two new adoptive children. My wife was too nervous to come with me.' We offered to accompany him as interpreters and an extra (two) pairs of hands. He told us about the children. One was a boy of two, and his sister, a baby girl a few months old. 'You should see the little boy! He has those huge dark eyes like that artist – you know the one – who paints those doe-eyed children.'

The orphanage was run, of course, by nuns, and the process was very efficient. It occasioned an experience I never expected to have: a baby was placed in my arms and a smiling nurse introduced me as 'Mama'. I explained. At the airport I led little Pablo by the hand while Roy, the new father, carried Susie. Pablo was indeed a gorgeous child, very serious, but alert to all his surroundings. When he saw the aeroplanes he stopped and stared and stared. A flight attendant took over and we returned to the city.

We spent Christmas Day eating fruit cake (bought from a luxury shop in Bogotá and saved, with great self-control, for this occasion) halfway up a mountain in Venezuela's Sierra Nevada de Mérida. The cable car which takes sensible climbers most of the way up Pico Bolívar, Venezuela's highest mountain, was closed, but the stations were open and the personnel stuck there over the holiday were glad of company. We had a very merry Christmas Eve celebration with quite a bit of wine. Of Venezuela, Ecuador and Colombia, Venezuela was the most developed, the wealthiest, and the one with a sizeable population of local hikers who kept the trails well maintained.

Totally different, in fact, from the other two countries, where trails were worn smooth by the bare feet of *campesinos*.

Colombia provided our biggest challenge, the magnificent Sierra Nevada del Cocuy. And another failed trek. So near and yet so far, so frustrating yet so rewarding, so very, very wet.

The Cocuy mountain range is pressed up against the Venezuela border, so we did this trek on our way to Venezuela, saving the rest of Colombia for later. Our 1:100,000 scale map showed an enticing trail going over three high passes (the highest one more than 14,000ft), crossing a large valley and heading up to a further snowy pass between glacier-covered mountains. If that pass was indeed ice-covered it would be too dangerous without proper equipment, so we had plotted an alternative route, following a descending river before looping round to join the glacier trail on the far side of the pass below the snowline. The map had one flaw: the part we most needed was blanked out with the word '*Nubes*'. In other words, there were clouds obscuring that part of the landscape when the aerial photo was taken.

The mountain scenery was surely the best in Colombia, with towering snowy peaks contrasting with dragon's teeth of black rocks and gigantic slate-grey slabs propped against each other. Approaching the range in a rare clear spell the view was so fine we asked the bus driver to stop the bus so I could take photos. The other passengers were aghast at our plans. We would be very cold, they warned. They didn't warn us about rain. It poured every afternoon so we learned to pitch our tent soon after lunch and wait it out. This was our first trek in this region, so by the afternoon our lack of fitness anyway meant we welcomed the rest. From the top of the last pass we saw that the route on the other side of the valley was indeed covered in snow so we followed Mouse River (Río Ratoncito) down, down and down. We spent three days looking for a trail to bypass the glacier before giving up and returning the way we'd come. I vividly remember that decision.

It was raining when we packed up our tent and we were both in tears. If you've packed up a soaking wet tent knowing you have two or three days uphill climb in the rain, you'll sympathise.

However, the backpacking gods decided we'd had enough punishment and quite suddenly the sky cleared, the wonderful Pico sin Nombre poked its white spire through the mist, and our climbs back over those three passes were rewarded with the most breathtakingly wonderful views.

Of course we gave our usual upbeat description in the book, even though it was a there-and-back trek. I've spent forty-five years thinking I might go back and succeed in doing the circuit. I didn't, I won't, and I regret it.

If Cocuy was the most spectacular of the Colombian hikes described in the book, the Río Magdalena trek was the most successful, one we could describe with confidence, having enjoyed a superb walk from San Agustín, with its monster statues which we had so admired in 1973, up to Laguna de Magdalena, the source of Colombia's most important river, and on to the colonial town of Popoyán. Four days of variety and we were never lost. Wow!

'Never lost' was not the usual situation, and not ideal for guidebook writers. Here's my introduction to an account of an ambitious hike to Volcán Antisana in Ecuador:

"I don't think we should write up this hike for our readers," I commented, watching George flounder toward a three-metre barrier of luxuriant growth. His technique was to fling himself full length on the tangle of vegetation, roll around for a while, then crawl over the top of the flattened bit, leaving me to follow. It didn't always work, and when it failed there were exciting drops down one-metre gaps in the lava floor. George had to go first because it was his fault that we were battling jungle. (Like hell it was, why were we here in the first place? -G.) I had been daintily stepping out over a lava field, an exercise needing concentration and balance and a high pain threshold for the occasions when moss turned out to cover a deep hole rather than a firm rock. George had soon given up and descended to the valley where he thought he'd seen a path. "Well, how is it?" I shouted. "Fine! There's a good horse track." It was difficult to imagine horses making their way through this sort of vegetation, but when I got down to his level I had to agree; there were horse droppings and a well-beaten path through the high grass. It was only when we entered giant reeds that I began to have my doubts. How could horses make tunnels? And tunnels only high enough to allow us to crawl on hands and knees? It wasn't my favourite type of backpacking, and when the tunnels wandered up the mountain and we had to resort to the bulldozer method, I liked it even less. A lake edged with soft mud provided relief and the answer to the tunnel question. Animal tracks criss-crossed the mud, but no ordinary animal. Each print showed three or four large toes. Mountain tapir! This furry relative of the jungle tapir is very rare, and the possibility of seeing one made all our efforts worthwhile. We set up our tent for optimum tapir viewing, but were not rewarded. Of course no tapir in its right mind would visit the lake after listening to us crashing along its paths all afternoon. At least the next day we had the sense to follow the lava, and our cross-country trip ended in the best hot bath in South America. Near Papallacta there's a river of hot water running through green fields. Part of it has been dammed to provide a deep hot pool. Sitting in the pool under a hot waterfall, we agreed that it had not been such a bad hike after all.

This may not have been the easiest hike we describe in the book, but the Ecuador chapter was actually full of useful advice because this country was teeming with climbers heading for Cotopaxi and Chimborazo and backpackers planning to stay a few weeks in Otavalo just to catch up on some serious eating. We gleaned plenty of information from them. Otavalo, as most travellers know, has the best Indian market in Ecuador and one of the most famous in South America. For a pig enthusiast like me, this market was bliss.

> If you get to the livestock market at dawn you'll hear a tremendous commotion as pigs are unloaded from trucks and squeezed under the barbed wire and into the paddock. The whole area is filled with milling Indians and their complaining animals – sheep, cattle and goats but mainly pigs. There are huge pigs and tiny ones; pigs with long combed auburn fur, and pigs covered in dense wool. There are pigs sleeping, pigs squealing, and pigs escaping; altogether a delightful place [one of us is a little less pig-enraptured].

We stayed a few days in a typical Otavalo *hostal*, with rooms clustered around a courtyard. As we were getting settled a middle-aged woman emerged from one of the rooms and greeted us in a strong Irish accent. She told us about a shop that sold good yoghurt. When we were alone, George said, 'Do you think that's Dervla Murphy?' We had heard that she was in Peru with her ten-year-old daughter Rachel. 'Oh no,' I said, 'she's a proper writer, she'd stay in a proper hotel.' When we met the woman again George asked, 'Are you Dervla Murphy?' She looked a bit alarmed and discomfited, but agreed that indeed she was. We spent the rest of the evening drinking rum and reminiscing. Thus began a lifetime friendship which only ended when Dervla died in 2022. A truly remarkable woman and a great travel writer.

❖ ❖ ❖ ❖

We returned from South America in the early spring of 1979 and, as before, we accepted hospitality from unsuspecting friends in Boston – this time Jim and Kathy. In a short period of time we wrote, mapped, drew and designed our next book. *Backpacking in Venezuela, Colombia and Ecuador* was more professional-looking than our previous Latin America guides, still typed, but with a Selectric typewriter, and with an improved font. There are plenty of maps which look rather good to me, and lots of photos. Chapter headings are still Letraset. The format of this title became standard in later guides, with illustrated sections on natural history, along with culture, conservation and so on. Another damned good book? Well, the words were (mostly) good, although I must admit that there were too many descriptions of failed routes that we were jolly well going to include because of the efforts we'd made to walk them, and there were plenty of spelling mistakes – and worse.

We had a very tight deadline. This time we were able to finance the printing ourselves, helped by the sale of advertising, and booked it in with a printer in Boston. I remember being driven to the printer's by Kathy and doing the last bit of proofreading and page sorting from the car's back seat. Not ideal. The second printing in 1980 had an Addendum: 'We apologise for the variety of misprints in this book and for the misplacement of page 56 which should have been page 43.' For the second printing we took the advice of a publisher friend. It had a laminated cover and – gasp! – an index.

We needed to sell our books. Normal publishers use a distributor; we used long-distance buses and a Eurail pass. In 1979 the Greyhound bus company sold coast-to-coast travel passes for $99 as a 'Thank you Canada' gesture. Canada, or rather the Canadian Embassy, had helped six American diplomats escape when the US Embassy in Tehran was seized. We weren't Canadians so I'm not sure how this worked but it meant that we could travel throughout the US for an unlimited amount of time, stopping in all the major cities to sell books. I can't pretend I enjoyed it. Most nights we slept on the bus or pitched our tent in city parks or vacant lots. Occasionally we'd stay at a YMCA to get cleaned up. But we had a unique product at a time when Americans had embraced walking and travel with equal enthusiasm, so we sold lots of books and made lasting friends with bookshop owners. To make the journey worthwhile we had added some books published by Roger Lascelles. (Yes, the same man who had sensibly turned down the opportunity to become our publisher. We were now his rep in America, which worked rather well for all of us.)

I bought a Eurail Pass in the US (not officially available to British citizens but no one asked) and did the same thing in Europe, travelling by train throughout the continent, staying with friends or sleeping on the train, and selling plenty of books. I didn't enjoy this either. It was a bit hit-and-miss, getting out in a new town or city, finding a telephone box and Yellow Pages, and guessing what the word was for bookshop. 'Do you speak English?' Then I'd launch into who I was and what I had to sell, and most would agree to see me and most bought books. And I made good friends in the specialist travel retailers who looked forward to my annual visit and reordered regularly. It could be a bit humiliating, however. Having made the appropriate phone call, I took the night ferry across to Helsinki from Sweden to visit the very large and well-known bookshop there. It had not been a restful night. No beds, we just sat in our reclining seats all night and one man had, I suppose, nightmares and kept us all awake by shouting. So I wasn't at my best when I met the buyer of the Academic Bookstore. I proudly showed him our four books. 'Oh dear, no,' he said, shaking his head, his long face the picture of disapproval. 'Not at all what I expected. No.' To my mortification I started to cry; I was very tired and it was the last straw.

Another time I had an appointment to see the buyer in a large Brussels store selling English-language books.

'What company are you representing?' asked the sales assistant I first approached.

'Bradt Enterprises.'

'What an unfortunate name! And your name?'

'Hilary Bradt.'

She went very pink. I assume she thought they were children's books.

One year I nearly killed myself. But only because I public-spiritedly stayed on the German train past its final destination in Kiel to put out a fire in a litter container. Someone had dropped a lighted cigarette there. The train moved on into a siding, so I got out and started trundling my case of book samples along the tracks. The case was strapped to a metal trolley (wheeled suitcases had yet to be invented), and I became aware of a railway official screaming at me from the far side. 'Halt!' He had a very red face and was in quite a state. He added something about many thousands of volts. I didn't know what he was talking about and shouted back defensively in my best German that I had been putting out a fire, and continued walking. His face took on an interesting purple colour and his voice was hoarse so I waited for him to come to me. I then understood that I was only a foot or so from the live rail, which would not have done me much good if I'd trundled my trolley over it. He escorted me, and the case, to safety and I thanked him for saving my life.

These sales trips were unorthodox, but they worked. A BritRail Pass, bought in the US, also worked, as did driving around Britain with boxes of books in the car boot, visiting retailers and being paid there and then from the till. Our ignorance about the normal business of publishing ensured that our early days were reasonably successful. By meeting the buyers in all those travel bookshops, we learned what travellers are looking for in terms of guidebooks, and made lasting friends in the places that mattered.

❖ ❖ ❖ ❖

We were at something of a crossroads. The only new book we had in the pipeline was *Backpacking in Chile and Argentina*, for which we already had a co-author, John Pilkington, a fellow backpacker who had contacted us before his nine-month exploration of South America. He offered to update our Peru and Bolivia treks and to write most of the Chile and Argentina guide. We wanted to go back to the central Andes ourselves before doing the third edition of our most popular guide (OK, the *only* popular guide). Now that trekking in Peru was offered by several adventure travel companies we needed to contact them and see how our hiking experience might meld with theirs and make us some money.

We met Hanns Ebensten for dinner in New York. Hanns ran luxury treks along the Inca Trail, but treks with a difference. They were exclusively for 'discerning gentlemen', and Hanns was every bit a discerning gentleman himself in his white linen suit, his single gold earring and his impeccable manners. He wondered if we might be suitable joint leaders because, as he explained delicately, his male leaders were sometimes inconvenienced by unwanted night visits by his clients. This was tempting. I liked the idea of being a joint leader (ie: I could still be a follower, a role that suited me perfectly), and the idea of a luxury trek was enticing. But we knew nothing about tour leading. What, George wanted to know, were we supposed to do if a client arrived ill-equipped for trekking? Hanns raised an elegant eyebrow. 'You would take him shopping, of course.' George looked stunned. 'You mean to say that we would have to waste a whole day because some asshole was not properly prepared?' A few days later the letter arrived. 'Dear George, the fact that you called my beloved clients assholes makes me wonder if…' A relief, actually. I'm not sure we would have fitted in.

Hanns wrote a charming foreword to *Venezuela, Colombia and Ecuador,* so I suspect that his response was somewhat tongue in cheek. His foreword was typical of the man, referencing Goethe backpacking through Italy in 1786, and his own journeys through the Magaliesberg mountains of South Africa in the 1930s.

May was a significant month. We had boldly booked a booth at the American Booksellers' Association annual convention in Los Angeles, and it was wonderful – extraordinary! Totally unlike the equivalents in London and Frankfurt, although admittedly our days were considerably enlivened by our near neighbour, a feminist publisher specialising in books on sex. On display was *I am my own lover: a woman's guide to masturbation,* among similar titles. The women running it were dour and rather fierce so of course none of the men who passed, goggle-eyed, and passed again, dared thumb through their books. So they hovered at our booth, examining our oh-so innocent titles and casting furtive glances to their right.

Booksellers wore blue labels, which made them particularly vulnerable. George would spot them at 50yds and launch an attack. Only the most determined got away – the others followed him back to our booth like lambs and usually ordered some books. I absented myself for long periods to browse possible titles that I could sell in England and Europe (my visits to European bookshops and effective mail-order business was proving to be quite profitable, and supplemented our still meagre list). I also made a beeline for the cookbook publishers, to gobble up the free samples, and enjoyed more outlandish titles such as *Madness and sexual politics in the feminist novel.* Thanks to George's salesmanship the ABA was a great success. We sold about five hundred books and easily made back the cost of the booth and our living expenses, as well as gaining loads of valuable contacts.

Everything was going well. We arranged a drive-away car to deliver in San Francisco – a simply enormous Oldsmobile with only eight miles on the clock. It was like driving a small house, and there was plenty of room to sleep in it at night.

Stung by Hanns's rejection, George was determined to contact all the Adventure Travel companies he could find in the Bay Area. He remembers that I didn't totally share his new enthusiasm for tour leading. 'We were in an ice-cream parlor which had a phone booth, remember? You didn't want me to make those calls but I changed $1 to dimes and phoned every one I could find in the Yellow Pages. The last dime went on a call to South American Wilderness Adventures.'

Bill Abbott and Bob Wolfson agreed to meet us in their Berkeley office. They had only been there a week, and their 'desk' comprised some packing cases covered with a Peruvian *manta*. I was hoping they would hire us as consultants but they politely told us that they had all the information they needed on the hiking trails, thank you. However they were looking for leaders for that summer's Cordillera Blanca trek.

'The very thought gave you the shits and you scuttled off to the toilet. When you reappeared you were fine with the idea and Bob and I had sorted out all the details.'

Because of my pathetic lack of confidence, they agreed that we could lead this first one jointly, and if it went well and they were willing to ask us again, then we would need to split up and do separate treks. Of course it was also a splendid opportunity to add some fresh hikes to the new edition of our Peru and Bolivia guide and produce the comprehensive book those countries deserved.

In August 1979 George and I met our group at Lima airport and escorted them first to Cusco and Machu Picchu, then to the Cordillera Blanca. Tour leading was a revelation. I found that I loved getting to know these feisty Americans, that I could just about cope with the bossy New Yorkers, and that doing Machu Picchu the comfortable way, staying at the hotel just outside the ruins, was a splendid opportunity to get the most out of the place. Very different from sleeping on straw in one of the ruins, as I had done a decade previously, and different too from getting soaked on top of Huayna Picchu. I liked trekking even more, doing the stunning Llanganuco to Santa Cruz circuit in the Cordillera Blanca with pack animals (albeit reluctant donkeys which needed group persuasion to cross boggy ground) and a camp crew who set up our roomy tents, cooked meals, played music on traditional instruments and improved our Spanish.

The third edition of our book was going to be the best so far. We conscientiously filled all the regional gaps in Peru, if not with our own newly researched routes, then with contributions from other backpackers. The Bolivian chapter was expanded and, best of all, Dervla Murphy agreed to write a foreword.

We based ourselves in the cheap gringo hotel in Cusco. In the six years since we were last there the town had been transformed. It was now heaving with tourists (and infested with thieves) but with the associated goodies that we craved such as pizza and chocolate cake. There was no longer the all-pervading smell of stale urine and the litter problem had been largely dealt with.

A day in the public library, where they had some rare English-language books about Peru, introduced us to Annie Peck, who was probably the first person to climb Huascarán, in 1908 – although her claim is disputed (well it would be, wouldn't it?). There is a wonderful reconstructed photo of her 'on the summit', with such a determined gleam in her eye that you find yourself believing that she really did reach the top but just had no photographic evidence. However, it was in the library of the Archaeological Museum that we found Ephraim George Squier's Peru: *Travel and Exploration in the Land of the Incas*, published in 1877, long before Machu Picchu was discovered but describing the ruins of Raqchi which became the focus of our Cordillera Vilcanota trek.

As tended to happen with our hikes, this didn't go according to plan. We planned to walk north from Raqchi to the snow peaks of Ausangate, but didn't have a topographical map of the route, only one showing the start of the trail. We'd managed without maps before so surely we could do it again? No, we couldn't. With no real evidence we decided we were 'on the right path' as we followed a river in roughly the correct direction. George described the experience in the next edition of our book:

> As dusk approached we hurried through a village, after saying goodbye to a boy who had shown us the trail over the ridge and into the next valley to the north. Minutes later he was hurrying towards us, waving his hands, shouting, and running all at the same time. "Please come and eat supper with us," he begged, "then you can walk with strength and sleep deeply." Without giving us a chance to think about it, he herded us through a gate in an adobe wall, and we found ourselves in the small courtyard of a typical Andean house. The cooking hut was tiny and too humble for such exalted visitors, so we were motioned toward two stones covered with a blanket in the courtyard. The boy's parents came out and shyly greeted us. Soon two earthenware bowls of food arrived, along with apologies; they needn't have worried, it was the most delicious meal we'd eaten since leaving Cusco. Would you complain about small tasty potatoes fried in pork fat with cheese? While we ate they whispered about us and we whispered about them. How could we repay them, we wondered. We decided on presents of a box of matches for father, a picture postcard of San Francisco for the son, and

Above: The map business: how to get all that luggage back from Peru?

Below: We published our first map in 1985. In 2022 it was selected for the book *Maps That Made History* (Belgium).

Below: I was thrilled with this new edition! The first with a colour cover, which I created with scissors, brown paper and a photo, and which Janet Mears (*inset*) typed.

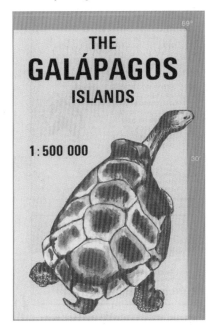

Above: Each summer I escaped to lead tours for Wilderness Travel. Peru's Cordillera Huayhuash was the toughest but most spectacular trek of them all. Normally I was backpack-free, but posed for this photo for the cover of the fourth edition of *Backpacking and Trekking in Peru and Bolivia*.

Above: I found the Inca Trail porters reading my guidebook, which gave me an idea…

For several years our catalogue covers followed the same theme, and authors had the additional responsibility of providing suitable photos of their book being enjoyed by locals. The most challenging photo (*below right*) was taken with special permission in Johannesburg Zoo by Philip Briggs.

Above: Frankfurt Book Fair, 1990

Below: Display at London Book Fair, 1992

Above: The back of our 21st anniversary catalogue says it all!

Above: Celebrating our Small Publisher of the Year Award (1997) with Tricia Hayne (left) and Janet Mears (right). The cheque for £1,000 certainly came in handy during those straitened times.

Below and opposite: These cartoons by Bill Stott appeared in the catalogue celebrating our 21st birthday in 1995

THE TEAM
Hilary Bradt

Boss. The buck stops here. The trouble is, Hilary keeps wandering off to Madagascar and beyond… Her staff's 1994 Christmas card said it all:

"…it doesn't seem like five minutes since last Christmas – time sure flies when you're having fun… it passes fairly quickly for the rest of us as well!" Hilary lives and works in Farnham Common with Chico the guinea pig, who has an insatiable appetite for electrical cables and laminated book covers.

Janet Mears

Office manager. In 1977 Janet answered an advert for someone to do a bit of typing for a part-time publisher. Life hasn't been the same since – even her house in Chalfont St Peter has been taken over by Bradt. Janet holds the financial side together – actually she holds everything together – and runs the show when the boss is globetrotting.

Dilys Saunders

Publicity and direct sales manager. Dilys spends a lot of time on the phone, chatting up customers… I mean dealing with customer orders and chasing overdue payments. But late payers beware – beneath the happy exterior lurks a Welsh dragon!

Tricia Hayne

Editor and project manager. Together with a fantastic team of editors, typesetters, illustrators and cartographers, not to mention the devoted attentions of a hyperactive dog, Tricia makes sure that well-written, accurate books are published on time – no mean task when one of the authors is THE BOSS.

Cartoons by Bill Stott (Tel: 0151 608 3812)

Above: Receiving the MBE from the Queen in 2008. 'And I saw why people had said I should wear a small hat.'

Below: Leaving the Presidential Palace in Madagascar after the surprise of being made an Officer of the National Order of Madagascar, 2018

Below: Whatever happens, keep smiling!

decorative hair grips for the mother and little daughter. That gave us an excuse to enter the kitchen and distribute the gifts. The small stone-and-adobe hut had a cooking area where a fire continuously burned, a crude table with a maize grinder, and an adobe seat covered with sheepskins. The base of the seat was honeycombed with holes through which scuffled and squeaked a large number of guinea pigs. The family were thrilled with their gifts, although they only recognized the matches. The postcard fascinated them; after we'd turned it right way up and pointed out the high buildings and the huge bridge they gasped in amazement, but they couldn't understand the scale of it all. And how could they when their world was made up of adobe houses, llamas, streams and footpaths?

We continued the next day up another valley through some of the best scenery and most interesting country life we've seen in Peru. Fantastic dark limestone formations spiked into the blue sky, little *molinos* or waterwheels crouched over the valley's stream, and we saw our first herd of pure white alpacas. As we got higher we could see the hills had had a sprinkling of snow during the night, the slopes were bare from overgrazing, and the purple-red earth glowed in the afternoon sun. Our path snaked up a series of hills, and we always thought the pass would be just over the next one. Not until we reached an enormous valley tumbling down on our left did we realize the pass was still a long, long way off. It was getting late, and frankly I was whacked. We'd gained 1,300m that day, and I was all for camping below the pass, but Hilary wanted to push on up into the gloaming. She hoped to see our river and the Ausangate range from the top of the pass, and sleep soundly with the knowledge she was 'found' on the map at last. There was no holding her back, as she slogged up the windy pass. I watched her stand motionless at the top, fling her backpack off and scamper down toward me.

"George," she shrieked, "guess what you see from the top!" I stopped, got my wind and waited until she reached me.

"Cusco?" was all I could think of that would explain such behaviour.

"No, no, you simply won't believe it!"

"Lima?"

"No, we've landed on Mars!"

When we got to the top I had to agree with her. Off to our left, at the very crest of a mountain, was a ribbon of defiant rock weathered into fantastic shapes and spikes, some as much as 30m high. Straight ahead every hill and mountain seemed to be wearing a multi-coloured striped poncho. And the colours were amazing: lilac, green, dark yellow, and a rich variety of reds. There was not a living thing as far as the eye could see.

We had stumbled on an unknown neighbour of the now famous 'Rainbow Mountain', which was only discovered in 2013 when the ice melted, revealing its colours.

In contrast, our highest trek yet, under the glaciers of Salkantay was, in terms of having a new hike to add to the book, totally successful, and we declared it our favourite in Peru. I think I would still agree. Salkantay is, or was, just about a perfect mountain, the pyramid shape that we all require, and (in those days) completely snow-covered. We walked from the low-lying village of Mollepata up a citrus-growing valley where parakeets shrieked and hummingbirds buzzed, to a peaceful campsite at the foot of two great white mountains. Next day we gasped our way up to the top of a 16,500ft pass, skirting the glacier and investigating ice caves, before descending to admire a little-known Inca canal and to meet the early part of the Inca Trail. And it was our discovery. It's now well known, of course, but we never knew if we were going to succeed in completing the circuit, which added some spice to the adventure.

It also allowed us to quote from Squier's book, describing Mollepata, at the start of the trek, as 'a place unsurpassed in evil repute by any in Peru'.

Apart from one abortive hike – which we included anyway – our time in Bolivia worked out well in terms of research for the book, with the lovely Takesi Trail a definite find. It rivalled the Inca Trail with its pre-Columbian paving, but was a much easier walk. Just one pass to show off the changes in vegetation, and then down into the jungly Yungas with all its tropical heat and colours. We added another mixed-altitude trail to the book – the Gold-diggers Way, researched by John Pilkington – which I experienced myself on a disaster-ridden tour a few years later.

Treading familiar ground in the Cordillera Blanca and the Cusco area brought home to me one of the least-considered harmful effects of tourism. Not only litter, which was too visible to ignore, but the much more subtle legacy that well-meaning tourists bring to rural communities. The third edition of our book was the first to address this issue in detail. I devote two pages to 'Minimum Impact'. If we were the first to bring foreigners to remote areas of the Andes, we had a responsibility to minimise the damage they might unwittingly cause.

> Another indication that a trail is a popular gringo route is that children rush up to you and demand sweets or money. Before you offer a child such presents, reflect on the consequences of your action. You are giving him a taste for sweets which he would otherwise not have acquired, and which he can only satisfy by begging. You are teaching him that begging is rewarding and that he can, after all, get something for nothing. The child that appears so endearing to you will seem like a damn nuisance to the gringos following you. His increasingly insistent demands for *caramelos*, *dulce*, or *plata* will irritate future trekkers and help

widen the gap between gringo and *campesino*. There are so many ways of interacting with children. We've watched a trekker sit down with a group of kids, and draw pictures for them. They reciprocated with some charming illustrations for her diary. Cat's cradles is a good game to teach rural children. Most can get hold of a piece of string, and the variations are endless. A frisbee also gives lots of pleasure. The idea that gringos are so rich that they can simply give valuable things away fosters deceit and perhaps robbery. Reciprocity is the foundation of village life; presents and labour are exchanged, not given. Give a smile and a greeting instead.

That was written over forty years ago, and was the first in a regular section on the subject in all Bradt guides. Having initially been called 'Minimum Impact', it changed to 'Responsible Travel' and then 'Giving Something Back', but whatever heading it falls under, our early guidance on how we visitors should behave in such a different culture, and perhaps make our own contribution, is something I'm most proud of.

We were back in the US selling books, staying with friends, and writing the third edition of what was now grandly called *Backpacking and Trekking in Peru and Bolivia* because we had added a chapter on organised trekking. This edition would be the most professional ever. We knew the sales would be healthy so decided to have it typeset rather than typewritten. It would be thoughtfully organised, have an index, good maps, and look like a proper book.

All was not well with our relationship, however. The couple who had travelled so agreeably together for seven years found that jointly running a business was a different matter. We had conflicting views of how our publishing company should develop and arguments went unresolved. I suppose I turned a blind eye to reality, helped by a lovely holiday in New England where we walked and cycled and all was harmonious. In September 1980, a few days before our eighth wedding anniversary, I went to England alone to sort out the business on that side of the Atlantic, and to look for a typesetter and printer for the guide.

My parents had arranged a dinner party on the evening of my arrival, something of a custom since I used to bring live lobsters back with me from Boston. I don't know if it was legal but the box was clearly marked and no one ever stopped me.

As I unpacked my suitcase before dinner I found a sealed letter from George. It told me that our marriage was over.

22

THE 1980S AND BEYOND

I told the letter-in-the-luggage story to someone the other day. He asked, 'So what was your reaction?'

'I cried for two years.'

I was helpless to change things. I didn't know if George was still staying with friends and I didn't want to phone them and weep down the line. I sent a short pleading telegram and a longer letter. His response, eventually, was that he felt I had been using him as a crutch and that he'd grown tired of my lack of confidence. 'Eight years is long enough.'

George assumed that we would go on working together, but that just wasn't going to happen, not long term, anyway. However, in the short term – actually two years – we were in the unreal situation of each publishing our own choice of books, and sending part of the print run across the Atlantic for the other to sell – much to the confusion of our respective authors. And in the immediate term I had *Peru and Bolivia* to finish off, and a Georgeless publishing future to try to come to terms with. If I hadn't had the support and help of Janet Mears, and of course my parents, I'm not sure how I would have coped. But cope I did, because there was so much to do.

I found a typesetter to rekey *Peru and Bolivia*, though I drove her – Vera – mad with my indecisiveness and emotional chaos. At least it was printed in the UK so I didn't have the additional challenge of getting a thousand or so books from George's 'warehouse' (where he was also sleeping on a bed created from a pile of book-filled boxes) to the UK as I did with the other South America titles.

Getting books from the UK to the US quickly and cheaply also presented a problem, but I had a neat, if rather dodgy, solution.

After filling one of my US mail sacks – I've no idea how I acquired these rugged canvas bags, but they were perfect for the job – with boxes of books, I'd heave them to Heathrow and check out the queue for the next flight to Boston. Having spotted an individual or couple with only hand luggage or one small bag, I would ask them, ever so nicely, if they would check in my mail sack, assuring them that they need do nothing else but give me the luggage receipt before going through Security. In the early 1980s, before computers, one could get away with that sort of reprehensible behaviour. A few days later George would receive the luggage tag in the mail, assume an expression of innocence and tell the baggage enquiry people at Logan airport that he had flown in a few days before but hadn't been able to collect his luggage because of a family crisis. He would be led to the luggage depository, collect the bag and – free transport for our books. I think we did it at least once in reverse, as well, because I remember picking up a couple of sacks at Heathrow. They contained copies of the final title in our lookalike backpacking series: *Backpacking in Chile and Argentina, plus the Falkland Islands.*

This had been typed by Janet while I was in the US, and was the first of our books to be produced with the help of another co-author: John Pilkington, whose name appeared alongside mine on the cover. He had not only covered Chile and Argentina exhaustively, but was a meticulous editor and credited as such in the book; the first we'd had (which of course is obvious to anyone who looks carefully at its predecessors). John came to Janet's house to check and proofread the final typed text. She fed him when he was still there at dinner time, retired for the night when he was still there at bedtime, and gave him breakfast when he was still there in the morning. The result is undoubtedly the best-looking of all those early guides and actually one of the best-looking, to my mind, for several years. I like the typed text, and a friend of John's had drawn some beautiful maps, infinitely better than my efforts.

John has a distant memory of driving into the cargo area on Heathrow's south side, rather to the concern of the security people there, and putting the carefully packaged camera-ready copy – the finished pages, as they will appear in print – on a flight that was leaving for Boston that afternoon.

There was no time to succumb to my grief. Earlier in the year we had booked a slot at the London Book Fair in the Grosvenor House Hotel in Park Lane. In 1980 it was an affordable tabletop affair held in October, just before Frankfurt. I made a batik Bradt Enterprises banner and Janet sewed a rather classy table covering. The artistry made up for our rather meagre display of books.

'How's George?' everyone asked.

'He's fine.'

'Why isn't he here?'

I invented various events in the US that had prevented him from coming. No way could I tell them the real reason without bursting into tears. I kept up this lie for months. It was two years before I could bring myself to remove my wedding ring.

Three things happened in the next few months to lighten my spirits. One was the news from John Pilkington that we were to be interviewed about *Chile and Argentina* on the local TV news by Cliff Michelmore, who was, I read years later in an obituary, enduring 'a brief and unhappy spell with Southern Television in 1980'. Perhaps it was being forced to interview nonentities like us after being such a well-known face on BBC's *Tonight* programme (he was the first to break the news of Kennedy's assassination and the Aberfan disaster). I don't remember whether we were articulate or struck dumb, but it was certainly morale boosting. The other, really very splendid, thing was being shortlisted for the first ever Thomas Cook guidebook award for *Peru and Bolivia*. It felt like we'd made it as publishers – that I had made it as a publisher – and I loved meeting others at the award ceremony. Finally I received a letter from Delphin in

Germany announcing that they'd like to buy the translation rights of another of our books – in fact three of our books – to create *Mit dem Rucksack durch Süd-Amerika*, a compilation of all our Andean guides. Published in 1981, it's a lovely chunky volume and it sold well – as you would expect. Germans are great walkers and this was the first guidebook to take them along the trails of South America.

In 1982, with no prospect in sight of their elder daughter moving out of the house, my parents took the only option available to them: they built a smaller house in the back garden, sold the family home, and told me firmly that there would be no spare room in their new abode. Or not for me, anyway. No problem, I simply moved in with my sister, Kate, who had made the mistake of reversing the trend by moving to a larger house which happened to have a Granny Annexe.

Meanwhile Janet found, perhaps to her surprise, that her house was now our official office address. I allowed her to recruit a helper, Dilys, to take orders, chase debts and keep an eye on stock levels, especially the all-important South American maps. As I say rather grandly in that year's 'catalogue' (four stapled A4 pages): 'We are the sole European importers of many South American maps, including topographical maps for hikers and mountaineers.' As indeed I was.

This is how it worked. I was now an established tour leader, sent to South America each year by Wilderness Travel (South American Wilderness Adventures had expanded to cover other countries and changed their name). There were always a few free days between groups and this was when I would visit the Instituto Geográfico Militar in Quito, Lima or La Paz and buy a hundred or so maps. The most valuable were the topographical ones, scale 1:100,000, to the most popular trekking areas of the Andes, but the country maps sold very well too – there were few decent maps of South America available in Britain and Europe in those days. I had learned that a rare commodity can carry a high price so the topographical maps I bought for under a dollar each could retail for £5.45 (a Bradt guide, in the 1980s, was £4.25) so I was on to a winner, but it did take considerable effort. First I had to book an appointment with a military man at the *Instituto*. I got to know most of them over the years so the red tape of showing my passport and explaining my business in poor Spanish became unnecessary. I particularly remember one colonel in Quito; I was transfixed by his name on a brass plate on his desk: Col Hitler Velasquez.

Because the topographical maps of popular trekking areas in Peru were so sought after, they were my biggest purchase and I had to set aside a full day to buy them. The morning was taken up with selecting and ordering what I wanted and the afternoon with picking them up by taxi to transport them back to my friends' house in Lima where I stayed between trips. These maps were sold as large flat sheets which we would roll into sturdy cardboard tubes. I travelled prepared with these, plus our trusty US mail sacks, and I could usually get all my purchases into two sacks. But this meant my total luggage for the return to England was now three or four large pieces rather than the permissible two. So what to do? This was pre-computer ticketing, so for a couple of years I would go to the airport as early as possible and check in with two pieces and collect my boarding pass. Then I would return shortly before the check-in deadline, very apologetic, saying I had checked in earlier but not been able to bring my luggage and here it was. Amazingly this was successful until the first computers were introduced, at which point I found that I had some difficult explaining to do. I got away with it – just – but that was the last time I used that technique.

So, yes, it was thoroughly dishonest but maps were what kept us solvent, and popular, during the 1980s. They were the mainstay of my regular selling trips to Europe. 'What have you got for us today?' my favourite travel buyer, Frau Fenz in the Berlin travel bookshop, would ask, leaning forward in anticipation. She was polite about the growing number of Bradt guides but it was the maps she wanted.

It was the maps that everyone wanted. Janet once had to do a doorstep sale of some Peruvian hiking maps to a pair of backpackers who were on their way to Heathrow. It was 7.30 in the morning.

During the '80s life settled into something of a routine. I published a few books and started taking a shared stand at the Frankfurt Book Fair, but it was tour leading that brought me the income I needed to keep publishing, putting me in the right places to do updates or, in the case of Madagascar, a new guidebook. It also enabled me to save enough money to take a few months off in 1984 to fulfil a childhood dream and ride a horse around western Ireland, which I later described in my book *A Connemara Journey*. In 1985 we changed our name to Bradt Publications to cover our broader publishing output, including maps, which we had now started producing under our own imprint.

Despite my successful European sales trips and our displays at the two book fairs, London and Frankfurt, I wasn't a natural saleswoman. What I liked best was creating books. Potential authors would contact me with their ideas and sometimes, if they fitted with my narrow vision of what we should be publishing, I said yes. *Climbing and Hiking in Ecuador* was an obvious one, but then came the proposal for *The Trans-Siberian Rail Guide*, a book which launched another series: guides to foreign railway journeys. I liked the idea of including anecdotes from people who'd done this famous journey, so I placed an advertisement in the personal column of *The Times* asking for stories and first-hand experiences. It was such fun! I received a dozen or so letters, many of which included amusing or inspiring stories that were inserted into the book. This guide was our best seller for several years.

The book I'm most fond of (that's a bit different from proud – that honour goes to *Ethiopia* by our star author, Philip Briggs) is the second edition of *Backpacker's Africa*, published in 1983, because Janet and I created it between us. Typesetting was an expensive business, with the entire text needing to be rekeyed, which seemed such a waste of money. I'd always liked the look of our typewritten books, and since Janet loved copy-typing she was in charge of the text, taken from our original *Backpacker's Africa* but extensively updated and augmented by the many people who'd written to us over the previous five years. I worked on the illustrations and maps, which, along with the typeset headings, were pasted in position with Cow gum.

Ah, Cow gum! I was chatting with Pat Underwood of Sunflower Books the other day – she was also shortlisted for the Thomas Cook guidebook award in 1980 – and we were recalling this essential for self-publishing in the early 1980s. A quick check on the internet shows used tubes of the stuff for sale on eBay for £35 and nostalgic recollections of the days when 'cut and paste' meant just that. I always thought this glue came from cows, perhaps because I remembered hearing of a horse in the Falkland Islands called Evostik because it had been saved from the glue factory. But no, Mr Cow the inventor put his name to good use and we oldies remember the tubs and tubes with a mixture of affection and relief that creating a book is so much easier these days. Cow gum was a rubber-based glue used to stick paper on to paper, so that's how all those bits and pieces were put in place. In the mid-1980s it was replaced by Spray Mount which, when you made a mistake – most of the time, it seemed – allowed you to peel off the misplaced text or picture and reposition it.

I used these two adhesives for years, and one thing I remember is that after an entire night of pasting up you were high as a kite from the fumes. In my case not pleasantly so. I remember after one all-night session I went to my computer and found myself staring at the keyboard, with no idea how my fingers were supposed to engage with the keys. I made the mistake of phoning my friend, speaking gibberish, then going to bed to sleep it off, leaving her to assume, quite reasonably, that I had finally gone mad.

Back to the mid-1980s when the simplicity of typewritten text had to end. Competition was creeping in and guidebooks had to look professional – and that meant typeset. A couple of our books during that era were retyped by professionals on a dedicated typesetting machine, but this was not only very expensive and time-consuming but a source of errors. In 1985 I bit the bullet and bought a chunky computer installed with WordStar and took a few lessons in word processing. In my late teens I had taken a typing course, as all young ladies did in those days of limited employment, so in theory I could touch-type, but had forgotten how. I couldn't get the hang of word processing, and I hated my computer and the questions it demanded of me which I couldn't understand. WordStar presented something very different to what I see on the screen as I type this. You peered at white or green letters on a black background, and any variation, such as italics or bold text, had to be marked up with a special code. The printouts emerged in fuzzy dot matrix. I yearned for a laser printer which would give me nice clear black lettering, but that sort of luxury was for the future. However, when I splashed out on the computer – I think over £400, which was a lot of money in those days – I promised myself I would earn the money back within a year through my published articles. And I did. My knowledge of Madagascar and South America was in demand.

I could now make the challenging leap from sending an author's typed and edited manuscript to a typesetter, to finding someone who could create a typeset book from the author's floppy disk after it had been edited. I had read about this miracle and it made perfect sense – no need to wastefully rekey the text, no risk of new errors creeping in, and the opportunity to make last-minute changes. Plus a massive reduction in costs.

Wrong. There were several eye-watering disasters before I got to grips with this, learned how to accurately put in the necessary codes, and found typesetters who I could trust to work efficiently from disk.

I learned the hard way that it was important to get a set of laser-printed proofs to ensure that I hadn't made any coding errors before the final shiny roll of printed text, bromide, dozens of feet long, arrived through the mail in a cardboard tube. It cost £3 per foot and I still had to do the (literal) cut and paste. I bought a light box, marked up a template for the text area, and cut the bromide into pages, pasting them on to A4 sheets of paper, along with the page numbers, running heads, photos, maps and illustrations. Inevitably I discovered spelling mistakes and had to use a craft knife to correct these. Sometimes I needed to create new words, letter by letter, out of discarded text (tricky!).

I can't hear Paul Simon's *Graceland* (released in 1986) without being cast back in my memory to the dining room table in my little flat (I had finally stopped sponging on relatives), which was never used for dining but mostly for that final-night paste-up to the accompaniment of those soothing/stimulating lyrics. At 4am I would set off by car up the empty motorway to Paddington Station to hand over the package of camera-ready copy to the Red Star office for express delivery by the first train to our printer in Exeter.

Despite the lack of sleep and stress of meeting deadlines, I loved making books. I enjoyed designing every page, sticking in the illustrations, and using fillers (travel hints or literary quotations) or in later books, feature boxes or adverts, to use up every available bit of white space. I also loved working closely with authors, commissioning, discussing, editing… the whole process.

Looking at my collection of catalogues, I seem to have done remarkably little publishing during the '80s. The catalogue of 1988 is pretty basic, a black-and-white paste-up of poorly reproduced covers. Mostly the imported books, but the slowly growing Bradt list did have some interesting titles, all unique with no competition. By this point I had ventured into the country guides that made Bradt distinctive during the coming years with the first English-language guide to Madagascar (which is now in its thirteenth edition) and Mauritius (now heading for the eleventh edition). Czechoslovakia complicated things by becoming two different countries, as did Yugoslavia, which spawned seven separate titles. And I managed to regress back to typewritten books by introducing a series of No Frills Guides: 'Every traveller knows that it's hard to find guides to offbeat parts of the world, and when there *are* guide books they are often woefully out of date because new editions are too expensive to produce. *No Frills Guides* beat this impasse by dispensing with all the gloss that makes a book attractive to the impulse buyer, and all the built-in delays which are part of normal commercial publishing. They are not typeset, they have no photographs, and have no colour cover. They are factual, informative, and written by recently returned travellers. They are constantly updated.' Putting the traveller first seemed a sensible, and rather original, thing to do.

This relapse aside, we were inching towards becoming normal publishers. I joined the IPG (Independent Publishers' Guild) and started the Small Publisher's Group for people like me who had come into publishing from another route and wanted to gain and share knowledge. And no more visiting bookshops in Britain – we got ourselves distributors both here and in the USA.

In 1988, during its first year of operation, I also joined Tourism Concern. Because I had the privilege of returning every year to Madagascar and South America as a tour leader, I could experience first-hand the growing impact of tourism on remote communities, and could also see how tourists might be a powerful force for good by becoming involved with local charities. It was so easy, especially in Madagascar. On the last day of each tour I would take my group to visit the nuns at the Street Kids Centre to donate their leftover medications, local currency and so on, and be taken on a tour of the centre. Very few left dry-eyed and clients frequently cited this as one of their favourite days on the trip. The Madagascar guide had, and has, pages of descriptions of organisations which welcome tourist visits and donations. With so little effort we could make a real difference.

In 2008 I was introduced to the oh-so simple concept of Stuff Your Rucksack, initiated by broadcaster and writer Kate Humble. Travellers to the developing world often have space in their luggage for items that are sorely needed by schools, orphanages or other charitable organisations. Heading off on holiday to Namibia with family and friends, I checked the Stuff Your Rucksack website, where I found a place just outside Windhoek which appealed immediately: 'MaryBeth is a volunteer at the centre, but pretty much runs the whole thing. The Children's Hope Initiative Project is a day program for orphans and vulnerable children...' With MaryBeth I had both a name and a personality, reinforced by her response: 'Thank you SO MUCH for offering to haul stuff over for us! If you want to know my ABSOLUTE NUMBER ONE DESIRE it is: SHARPIES!!! That is a brand name for permanent markers.' She used them to make educational games from recycled materials.

A phone call to the Sharpies manufacturer resulted in the gift of a large box of pens. A trawl around the charity shops produced some football shirts and a fellow publisher donated some children's books. MaryBeth met us at our hotel, an American as exuberant and upper case as her emails, and drove us to the centre where we spent the morning interacting with the children. It was an eye-opening, endearing and gratifying start to the holiday. It also put the rest of Namibia into perspective. We had a splendid trip but of all our experiences in the country, this is the one we talked about most. And it didn't have to be a one-off experience. The author of our Namibia guide was happy to add a page about the project (now renamed the Bernhard Nordkamp Centre), which has been repeated in all subsequent editions and ensured a steady flow of donors, visitors and volunteers – and periodic emails from MaryBeth, still larger than life, still upper case, still working at the centre, thanking me for 'the gift that keeps giving'. Such a very easy gift, with such far-reaching results.

Tour leading led me to stints lecturing on expedition cruises. I was away for longer periods, and having a very happy time, but it was not compatible with running a growing publishing company. In 1992 a real, proper editor browsed our stand at Frankfurt and suggested that we might like to employ her since she lived near our office. Tricia Hayne became the fourth member of the Bradt team and insisted that things were done properly.

And that was it, really. Gradually 'I gave away the things I loved', to paraphrase Carly Simon's song, my years of happily creating books drawing to a close and Tricia taking on my favourite tasks of commissioning and editing. As a result the company ran smoothly and profitably, and I learned the value of delegation. In 1994 we found an American co-publisher, Globe Pequot, which remains Bradt's partner to this day.

In 1995 we celebrated our twenty-first anniversary in style, with a splendid lunch in a Windsor hotel and a boat trip down the Thames. It was an opportunity to thank my parents, my sister Kate, and our authors, cartographer and distributors, for keeping us in business during quite a few dodgy years. I had a lot to be grateful for.

The year 1997 was very special because we won the Sunday Times/IPG Small Publisher of the Year Award – the first travel publisher to do so. This was a huge morale boost, and I treasure the judges' citation: 'Bradt Publications has been built up by the flair and dedication of Hilary Bradt to become a recognised brand name, publishing attractive and clearly targeted books. The list combines professionalism and focus while keeping a personal flavour.' *And* it came with a cheque for £1,000!

Seventeen years after the split with George, I – we – had made it. This seems like a good place to stop these recollections. This isn't a biography of Bradt Guides, it's my own personal journey. Since then twenty-six years have passed, and Bradt is now a sizeable and successful company run by a terrific team and ably headed by Adrian Phillips who joined us as editorial assistant in 2001.

I sometimes find it hard to believe how fortunate I have been.

Before I come to the end of the chronological story, though, there is one more tale I'd like to tell. In 2008, the year that I moved to Devon and into semi-retirement, something extraordinary happened, as I described in my Christmas letter that year:

> Something so big and so surprising happened in the spring that it chases all other events into the background. I'll begin at the beginning with the arrival of an envelope in mid May that looked like a tax demand. It also stated that it was from the Cabinet Office which frightened me; I wondered what I'd done to upset Gordon Brown. Inside was a letter from a man who signed himself my Obedient Servant, suggesting that 'The Queen may be graciously pleased to approve that you be appointed a Member of the Order of the British Empire (MBE)'. The Prime Minister, he said, would be glad to know if this would be agreeable to me. If so I needed to fill in a form stating my ethnicity, disability, background... The rest of the sentence had stuck to the envelope flap and torn off. I was also sworn to secrecy but I did phone my MD, Donald, and ask if it was a joke. He thought not. The citation is 'For Services to the Tourism Industry and to Charity'.

> I kept the secret pretty well until the Birthday Honours were announced on June 16, and there indeed was my name. I still have difficulty believing it, but I've decided to banish all thoughts of unworthiness and just enjoy it. The investiture is at Windsor Castle (apparently the Queen prefers it to the Palace).

It's in two days' time, on December 12, so I'll finish this letter with a description of the actual event.

Meanwhile I'm worrying. Mostly about clothes and my fingernails. When I got the news in the spring I headed for the charity shops and bought a rather nice summer outfit. It's still in the wardrobe. Now it's winter I'm borrowing Inge's red velvet jacket and Daphne's black trousers. And I'm hiring a hat with a huge brim (everyone I speak to says that it should be a small hat) so I'm sure I shall knock Her Majesty over with it. Or fall over myself when I try to curtsy. Or fail to recognise HM. Or... And the fingernails! I painted my new fireplace today with heatproof black paint. I should have worn gloves, or at least not smeared permanent black paint under my nails. So I'm going to have to ditch the red jacket and hat, switch to faded black, and go as a Goth.

Dec 14. So, it's happened. I got invested and it was literally awesome. I and my guests, Kate, Janice and Inge, were ushered up a magnificent staircase past a line of household cavalry chaps all dressed in silver, red and gold and at least seven feet tall. Then the recipients were separated from the guests and herded into a room with refreshments (wisely non alcoholic) and we mingled. I talked to a jolly woman who got hers for Services to Netball and a conspicuously caring woman who'd done thirty years at Great Ormond Street Hospital. And a woman who will have intrigued the Queen since hers was for Services to The Caterpillar Club. Disappointingly it turned out to be connected with parachutists in the War. And there was a man called Dr Drain who got his for Services to the Environment (bet HM had a giggle over that). Then a beautiful Mr Darcy-like man came in, scarlet jacket all hung about with plaited gold braid, and wearing spurs, and talked us through what we'd have to do. My brain immediately went into No Memory mode and although I could hear the words they didn't seem to refer to me: walk to Mr Foster and stand at his chest (what?) then turn 45 degrees and walk towards the Queen (oh Lord), stop and curtsy (demo of a curtsy, with spurs clanking), then forward to HM who would say a few words. We were to address her as Your Majesty the first time and Ma'am to rhyme with jam the second time. Then step back three paces, another curtsy, and leave the room. 'One warning,' he said. 'Don't forget to let go of the Queen's hand.' Nervous giggles all round as we visualised dragging HM along the floor.

Far too soon, I found myself at the head of the queue. I could see this little blue figure with white hair, and I became rooted to the spot. 'Go on,' said the scarlet-jacketed man, giving me a little push. I couldn't remember what you are supposed to do with legs to create a forward motion. Kate said I looked like the waitress in Victoria Wood's 'Two Soups' sketch, weaving my way across the floor in the rough direction of the Queen. But I did my curtsy and wobbled forward. She popped the medal on to me (they pin a hook on beforehand to make it easier) and said 'Is it children?' I couldn't think what to say. 'No no,' I blurted out, 'I publish guidebooks. For adults'. Then I realised she was talking about the charity part. 'Oh yes, Children. Madagascar', and did a huge gesture to encompass the Indian Ocean and all the children thereon. At that she looked rather frightened and held out her hand. I managed the second curtsy and fled, realising that I hadn't addressed her as Your Majesty nor Ma'am. So will probably be stripped of my Award.

Then official photos and a delicious lunch with the lovely people who had nominated me. The photo of the actual medal pinning arrived by email that evening. And I saw why people had said I should wear a small hat.

23

TALES OF A TOUR LEADER

'I can't think of a person less suited to the job of tour leading than you!'

This wasn't a malicious comment. It was borne of long acquaintance, and my friend was absolutely right, just agreeing with me when I said it was time I stopped. I'd had a wonderful thirty years or so, despite not being a perfect match for the task. In those days I could accurately describe the job as giving people the impression they were having an adventure while trying to ensure that they did not.

So why unsuitable? If you've read this far you will know about my prosopagnosia (face blindness) and propensity for getting lost, so let's start with those.

Having greeted my group at the airport in Nairobi, Lima or Antananarivo, I would ask them to wait in a huddle while I located the bus to take us to the hotel. On re-entering the airport I had no idea which of the various tourist huddles were mine. To prosopagnosiacs all faces look the same. I once managed to herd the wrong group on to my bus and only realised the error when one woman rather crisply asked where we were going. And even if I got the right group on to the right bus, by cunningly noting clothing or luggage that would identify them, there was the nightmare of the hotel breakfast the following day. Now they were wearing different clothes, how on earth was I to know which of those diners were mine?

Having no sense of direction was actually not as problematic as you might think because we usually had local guides to take us around and show us the way. And on treks I always made sure I was at the back, 'supporting the slow walkers' as I explained. It was harder to give a reason why we had walked three sides of a square to reach the restaurant in Quito that I'd booked for dinner. The real crunch, when I knew I had been found out, came when I took on the job of leading a delightful group of American hikers along England's Cotswold Way. If I had been happy to stick to the plan and actually follow that national trail we would have been fine, but I couldn't resist suggesting that I could vary the route to show the group some of my favourite places. So much more interesting, I told them, than the well-trodden Cotswolds Way. (I was totally wrong here, as I found out this year when I finally walked the trail.) I should have recognised that this plan was doomed to failure. On the last day Bob told me how the group had entertained themselves.

'Each day we took bets on whether you would get lost. And – oh Hilary – I was the only one who bet you wouldn't get lost today. But that hundred-yard "diversion"… I lost my bet!'

Also I'm absent-minded. Vague, my mother called it. Easily distracted, I would say. My mind's never absent, just gone off along another path. A good tour leader counts them all out and counts them all back. On our Peru treks we always started in Cusco with a tour of the ruins of Sacsayhuamán; one time, as we drove back to the hotel I was busy explaining some subtlety of the Inca Empire when I felt an urgent tap on my shoulder. 'Just a minute,' I said airily, 'I'll finish this explanation then I can answer your question.'

'But it's Mary! You forgot her and she's running behind the bus!'

Whether a trip was a success or a disaster depended mainly on the clients, and most were extraordinarily forgiving and enjoyed the genuine adventures when they cropped up. And fortunately I had a really splendid group when we were stuck in Lago Agrio, an Ecuadorian oil town, with a transport strike blocking all possible means of escape. The strikers had dynamited the one road leading to Quito, the plane was fully booked for a fortnight, and the group was expecting to fly home to the US in two days' time. I had to do something, but what? It transpired that my only hope was to talk to the Shell people in their headquarters on the outskirts of town; they had a small plane which they used to commute to Quito for supplies. For moral support I took with me my favourite client, Mike, a distinguished-looking man with a mane of white hair and matching beard. At first my pleas and explanation about our plight fell on deaf ears.

'I have to get back to Boston really urgently,' chipped in Mike.

'Yes,' I burbled. 'Dr Clarkson is a professor at Tufts University!' (A complete lie, it just popped into my head.)

'Oh, Tufts!' exclaimed the Shell executive, breaking into a smile. 'My daughter's there! I guess we could give you guys a lift tomorrow.'

So it was that we flew back to Quito for free, in time for a slap-up farewell dinner and for the flight home the following day. And Mike, who had a far more humble job, sent me love letters for the next decade.

Most of my more taxing trips were in Madagascar. It's one of the characteristics of that delightful country that the more things go wrong, the more the gentle Malagasy people smile. This doesn't always work. I remember once spotting our local guide frowning at himself in the mirror. When I teased him about it he said, 'As a Malagasy man I smile a lot. I can see that if I want to work with Americans I must learn to frown.'

I didn't need to learn. It was sometimes difficult not to burst into tears of frustration, or into helpless giggles at the ludicrousness of the situations we found ourselves in. Or the eccentricities of the clients. Maria, a rich Colombian girl, stands out from that exclusive crowd.

On our first night in Tana (Antananarivo, Madagascar's capital), she woke me in tears at 4am to say she must return home immediately. 'I had my Tarot cards read last month. The lady predicted a long journey followed by a death. I've made the long journey, and now (sob) my parents are going to die!' A phone call to the still hale and hearty parents did nothing to allay her fears so I spent the next morning arranging a flight home. As I was recovering over a cup of coffee the taxi returned with Maria. 'Hilary, I can't go back. *This* will be the long journey, so my parents will die if I go home!' She spent the rest of the trip in a tranquilised state lying topless on the beach, much to the delight of the local fishermen.

The number of disasters that Madagascar could cram into one trip is exemplified by what happened in 1993. I had a cheery group of twelve, a mixture of Americans and Brits, and for two days everything went swimmingly. The hotel was nice, the food was good, the sun shone, everyone was happy. Then, as we prepared for the drive south, I spotted Roland, the local guide, loading tents on top of the bus.

'But we're booked to stay in the hotel at Ranomafana!'

'It's just in case it's double-booked. You know, to be safe.'

We arrived at the reserve to find a group of Brits sitting disconsolately outside the hotel drinking warm beer while their leader scurried around putting up tents. I muttered consoling words to him. 'Don't worry, I can see your group are pretty miserable – oh, ill are they? – Well, we've got rooms and my folks are so wonderfully sporty some of them probably *want* to camp, so your sickest people can have our beds.' Roland returned to say there were no rooms. The hotel was treble-booked. We put up the few tents that we had brought and Roland and I slept in the bus.

After that it was downhill all the way. Tight-lipped and hollow-eyed, the group suffered the gorgeous dawn walk with a plentiful supply of lemurs and birds, and tight-lipped they packed up for the journey to the coast. Our bus driver made it his mission to reach the Air Madagascar office before it closed so we could confirm our flight the next day. We made it, though several chickens lost their lives in the process. No problem, the staff told us, our seats were confirmed on the Twin Otter, but we were to be weighed with our luggage. Only hand luggage would be permitted on the plane; the rest had to be sent back with the bus. A rustle of alarm went through the larger members of the group.

Next day everything was going beautifully and the group relaxed a little. A shiny little Twin Otter landed and Roland handed us our boarding passes. Then, 'Can I have a word in private?' There was a problem. Yes, there were seats for all of us, no problem there, but we couldn't actually sit in them since the weight limit was used up with the kerosene they'd loaded on board. Drastic action was needed. I beetled over to speak to the pilot. No, he couldn't unload the plane. No, he couldn't do anything to help. All right then, he'd just taxi over to the far side of the airstrip where the radio reception was better and talk to his boss. He taxied over… and took off. I was not popular. Air Mad was not popular. Roland was popular because he spoke to the Right People by radio and they promised a plane the next day.

Fortunately the one hotel still had rooms available, and the plane did indeed arrive. And took off – with us on it. We now only had one day in the private reserve we had planned to visit, but the lemurs arrived on cue and things were almost as they should be – except for the group mood – so I arranged a rather sumptuous lunch at Fort Dauphin's finest restaurant. We would eat there prior to catching our flight back to the capital, I told them. Then Air Mad put the flight forward three hours, giving us just fifteen minutes to eat the three-course meal.

Things were falling apart. In Tana if people weren't too angry to speak to me they were too ill. I had to fetch a doctor. She cost a little less than a bottle of wine and had about the same effect. Never mind, I said to the eight or so who were still turning up for meals, it's Nosy Be tomorrow and that's a *real* holiday. We got to the airport. No flight. Go to the Hilton, said Air Mad, we've arranged for all passengers to stay there. 'Now isn't that lovely!' I squawked. 'You've been saying, Christopher, that you wish we'd stayed at the Hilton!' When we got there it was full. We were sent to the Panorama, driving across town through torrential rain. We were the only guests –

perhaps for months – and squelched down the corridor to the rooms which smelled strongly of mildew. Carol shot out of her room.

'There are three of them in the bathroom! One is spreadeagled across the sink!'

'What?'

'Cockroaches!'

We were up at 3am to get to the airport for the 5.30 flight. Jane was very ill. In between being sick, she lay semi-comatose across three seats. Two Air Mad ladies materialised, waving a piece of paper. A waiver. If Jane dies on the flight it's not their fault, she flies at her own risk and will she sign it please? Jane sat up briskly. 'Certainly not.' They giggled and melted away into the dawn. Jane survived the flight but it was she who fell into the sea a few days later when trying to board a boat. She was carrying her very expensive video camera.

I used to give a talk entitled 'Tales of a Tour Leader'. These, and the story that follows, were only a few of the rich collection of disasters I accumulated during those decades of leading tours. Once, when I asked if there were any questions, a woman put her hand up. 'How can I ensure that I *don't* come on one of your trips?'

INTERLUDE
A PERFECT STORM

It's the recipe for a Perfect Storm: an ill-sorted, ill-prepared group signs up for a tough trek in a country which is only just getting the hang of tourism. That was Bolivia in 1982, a fragile democracy with more changes of government than years of independence, and with inflation well over one hundred per cent. Add to that the fact that this was the first time their leader had been in charge of a group in Bolivia and... what could possibly go wrong?

Weeks before this trek I had felt a twinge of uneasiness. The tour operator had emphasised that this would be a true adventure (in other words it was the first time they'd run it). The trip roster showed me that I had eleven passengers: ten women, one man. My fears were not allayed when I met the group and asked them conversationally what had attracted them to this particular trek, which would take them over the high Andes and down into the jungle. Five women were committed feminists from the mathematics department of a well-known university. They'd chosen this particular trip because they wanted a woman leader and I was the only one on offer. Then there were three young women, whom I soon thought of as the Normals, who'd signed up hoping that a strenuous trek could lead to some possible romance. James, the lone man, remained silent despite my efforts, except to ask where he could buy coca leaves. Then I learned his reason for joining the trip: he'd become happily familiar with coca (the main ingredient of cocaine) on a previous visit to South America, and was the only tourist I've ever met who succeeded in getting high on coca leaves. But then he did chew them continuously for all his waking hours.

As we toured Cusco and Machu Picchu, things went reasonably well. I bought a birthday cake for James to enjoy on the train journey over the high Altiplano to Puno, the chilly town on the shores of

Lake Titicaca. This was when I first had doubts about the group's capacity for enjoyment. The ten-hour train ride is considered one of South America's most spectacular rail journeys, and we were travelling not just first class, but special class. James's birthday party was a bit of a flop; he'd taken several Valium tablets and slept soundly the whole way, just needing an occasional shove to prevent him falling off his seat. The militant women, however, were awake and unhappy: 'Why didn't we fly this stretch?' asked one impatiently, as we glided past herds of alpacas, their fluffy coats golden in the setting sun, and backed by snow-covered mountains. I comforted myself with the thought that maybe they felt that good scenery could only be enjoyed on foot, but this hope was dashed when I explained that in order to help them acclimatise various optional walks around the Bolivian side of Lake Titicaca had been planned. They opted out.

Then Douglas arrived. I'd been asked by the local tour operator whether we minded if a journalist joined the group to take the place of a last-minute dropout. 'No problem,' I said, 'but I'll check with the group.' (This was before I learned that tour leaders must be dictators, not democrats.) A meeting was called. The group that assembled was amicable, chummy and cheerful. The group that left was divided, bitter and angry. The Militants had been adamant that no man should join the group. 'He'll spoil our sisterhood. Besides, he'll always be writing down what we say to print in his stupid paper.' The Normals put up a spirited case for Douglas but were outnumbered and lapsed into angry silence. James chewed his coca leaves and was ignored by both sides.

Next morning I telephoned the office in La Paz to tell them Douglas would have to join another group.

'But he's already left! Don't you know about the strike? There is a blockade around La Paz and no transport is allowed to leave.

We just managed to get your bus out in time. Douglas is on it. He will be arriving very soon.'

I put this little difficulty aside and sorted my luggage for the trek. The bus that was bringing Douglas would stay to take us to the trailhead in the afternoon. Soon I was introducing myself to this very pleasant and unassuming Englishman, and asking if I could have a word in private. It was not easy explaining that previous evening's discussion but I reassured him that although the atmosphere might be a bit tense at first, I was sure he'd soon be accepted. Then I led him on to the bus where the group was already seated and introduced him. To an icy silence.

The atmosphere when we began our trek was grim. The leading Militant handed me a note saying what she and her friends thought of me, but I had two more pressing anxieties. One was our guide, Jean-Pierre. He was French, a mountaineer and a poet. He had flared nostrils like Rudolf Nureyev and was strong, handsome and sensitive. And he told me the first evening that he didn't think much of women and hated Americans. Perhaps it was a good thing that he spoke very little English. We mostly communicated in French and Spanish. The other anxiety was the inescapable realisation that two of the Militants had never really walked anywhere and were totally unprepared for a tough Andean trek.

The first evening Donna and Ann struggled into camp at dusk, exhausted and furious. Once over the pass Donna's (borrowed) boot had started to disintegrate. Fortunately I had my mainstay for all repairs – dental floss and a strong needle – in my daypack and was able to sew the sole back on while Donna stared silently over my head. It was hard to be sympathetic. A Grade 4 trek in the mountains is likely to involve some walking, and we'd had some stunning mountain views and a rather delicious lunch provided by Jean-Pierre who was in full charm mode. It didn't last. The second day we didn't stop for lunch. No one went hungry — there were trail snacks aplenty —

but it was not going to ease the tension. A meeting was called once we'd all arrived at camp. My role as interpreter was severely strained.

'Why didn't we stop for lunch, Jean-Pierre?' I asked.

'These women, they are stupid. When I served them food they just take. They don't say thank you. They are animals.'

'What's he saying, Hilary? No, tell us *everything* he's saying!' the group chorused.

I also had to decide how much to tell them of what Jean-Pierre had reported he'd heard on a villager's radio. He pre-empted me.

'There's been a revolution,' he announced melodramatically (and not very accurately, I learned later). 'La Paz is full of tanks and people are dying in the streets.' This had a noticeable effect on the group – apart from James, who wanted to show me his sock, which was soaked in blood. Coca had numbed his feet and he'd been unaware of the blisters until too late.

Next day, for a reason obscurely connected with not having had lunch, four people – including James, who was now in search of more coca leaves – left at 6.30am. I told them, as best I could, where the next campsite was, and warned them not to get ahead of the guide. I reached the camp (which was not where I expected) hours after the others, having stayed back to offer (resented) succour and support to the two non-walkers.

'The four people, they went on ahead,' said Jean-Pierre airily. 'I called to them but they took no notice. They are stupid.'

'How long ago?'

'About two hours.'

It was now almost dark. I set out with an *arriero* (muleteer) and Douglas, who was properly fit. Soon I was left far behind as I picked my way along the rough trail by torchlight. After half an hour the two returned with a note. 'We waited here an hour and are going to Bella Vista [the next settlement]... please bring our sleeping bags and some food...' But how? Bella Vista was at least three hours from the camp and it was already dark. They would have to manage as best they could. Which they did. I learned later that James, who spoke Spanish, had arranged for them to spend the night in the village school, with the added bonus of his Valium to ensure they got a good night's sleep. The schoolteacher had brought some boiled rice, but retreated in some confusion at the sight of James dressed in a borrowed tank top edged in frills. It was not very cold, and they might have considered it an adventure had Jean-Pierre not found them the next day, before I had a chance to tell them how inspiringly brave they had been. Tact was not his forte. By the time I reached them they didn't trust themselves to speak, so handed me a note. It said roughly the same thing as the woman who was sharpening her Swiss army knife on a stone, spluttering, 'I'm going to castrate him!'

On a trip like this, when you think things couldn't get any worse, they generally do. We ran out of food because the *arrieros* had sold it in the villages along the way, and one of the non-walkers appeared to be going into a clinical depression. Because of our slow pace we failed to reach the designated camping areas and were forced to pitch camp in places where there wasn't enough room to put up all the tents. On one such night I awoke to find myself staring up into the private parts of a mule. On the last day of the trek it poured with rain. The *arrieros* said it was too slippery for the mules so they would stay behind with the luggage, and Jean-Pierre, until the rain had stopped.

There should be some sense of relief at arriving at a destination, but the gold-prospecting town of Unutuluni on Independence Day, in the rain, was not an edifying place. The streets were ankle-deep in glutinous yellow mud and excrement. Drunks lay in the gutter and horses drooped outside saloon bars. From time to time a door would be flung open and, amid a burst of laughter, another drunk would reel out to join his companions. Our arrival was greeted by friendly hilarity, and when I asked if our bus had been seen (it was supposed to be waiting for us here to convey us to a first-class hotel further up the valley) the mirth redoubled. *'No hay gasoline!'* No petrol.

I sat the group down to the best meal I could find (sardines and stale bread) and set out with a cube-shaped wad of pesos in my hands to find alternative transport. Soaring inflation meant that even the highest-value banknote was worth only a pound or two. No one could imagine leaving Unutuluni during fiesta time, and besides, there were very few vehicles. Finally I located a man who was prepared to take us, providing we left immediately, before the rain made the roads any more treacherous. That was tricky; Jean-Pierre had just arrived to say that the *arrieros* had been so unnerved by the rain they'd decided to wait until after lunch before setting out from the campsite. They wouldn't arrive until the evening. I didn't dare wait till then so I scurried around buying blankets and polyester trousers for my sodden group and told them firmly that I did believe that Jean-Pierre would keep his promise to get our luggage to us somehow, and that unless they wanted to spend another few days in Unutuluni they'd better be prepared to leave in a few minutes. The pick-up truck had looked fine; it was only when we started heading downhill that an oily liquid started trickling out from near the wheels. Brake fluid. We decided to walk down the hills and ride on the level and uphill. It helped keep us warm.

The idea was that we'd get to our destination by midnight. The misery of any truck ride in the rain is compensated for by the thought of a first-class hotel at the end of it. What I didn't know was that there was a river to cross before we got to Civilisation. The river was in full flood, and our driver told us regretfully that the ferry wasn't functioning. We'd have to spend the night in a small town which was even more decadent than Unutuluni. I checked out the two 'hotels'. Thinking it wise to withhold the information that they were also whorehouses, I got everyone fixed up with a bed. In one hotel the only loo was a stinking hole in the ground, and the toilet in the other had a monkey chained to the seat which wouldn't allow anyone to enter. I wedged my bedroom door closed, but the four women in the adjacent room had shown less ingenuity. At intervals through the night I was woken by shouts of 'Fuck off!' followed by a man's muttered apology and retreating footsteps.

Next day we did make it to our first-class hotel, were duly reunited with our luggage and Jean-Pierre, and finally reached La Paz, where I wined and dined and cosseted the group to the best of my ability. But to no avail. I learned from my boss that the Militants had filed a $300,000 lawsuit for 'mental anguish'. And what about their leader's mental anguish, I wondered.

24

SEEKING THE BUBBLE
REPUTATION...

In the 'Seven Ages of Man' soliloquy in *As You Like It*, Shakespeare describes the soldier as 'Seeking the bubble reputation / Even in the cannon's mouth'. The stories that follow, which round off my own (abbreviated) Seven Ages, are drawn from my annual Christmas letters to friends. They show how easily that ego-bubble can be burst – especially where the media is involved.

1989

In January this year I got a call from the posh magazine *Harpers and Queen*, saying that I had been recommended by their travel editor (a friend) as an expedition leader, and could they interview me for an article they were putting together? I explained that I didn't lead expeditions, only group tours, but they said that's what they meant anyway. So Lucie Double-Barrelled Name made an appointment to come and talk to me in my scruffy little flat, and I cleaned for five hours to prepare for her visit (convinced that my image as a fearless leader would somehow be diminished if she spied a speck of dust along the skirting board). I forgot about the loo, though, which looked distinctly grubby and had rows of knickers drying over the bath. She arrived with a full bladder...

The interview lasted an hour, and I was so nervous I talked non-stop. I thought that was that but as she left she said a photographer would be along sometime. A few days later the editor phoned and said they weren't coming here (probably after a hasty discussion with Lucie about the knickers) but they would have a photographic session in – wait for it – St Pancras station.

And did I have any 'Amazing Luggage'? I told her about the US mail sacks, stamped DOMESTIC, which I usually cram with Peru gear, and she said, rather faintly, 'Brilliant!' and arranged to meet me at the office. So I rose at 6.30 to catch a commuter train, with bags under both arms (and under both eyes) and a rucksack on my back. When I entered the Fashion Department to meet Camilla she gave a tight smile, looked at the mail sacks in disbelief, and told me they had decided not to bother with luggage, they were going to do clever effects with a toy train, hence the station as the perfect setting. I was introduced to a make-up girl, who was to do her best with me in the office then accompany us to St Pancras, but she was too despairing to do more than give me black beetle-brows and occasionally run her fingers through my hair to make sure I was fashionably untidy. I suspected that she wasn't sure if I was a man or a woman, so didn't dare suggest lipstick.

The rather dishy photographer, Chris, arrived and we set forth with Wendy (make-up) and Camilla. Being in fashion she looked a total mess, exacerbated by the fact that she had flu and had to keep nipping off to be sick. I was wearing Sensible Clothes (a bit too sensible – I had noticed to my dismay on the train that some years previously I'd apparently spilled soup on my trousers and then hidden them in a drawer, that they were unfashionably short, and that my bunion was starting to make its inexorable journey through the soft leather of my new lace-ups).

While I chatted to Wendy in the coffee bar – both of us struggling to find anything in common – Chris and Camilla explored the station and found just the right place on a puddled and windy section of the platform. Remember, this was January. We then spent a couple of hours getting just the right shots, only to find that the camera wasn't working (it was, after all, Friday the 13th). The two women looked absolutely miserable, particularly Camilla who, apart from flu, had tiny black culottes over thin black stockings and some sort of skinny top, and no buttons on her jacket. Their job was to hold the toy railway tracks so the *Flying Scotsman* could fly up and down a few inches above or below my face. I expect the effect will be like that Magritte painting, but instead of a train steaming out of a fireplace it'll be steaming out of my right ear.

Since the polaroid part of the camera wasn't working, they skipped the usual business of doing trial shots to show how I would look, but apart from the train and right ear bit, Chris specialised in zoom shots of my bunion until I asked him not to, muttering about my shoes. Camilla offered me her little black pumps but was rendered speechless when I told her I took size eight. No one told me what to do with my face, and after a couple of attempts at a smile I settled into a chilly scowl. Chris was very energetic, lying down in puddles to get just the right view of my feet. After four hours, when we were all quite rigid with cold, he declared that we were finished, but that he'd take a few at the other end of the platform where there was a public phone. This involved me 'making a call': astonished passengers looking on while I reeled off the names on a pub sign to make it look as though I was speaking to someone.

The resulting article was quite flattering (they said I had the sort of face you can trust) but the photo – not surprisingly – wasn't, and the toy train was too blurred to make out. I do wonder whether it was worth the total of five hours and three paid members of staff.

1997

This year I did a publicity tour through the western USA in a rather futile attempt to sell more guidebooks. I gave talks in California, Oregon and Washington, and in Dallas, Texas, where a TV appearance had been arranged. The publicity chap warned me, 'It's a show called *Home Life* and, yes dear, it is a CHRISTIAN show, but it reaches 55 million homes, no kidding, so I want you to be on your very best behavior.' The blurb about the TV show was a bit discouraging. It was not just a Christian station but a Southern Baptist one. '*Home Life* is a half-hour daily television series dealing with topics that focus on healthy lifestyles, family values and wholesome relationships within the home.' It went on to say that the hosts 'live victorious family lives'. I was to give tips on women travelling alone. Hardly a topic to 'celebrate and undergird family life'.

I asked my friend Julia's advice. 'Big hair,' she said. 'That's the only thing that matters on Texan TV as far as I can tell.' So on the morning of the show I got up at 5.30 to wash and fluff up my hair and drove to the TV station where I waited half an hour for it to open. I sat on a wall in the mist and my Big Hair got smaller and smaller. Eventually the doors opened and I met Dresden, the make-up girl (appropriately named after a bombed city). She looked at me despairingly. 'Do you normally wear your hair like this?' I confessed that I did. 'We'd better leave it, then.' She concentrated on filling the lines and hollows on my face with orange Polyfilla.

The first guests were already being interviewed. They were boy scouts promoting a book about an incident that had happened some years ago when the older boy had rescued the twelve-year-old (now a morose seventeen) from a bear. The older boy was beautifully dressed in scout uniform, the personification of family values. First the monosyllabic boy came alive and described, most graphically, what it feels like to be dragged by the head towards the bushes by a black bear. Vicki (looking victorious, and wearing very Big Hair) asked the older lad, 'And what happened next?'

'Well, I was sitting in my tent reading the bible when I heard a scream...'

I knew then that I'd lost it. Oh, I tried so hard in the few minutes that they gave me. I talked about family values and the happiness derived from bonding with people from other cultures. Thanks to Dresden my flawless face radiated a healthy lifestyle and wholesome relationships, but it wasn't enough. I couldn't compete. They never broadcast the interview, so 55 million households (no kidding) never learned ten tips for women travelling alone. So it goes.

1998

I made my BBC TV debut this year. Something to boast about? Well, actually no. To begin at the end... My friend Roz was channel flicking in September and came across this programme called *Trade Secrets*. 'Look,' she said to her husband. 'That's Hilary!' And they both watched silently. And at the end of the programme they said nothing. That's why I thought I'd got away with it. Since no one admitted to seeing it, I assumed no one *had* seen it. Not true – it was simply too embarrassing to mention.

Here's how it happened. Over two years ago I was phoned up by an independent TV company looking for tips from jungle explorers. People do that to me from time to time, I think of a few gems of information and they go away and that's that. But I was feeling a bit frivolous, so I said to the researcher, 'Well, I can think of ten uses for condoms...' She sounded interested, and I started to try to wriggle out of it (because I only knew of one, apart from the obvious, and that was that they made passable emergency water containers). She said I might be hearing from her, and hung up. I tried to think of nine other uses for condoms and failed, so put it out of my mind. A few weeks later she rang again saying the producer was very interested in the condoms.

I deflected her with other bright ideas but it was only a temporary diversion. 'So what *are* the other uses of condoms?' she asked. I said I'd get back to her the following week.

I went into our little local chemist and asked if they had extra-strong condoms. Yes? Could I have two boxes please. The young assistant looked quite impressed, I thought. I needed small ones too, but couldn't quite bring myself to ask if they made child-size ones. I went home and started trying out ideas. In quick succession I found that condoms are no good as catapults (too slippery), too big to protect an injured finger, and, despite what I'd been led to believe, too small to carry water. I felt a bit desperate. Yes, they sort of worked as a way of keeping a box of matches dry, but compared with a plastic bag, virtually useless. Tracy phoned again. She said they did indeed want me to present all these wonderful condom ideas, and that, no, they were not going to fly me to the Amazon because she'd checked out Birmingham Botanical Gardens and they were just fine for the purpose.

I arrived at Beaconsfield station in lots of time to catch the train to Birmingham, all kitted out as an explorer with several boxes of extra-strong condoms in my backpack. The train arrived and I settled down to read my book and try to avoid thinking about what I'd got myself into. The train stopped and everyone got out. I was in Aylesbury, not Birmingham. I'd caught the wrong train. I was now in a mega-panic, trying to phone Tracy (her mobile was switched off) and work out alternative ways of getting to Birmingham. There weren't any. I had to go back to where I started from and catch the next train an hour later. By the time I reached the Botanical Gardens I was gibbering with guilt and anxiety. Tracy was very nice about it and introduced me to the camera team who were all around fourteen years old and very hip. I didn't even have time to comb my hair...

One of the lads told me what to do. For the first take I was to stroll up the 'jungle' path, thrust aside a tropical tree, and say something reassuring about how we jungle explorers cope with day-to-day problems (in case you're thinking hang on a minute, when was she last in a jungle, you're right – it was rather a long time ago...). Trouble was, they hadn't closed the gardens to the public and every time I got ready to peer through the parted fronds a large family would saunter past behind me, and we'd have 'Cut!' and they'd be shepherded out of the way. Then we moved on to the condoms. At this point a group of pensioners shuffled into view. Some were on walking frames and some in wheelchairs, but they were thrilled to see the BBC TV cameras. 'May we stay and watch?' one of them quavered. They lined up behind the cameras but in my view as I did take after take of slipping a condom over a box of matches, leering at the camera, and saying, 'And then you can light your fire in *safety*!' The retakes were necessary because either the condom slipped from my trembling grasp or another family group appeared, mesmerised, in the background.

The final take was me plunging my nose into a tropical flower before moving off into the mist, my body language exuding misery. 'That was great!' said Tracy brightly, and gave me a paper to sign giving them permission to show the episode.

I rode back in the train in a state of numbed disbelief at what I'd just done. So for the last two years I've kept very quiet and hoped that perhaps they'd realise how awful it was and not show it. Or perhaps there'd be a national disaster of sufficient magnitude that they'd cancel all TV programmes. I was unlucky. Quite a few of my mother's friends wasted no time in phoning her up to say, 'Was that your daughter I just saw on television?' All I can say is, I won't do it again. Ever.

EPILOGUE

'The world breaks everyone and afterward many are strong at the broken places' (Ernest Hemingway, *A Farewell to Arms*). I've always liked that quote, and also Leonard Cohen's 'There is a crack, a crack in everything. That's how the light gets in'. The break or crack caused by George leaving, certainly the worst thing that's ever happened to me, did indeed make me strong. And let the light in.

We all gain from heartbreak; I learned to hug and be hugged, and to accept the kindness of others. And I learned empathy and how to provide comfort. I look back with sadness at one event, lodged in my memory, when my friend the poet Elizabeth Bishop sat and sobbed next to me on her garden steps in Ouro Preto, Brazil. As a 28-year-old I didn't know what to do. So I did nothing.

Would I have achieved what I have achieved if George and I had stayed together? No.

George was partially right that I often used him as a crutch – or a support, anyway – in social situations. Being married to such an extrovert made life, and travel, so easy for me. As will have been evident from the descriptions of our journeys together, our encounters with the locals enriched us and George was invariably the instigator. But I had already climbed out from under that metaphorical table when I made my first trip, on my own, through South America. It took a lot of courage. And I felt the fear and did it anyway.

I can now look back on my life with more clarity. George and I had ten years together and during that time we travelled in a way that I could never have done alone. And we started a successful business together. Perhaps the child who set out down Bournemouth beach was actually going in the right direction, looking outward, not towards family and home. Maybe George leaving me so abruptly allowed me to rediscover who I was all along.

George and I email often, share memories and discuss what happened when. I've used a lot of his writing in this book. We're now both octogenarians, and this is how it should be.

50 YEARS OF BOOKS AUTHORED OR CO-AUTHORED BY HILARY BRADT

The current editions of titles marked with * are still available from www.bradtguides.com.

1974 *Backpacking along ancient ways in Peru and Bolivia*

1977–2002 *Backpacking in Peru & Bolivia* (eight editions)

1977–1994 *Backpackers' Africa* (four editions)

1978–1982 *Backpacking in Mexico & Central America* (two editions)

1979 *Backpacking in Venezuela, Colombia & Ecuador*

1979 *Backpacking in North America*

1980 *Backpacking in Chile & Argentina*

1986–2020 Guide to Madagascar (13 editions)*

1996–2001 *Madagascar Wildlife* (two editions)*

2010 *Slow Devon & Exmoor*

2014 *Trekking in Peru*

2014–2024 *Slow Travel: South Devon & Dartmoor* (three editions)*

2015–2019 *Slow Travel: North Devon & Exmoor* (two editions)*

2016–2020 *Slow Travel: East Devon & the Jurassic Coast* (two editions)*

2019 *Slow Travel: Exmoor National Park*

2022 *Slow Travel: Mid & North Devon*

2021 *A Connemara Journey*

2024 *Taking the Risk*

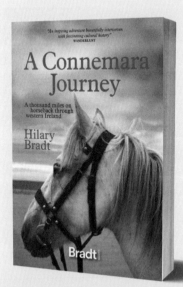